Tom:

Blessings & Peace

Ray Sarfield

HEALING JOURNEYS

Study Abroad
with
Vietnam Veterans

HEALING JOURNEYS

Study Abroad
with
Vietnam Veterans

Vol. 2
of A Vietnam Trilogy

Raymond Monsour Scurfield

Algora Publishing
New York

No portion of this book (beyond what is permitted by
Sections 107 or 108 of the United States Copyright Act of 1976)
may be reproduced by any process, stored in a retrieval system,
or transmitted in any form, or by any means, without the
express written permission of the publisher.
ISBN: 0-87586-404-X (softcover)
ISBN: 0-87586-405-8 (hardcover)
ISBN: 0-87586-406-6 (ebook)

Library of Congress Cataloging-in-Publication Data —

Scurfield, Raymond M.
Healing journeys: Study abroad with Vietnam veterans: Vol. 2 of a Vietnam
trilogy / Raymond Monsour Scurfield.
    p. cm.
Includes index and bibliographical references.
    ISBN 0-87586-404-X (trade paper: alk. paper) — ISBN 0-87586-405-8
(hard cover: alk. paper) — ISBN 0-87586-406-6 (ebook) 1. Post-traumatic
stress disorder—Treatment. 2. Veterans—Mental health. 3. Vietnamese
Conflict, 1961-1975—Veterans—Mental health. I. Title.

    RC552.P67S374 2006
    616.85'21008697—dc22
                        2006005328

Front Cover: *Veterans in a boat on the River Song Trol, which they flew over when they bombed the Ho Chi Minh trail.*
Image: © Les Stone/Sygma/Corbis
Photographer: Les Stone
Date Photographed: March 1, 2000

Printed in the United States

TABLE OF CONTENTS

SOME TERMS AND DEFINITIONS

Afghantsi: Veterans from the Soviet Union who fought in Afghanistan from 1979 to 1989. The bitter guerilla warfare and the global politics behind the war, the unpopularity of the war back home, and the high rate of drug addiction that resulted among soldiers were just some of the similarities to the US war in Vietnam.

American War: The term used in Vietnam today by the government and the people to refer to what the United States calls "the Vietnam War."

ARVN (Army of the Republic of Vietnam): The army of "South Vietnam," the Saigon-based government, during the Vietnam War. The US allied with them in fighting against the Communists.

Boot Camp: The US basic training course for all active duty military personnel.

Corpsman: A US Navy medic attached to a Marine unit.

Cyclo: Vernacular referring to Asian pedal-driven two-wheeled carts that carry two or three passengers.

DMZ: Demilitarized Military Zone. A narrow strip of land that was designated as the buffer zone dividing North and South Vietnam. US ground troops were prohibited from crossing to the north. (It was also called the "Dead Marine Zone," because of the high number of Marines who were killed in the DMZ.)

DOD: The US Department of Defense.

Evacuation Hospital: An "evac" hospital is a military medical facility where wounded military personnel are taken first. The patient's condition may be stabilized and acute treatment is provided before he is transferred elsewhere.

Field Hospital: The most comprehensive US military medical facility in the Vietnam War. The author served in the psychiatric team attached to the 8th Field Hospital in Nha Trang.

1

Flashback: A phenomenon in which a trauma survivor "psychologically relives" a prior traumatic event through trauma-associated memories, mental pictures, feelings and reactions. In more severe flashbacks, the person fully experiences and believes he or she is in the actual event and has no consciousness of current reality. In less severe flashbacks, which are much more common, one may be aware of current reality to varying degrees while simultaneously re-experiencing aspects of the original trauma.

Friendly fire: An accident or error involving bombs, bullets or any other incoming ordnance fired at you by your own fellow soldiers or allies rather than by enemy forces.

Gook: A disparaging term for (enemy) Vietnamese.

Ho Chi Minh City: The new name given to Saigon after it was captured by the Vietnam Communist government.

Jar Heads: US marines.

KIA: Killed In Action.

MEDCAP: Medical Civil Assistance Programs (also known as Medical Civic Affairs Projects, Medical Civic Action Projects or Medical Civilian Action Programs). Programs or projects in which military medical personnel provide free medical services to local people, including immunizations, physical examinations and basic outpatient treatment. Frequently, MEDCAPs are conducted jointly with local providers.

Med-evac: The process of removing a casualty (an injured person) from the war zone or from one medical facility to another.

MIA: Missing In Action. Thousands of military personnel in various wars have never been accounted for, and their families still do not know whether they were killed or taken prisoner.

NVA (North Vietnam Army): The regular uniformed armed forces of the Hanoi-based Communist regime ("North Vietnam") during the Vietnam War.

98th Medical Detachment (KO Team): One of the two Army psychiatric teams during the Vietnam War that assessed and treated military psychiatric casualties. The 98th Medical Detachment had both an inpatient and outpatient mental health capacity. The author was the administrative officer of this team and provided outpatient mental health services.

Persian Gulf War: The US and Coalition invasion of Iraq, January-April, 1991, following Iraq's invasion of Kuwait. The same term is sometimes used in reference to the US-led invasion of Iraq on March 20, 2003 and its subsequent occupation, although the latter war is more properly called Gulf War 2 or the Iraq War.

Psychiatric casualty rate: Official figures from the Department of Defense regarding military personnel considered to be unable to perform their normal duty responsibilities. During the Vietnam War, a psychiatric casualty was defined as one who missed three or more duty days due to a psychiatric problem or illness.

PTSD: Post Traumatic Stress Disorder.

PTSD Clinical Team (also known as the "PCT"): Department of Veterans Affairs (VA) outpatient mental health teams typically comprised of three or four mental health professionals and an administrative support person. The PCT focuses on a range of mental health interventions with veterans who have a post traumatic stress history due to exposure to military trauma and/or to sexual trauma.

Re-Education Camps: Incarceration facilities established by the Vietnamese Communist government following the Vietnam War where former members of the Saigon-based government and military were sent for punishment and inculcation in Communist doctrine. Some inmates are reported to have been incarcerated for at least 15 years.

VA: The US Department of Veterans Affairs.

VC (Viet Cong): The irregular enemy forces (guerillas) indigenous to southern Vietnam who allied with the Communist North, and were opposed to the Saigon-based Vietnamese government.

VVA: Vietnam Veterans of America, a US veterans service organization (VSO) established in 1978 and exclusively dedicated to Vietnam-era veterans and their families. The VVA was established because Vietnam veterans sensed that the traditional VSOs were not welcoming or sufficiently responsive to their concerns.

WIA: Wounded In Action.

PREFACE

The following pages trace the experiences of Vietnam veterans as they work to reconstruct their lives and to handle the indelible effects of the Vietnam War and its aftermath, and a unique trip back to the scenes of their trauma with a study abroad course on Vietnam history.

This book is the second of three. The first, *A Vietnam Trilogy. Veterans and Post-Traumatic Stress, 1968, 1989 and 2000*, described the healing journeys of hundreds of veterans from Vietnam and earlier wars up until 1990, when I co-led a group of veterans on a therapeutic trip back to Vietnam to "face their demons." The current volume continues from 1990 to 2000 (including a discussion of the impact of the first Gulf War on veterans) and a second return trip to Vietnam in 2000 to help veterans in their healing process. A third volume, *From Vietnam to Iraq* (Algora, fall 2006), will complete the Trilogy, with a consideration of the experience of prior wars to help people who are now in the military or in the healing professions, and their families and communities, to deal with today's realities of combat and its aftermath.

It is not necessary to read the first volume in order to appreciate *Healing Journeys: Veterans, PTSD, and Study Abroad in Vietnam*. However, it is a helpful introduction to events and developments that characterized US military psychiatry in Vietnam, the nature of the traumas caused by the Vietnam War and the strategies Americans used to survive during war. It also explores the more immediate and longer-range impact on the in-country and post-war lives of hundreds of thousands of US veterans, and shows how veterans benefited from a return trip to Vietnam in 1989. (That visit was extremely different from, yet laid the groundwork for, the very successful study abroad course to Vietnam, accom-panied by US veterans, in 2000, described in the current volume.)

The third volume, *A Vietnam Trilogy Vol. III: From Vietnam to Iraq*, takes lessons that could have been learned in prior wars and applies them to current realities. These are lessons that absolutely *must* be learned by more recent US veterans, including veterans of the Persian Gulf War and the Iraq War, if they are to avoid decades of needless horror and suffering.

The first volume considers the stereotype of the "troubled war veteran." Is it an overblown myth, or reality? It is essential to set the record straight on this, particularly in regard to the "typical" Vietnam veteran about whom so much has been written and so much controversy generated over the last three decades. Ironically, much the same debate is currently going on about reported suicides and mental health problems of US troops in the Iraq War.

Chillingly, what happened in Vietnam in 1968-69 regarding psychiatric casualties has enormous parallels to what is happening today regarding US psy-chiatric casualties from the Iraq War. I served as an Army Social Work Officer on one of the Army's two psychiatric teams, the 98th Medical Detachment, attached to the 8th Field Hospital in Nha Trang. Our mission was to assess and treat psychiatric casualties from throughout the northern half of South Vietnam in order to "conserve the fighting strength." Our mental health team was ill-pre-pared to understand and treat acute psychiatric casualties of war and we learned what we could on the job. For me, this experience began what is now almost a 40-year career in mental health, focusing on PTSD treatment, education and research, with and on behalf of veterans from the Vietnam War, as well as from World War II, Korea and the Persian Gulf.

From 1979 to 1989, I was privileged to be a clinician and program leader in the development of several regional and national mental health programs for the treatment of war veterans. As such, I was both an observer and a participant in the midst of a powerful national political and social upheaval centering on vet-erans — including working in the bowels of the Department of Veterans Affairs Headquarters in Washington, D.C., and leading a counseling and outreach oper-ation during the national dedications of both the National Vietnam Veterans Memorial and Statue. Then I led the implementation of a 33-bed PTSD treatment program in the Pacific Northwest that quickly developed (and sustained over several years) a waiting list of more than 200. Veterans wanted and needed this internationally acclaimed program. Our experiences with innovative action-based activities like "helicopter ride therapy," Outward Bound Adventure-based programs, and extensive involvement with American Indian veterans and their healers and healing rituals, were direct precursors to the pivotal decision to undertake a veterans' return trip to Vietnam two decades after the war.

In 1989, I returned to Vietnam as a co-therapist, along with April Gerlock, on an extremely controversial, much publicized sojourn involving a therapy group of veterans with PTSD. Both the VA and the State Department refused to sanction this trip in any way. We flew to Vietnam with the hope of revisiting sites where each of us had served during our tours of duty, and we were accompanied by several film crews and extensive international publicity. We hoped that this return trip might help the veterans' recovery efforts.

Also, through a Public Broadcasting documentary of the trip, we hoped to offer a glimpse through the shrouds of time and diplomatic and economic embargo so that tens of thousands of Vietnam veterans and their families (who would never have the opportunity to return to Vietnam on their own) could see for themselves a peacetime Vietnam. By sharing the experiences of nine veterans attempting to heal their own ongoing pathos, perhaps others, too, could escape the trap of pain-filled memories and images of a country and a people, a long-ago war-ravaged Vietnam that was no more, and replace those visions with the reality of a peacetime Vietnam in 1989. Many war veterans who lead relatively successful post-war lives will still remain conflicted regarding their war experiences, whatever therapies may be provided. Indeed, some war-related problems and symptoms, which are troubling but which certainly are to be expected, are mislabeled as a psychiatric disorder. Some, however, are disabling and seemingly "incurable," partly as a result of the potency of the "combat cocktail": the indelible imprinting of the suffering and exhilaration of war combined.

This, the second volume, focuses on the decade 1990-2000, which brought many breakthroughs in understanding and treating veterans with war-related issues. As well, there were many lessons that *should* have been learned about medical evacuees, racism in the military, and the collusion of silence and sanitization of the full human impact of war — but were not. The Persian Gulf War had an immense impact on veterans of all wars. Yet, as a national faculty member for joint VA-DOD training programs to enhance mental health response readiness for receiving anticipated medical and psychiatric casualties from the Persian Gulf War, what I found was a resurgence of selective amnesia and denial about the true impact of war. Nevertheless, I participated in novel therapeutic "people-to-people" meetings between Vietnam veterans and Soviet veterans of the Afghanistan war, meetings that belied what our respective governments had been saying about each other for decades. Such interchanges offered a glimpse of the power a "healing circle" can provide, even between former adversaries; this would be replicated with veterans returning to peacetime Vietnam. Sadly, there was also a resurrection of racism that seems inevitably to accompany war, and is graphically described concerning the Vietnam War and the Persian Gulf War.

I returned a second time to Vietnam in May 2000 with a fellow college professor, Andy Wiest, and a clinical psychologist, Leslie Root, who co-led a Vietnam History study abroad course under the auspices of the University of Southern Mississippi. We took sixteen university history students and three Vietnam combat veterans. This unique program set a precedent by integrating the curricula of military history and mental health, with the added value of the personal Vietnam histories of each of the three veterans. There were many powerful experiences and learning moments when the veterans found themselves in a transformed Vietnam, a country and people that were markedly changed even from 1989 when I had co-led the first therapy group of veterans with PTSD to return to Vietnam. And, there were amazing incidents of mutually healing and beneficial experiences between the veterans and the history students and faculty.

This book concludes with a detailed analysis of the benefits and potential pitfalls for veterans returning to their former war zones as part of their effort to heal from their war experiences.

The third book of *A Vietnam Trilogy* will relate the Vietnam and Gulf Wars to 9/11 and Iraq. The attacks of September 11, 2001, like attacks in a war zone, triggered psychiatric reactions in a substantial number of people that must be understood as normal and relevant to our understanding of the impact of war. It is also important to recognize what happens when we dehumanize the enemy and use racism and xenophobia to justify national policies. The book discusses the ways in which personal emotional and cognitive reactions to an attack can fuel and complicate unresolved issues from prior traumas that we may have experienced, driving us to support or oppose various national and international policies.

Iraq is leaving America with mental health casualties that are strikingly similar to those from Vietnam; the parallels, in terms of war zone stressors, and the occurrence of and the acute treatment of psychiatric casualties by the military mental health practitioners, are mind numbing. And yet many active duty military personnel and veterans and their families are experiencing serious shortcomings and gaps in services that are to be provided by the Department of

Defense and the Department of Veterans Affairs. Combatants and their families deserve to know the truth about the shorter and longer-term impacts of war on its survivors. These include war-related blame, guilt and shame, and the return home from deployment "ricochet effect" in which the war veteran detaches from or rejects the family, and issues that the family members may harbor.

An expanding circle of healing is described in Volume III, with examples of an innovative model of treatment to promote recovery from the profound impact of war on combatants and on their families. I have lived and walked arm-in-arm with many of my fellow and sister war-zone veterans since 1968, in our joint journeys of recovery and healing, in Pennsylvania, Southern California, the greater Washington DC area, the Pacific Northwest, throughout Hawaii and the Pacific Basin, and in Mississippi. In addition, because of the regional and national scope of the programs in which I have been involved, I have had the honor of meeting and working with hundreds of veterans from across the United States, Canada, Australia and the Soviet Union.

We all have been a part of a long and continuing journey: the struggle to provide our war veterans, who have served in harm's way, and their families, with what they have so fully earned beyond any measure. And that includes respectful, enlightened and responsive medical, psychiatric and social services, and understanding and acceptance by our citizens and communities. All of this is required if we are to actually help former combatants and their families in their post-war recovery — as they and we strive to attain the most fulfilling and satisfying quality of life possible. All of us deserve no less.

And so, this is both our and my story. It needed to be told decades ago — but then, it could not have been a Vietnam *trilogy*.

Pax mentis, and in faith, hope and love,

Raymond Monsour Scurfield

(*Pax mentis,* Latin for "peace of mind," was the unofficial motto of our 98th Medical Detachment psychiatric team in Vietnam in the late 1960s and was inscribed on our unit patch.)

CHAPTER 1. VIETNAM, THE GULF WARS, AND BACK TO VIETNAM

Serving as a social work officer on a US Army psychiatric team during the Vietnam War in 1968-69 was a turning point in my life. That experience opened my eyes and my heart, as I witnessed firsthand and was immersed in the remarkable range of changes that occur to men and women in war. There is a popular saying that "war brings out the best in people," but it is much more accurate to say that "war brings out both the best and *the beast* in people."

Yes, war is something that can bring out courage, comradeship, caring, humanitarianism, heroism and adrenalin-pumping excitement at the most extraordinary levels attainable by human beings. Of course, at the same time war also brings the most horrific experiences of terror, grief, rage, inhumanity, murder, maiming and mayhem that human beings can do to each other.

This extraordinary paradox, inherent in any war, and what it takes to survive both at the moment of violence and later, involves a powerful and complex mental process. This process imprints combatants and civilians with indelible markers of experience and vivid memories that have an impact both during the war and, in many cases, for years, decades or a lifetime afterwards.[1]

Several large-scale studies have confirmed that about one in every six combatants shows signs of serious psychological and social difficulties or unresolved issues, months, years and decades later. And many such veterans have not found a path to even partial recovery. (It is this fact that inspired me to co-lead the first

---

1. I describe both of these phenomena in *A Vietnam Trilogy, Vietnam Veterans and Post-Traumatic Stress* (Algora, 2004).

11

therapy group of veterans with PTSD to return to Vietnam in 1989. Something new, something radical had to be tried, as we struggled to understand the nature of the continuing hurting from the experiences of war. Maybe, we thought, a return to former battlefields might be helpful.[2]) This book begins in the eventful decade from 1990 to 2000, when the US launched Operation Desert Storm and the Persian Gulf War. These events had a major emotional impact on Vietnam veterans and on their care-givers throughout the country, including at the American Lake VA PTSD Treatment Program in Tacoma, WA, where I served as Director, and on our veteran patients.

In preparing to help the VA (the Department of Veterans Affairs) and DOD get ready for expected Gulf War medical and psychiatric casualties, my close friend, colleague and fellow Vietnam veteran Steve Tice and I discovered that almost nothing of a practical nature had ever been written about the entire series of emotional (versus physical) experiences and trauma that occur during the entire time-line from the moment someone is injured in the war-zone and through the ensuing series of medical evacuation procedures and relocations within a war-zone and to a stateside hospital; and as soon as we began to study the question, critical lessons for how we treat wounded military personnel began to unfold.

This chapter contains information that is critical to what is happening today in the Iraq War, in which there have been well over 2,000 US casualties at the time of this writing — and increasing by the day. Most health care providers and veterans' families have little familiarity or sensitivity about much of what happened to medical and psychiatric casualties from the Vietnam War that may still be deeply affecting Vietnam vets today. And little has been done to see how this is relevant to medical evacuees of later wars, including today's and tomorrow's.

There is a collusion of interests masking the true impact of war. The massive media coverage of the war in Iraq, the pending forecast of major casualties, and a polished military and media coverage strategy, markedly downplayed the Iraqi civilian casualties in particular. Our country has historically tended to sanitize and to silence reports about the full impact of war and the human costs.

---

2. This first return to Vietnam in 1989 is described in detail in *A Vietnam Trilogy, Vietnam Veterans and Post-Traumatic Stress*, and is portrayed in a PBS documentary, *Two Decades and A Wake-Up*, which aired nationally initially in 1990 (Stevan M. Smith, Producer).

When several groups of veterans from the Soviet Union visited our PTSD program, we replicated in a microcosm other meetings that were being held between American and Soviet "Afghantsi" veterans here in the US and in Russia. Both the US and Soviet governments had exaggerated the progress, and minimized the human costs, of the Vietnam War and Soviet war in Afghanistan. Talking together about these situations promoted a remarkable discovery of common bonds between soldiers of two countries that had been at odds with each other for decades; and these interchanges laid further groundwork for the next return trip to Vietnam to face old enemies.

Racism was another troublesome aspect of both the Vietnam and Persian Gulf Wars. There were numerous reports of racist attitudes and behaviors in America towards people who were perceived to be of Middle Eastern ancestry. This development was personally upsetting to me, hitting close to home because of my Syrian-American heritage. It also hit me as a Vietnam veteran, arousing powerful emotions and issues related to what had been a terribly racist attitude among many Americans in the Vietnam War and continuing racial issues among many Vietnam veterans towards the Vietnamese people.

"They [all Vietnamese] are gooks to me. And the only good gook is a dead one."

"I would hear the word 'gooks' all the time, or 'chinks.' That was everyday language for the men that I worked with. The way I dealt with all these words, it never really dawned on me till I came home that these words were actually derogatory. It's like calling a black guy a 'nigger.' It's the same thing."[3]

These continuing issues are too important not to be discussed. The extent of such racism dynamics was brought to my attention even more clearly following my move to Hawaii in 1992, where I became the Director of the newly established Pacific Center for PTSD. We established the first-ever residential PTSD treatment program in the Pacific for war veterans from Hawaii, Guam, and American Samoa. Through the gut-wrenching stories of the veterans we were seeing, I became exposed to what has been one of the least-talked about and yet most problematic aspect of the Vietnam War — the terrible racism that some American active duty personnel in Vietnam directed towards fellow and sister Americans who happened to be of Asian-American and Pacific Islander ancestry — as well as towards African-American and Hispanic American military personnel. I also discovered how prevalent the issues still were among Asian

---

3. Holm, Tom, The National Survey of Indian Vietnam veterans, in *Report of the Working Group on American Indian Vietnam Era Veterans* (Washington, D.C.: Readjustment Counseling Service, Department of Veterans Affairs, May 1992), pp. 25-34.

American and Pacific Islander veterans. And the same thing is being done today in the context of the Iraq War, where the dehumanization of the enemy includes racial and ethnic stereotyping.

I took an early retirement from the VA after a 25-year career, feeling that it was time to move on to work that was not totally encapsulated with veterans, and I accepted a teaching position in the graduate school of social work at the University of Southern Mississippi.

To my great surprise, I soon discovered a unique opportunity that brought Vietnam back into the center of my life. I was asked to be a consultant in the planning for a unique university study-abroad Vietnam History course that would combine military history and mental health educational and therapeutic objectives for history students and Vietnam veterans together.

That involvement resulted in something that had been absolutely unthinkable to me since returning from Vietnam in 1989: I found myself persuaded to return to Vietnam again, to further the healing journeys of another group of Vietnam veterans — and me.

Vietnam History Study Abroad 2000 turned out to be extremely different from the 1989 trip. The combination of sociological and cultural experiences and student-veteran interactions produced an extremely positive set of experiences among all of the course participants — students, veterans and faculty. These experiences provide considerable food for thought as to what needs to be done, and can be done, to help veterans further heal from the trauma of war — and the experiences also identified some potential negatives for some veterans planning to return to their former war zone. Perhaps such a study abroad course is the best way, or at least one ideal way, for vets to re-experience Vietnam today: as a sub-group of a larger, supportive group that focuses on the military history of Vietnam, seeing and tasting Vietnam today, interspersed with visits to battlefields and other sites of personal interest, with some discussion of mental health dynamics.

Then, along came September 11; and then the Iraq War. I realized that America was still not doing its casualties justice; that all the lessons that had gone unlearned meant that we were still adding unnecessary pain and trauma by the way we treated medical evacuees, and we were still not adequately identifying or addressing these sources of pain; this only accentuates the post-war problems facing hundreds of thousands veterans and their families. How are we treating the casualties created by our participation in the Iraq War today? Are we, the public, still colluding with the media and Washington to downplay the full human impact of war, both short and long term? Are we mindful that racism that is engendered and exacerbated during times of war does damage to our society for decades to come, and have we calculated the costs?

If we don't think through and apply the lessons of Vietnam, we are leaving the tens of thousands of Iraq War veterans and their families to suffer needlessly in the coming months, years and decades. And our nation's war policies will continue to be promulgated without full consideration of the human costs of war, both short and long-term.

CHAPTER 2. MEDICAL EVACUATIONS FROM THE
BATTLEFIELD TO STATESIDE: A TRAIL OF TRIBULATION

"A guy next to me in the hospital died; and when I woke up, he was gone. When I asked where he was, the staff lied to me about his death. But I knew that he had died. They lied to us a lot. How was I to know what really was my medical condition? What could you believe?"
— A severely wounded vet at evac hospital in Japan, 1970.[4]

(Steve Tice contributed much of the content for this chapter, including this quote.)

While I was stationed at the 8th Field Hospital in Vietnam in 1968-69, I was exposed to many acutely wounded and psychiatrically disabled soldiers who had been evacuated from a battle area. The acute treatment focus naturally would be on stabilization and immediate treatment of their physical condition. These medical casualties either died or survived. If they survived, and their medical condition was successfully stabilized, there were two dispositions possible. They either recovered sufficiently to be returned to duty or to be reassigned to other duty in the war zone due to the nature of their wounds; or their condition was so serious that they had to be evacuated out of Vietnam, and we never heard or saw from them again.

---

4. Much of the following material concerning medical and psychiatric evacuees is derived from two sources that Steve Tice co-authored with me: Interventions with Medical and Psychiatric Evacuees and Their Families: From Vietnam through the Gulf War. *Military Medicine*, 157 (2), 88-97, 1992; and "Acute Psycho-Social Intervention Strategies with Medical and Psychiatric Evacuees of Operation Desert Storm and Their Families," 1992. The latter paper was distributed by VA HQ throughout the VA medical care system and was included in the "Operation Desert Storm Clinician Packet" prepared and distributed nationally by the VA National Center on PTSD in June, 1991.

Because of the total lack of any feedback regarding casualties medically evacuated out of Vietnam, we never knew what became of them. Where exactly did they end up once they left the war zone; did they live or die; did they recover partially or completely? Of course, quite frankly, we were too busy taking care of the next wave of acute casualties arriving at our door to spend much time speculating about what had happened to those who had been evacuated out, but it left my colleagues and me with a gaping sense of something incomplete.

It was not until the mid-1980s, when I came into clinical contact with many physically disabled Vietnam veterans who also were suffering from war-related PTSD, that I became aware of a startling fact. Most veterans who had become medical casualties in the war zone and who had to be medically evacuated from the battlefield (and then eventually out of Vietnam) had an extraordinary series of stressful and traumatic post-casualty experiences that were little known, recognized or considered by almost anyone in the military or in the VA health care system.

Indeed, their post-casualty experiences left such a profound impact that we instituted a special treatment strategy for them in our PTSD treatment program at the American Lake VA Medical Center in Tacoma, WA. Of course, all war veterans participated in "Vietnam focus" therapy groups. In Vietnam focus, each veteran had the opportunity to discuss traumatic experiences that were still troubling, such as guilt or rage over specific horrific incidents witnessed or otherwise experienced. Those veterans who served more than one tour of duty in Vietnam had the opportunity in war focus groups to discuss troubling experiences in each of their war tours, since a second or third tour oftentimes brought a markedly different series of experiences.

We then learned from veterans with amputations and other serious physical disabilities stemming from battle wounds that there was another entirely different series of experiences that they went through, and in most cases had never discussed with anyone at all. These were the traumatic experiences that they were subjected to in the course of the medical attention they received, from the moment they were wounded all the way through the entire evacuation, triage, stabilization, acute and initial treatment phases and subsequent stages of recovery. And these distressing experiences were spread over many months, if not years.

We began considering any war veteran who had become a medical casualty (medical or psychiatric) in Vietnam and had to be medically evacuated out of country as having in effect served a "second tour of duty," encompassing everything that happened to him from the moment he was hit or injured in battle, all the way back to his time in a military hospital in the United States. And then, ultimately, if the wounds or psychiatric condition were severe enough, his discharge from active duty and transfer to a VA medical facility.

"The whole evac process — people just don't know how traumatic the whole medevac process was. Each time we were transported somewhere else was a trauma in itself."[5]

The re-traumatization goes on and on. A severely wounded vet is repeatedly called upon to inform medical personnel of his/her history and how he or she was wounded. The VA for years did not systematically include meaningful military histories as a fundamental element in the assessment of veterans' problems. And private physicians did not (and could not be expected to) have a clue about it. As affirmed by many hospitalized medical evacuees, even when the military history was in the chart, VA doctors often did not review it prior to seeing vets and thus relied on the injured vet to "briefly" fill them in on the wounding. Steve Tice reports the following that happened to him:

"I had the experience of seeing a VA physician over a four-year period who rarely looked up from his computer to look at me. He just asked the appropriate questions and typed my response. Near the end of the four years that I saw him, I was complaining about my left arm hurting. he typed away and asked me, without looking up, if my right arm hurt in the same area. I told him no, I was an amputee. He hadn't realized this after four years!"

This entire process was, obviously, very stressful and traumatic, coming on top of what had happened in the war zone. And, naturally enough, during the entire process the medical personnel concentrated almost solely on life- and organ-saving emergency treatment procedures. The pace at which acute medical assessment and treatment had to be accomplished was usually so rushed, with wave after wave of casualties coming in, that the individual casualty often was left ignorant of his own prognosis and expected fate.

"No one ever told me how long I might be here, the actual severity of my wounds (or conditions), or what was going to happen to me next."[6]

In the midst of providing an intensive series of medical diagnostic and treatment interventions, usually in overcrowded facilities with harried and overworked medical staff, extremely few of the care providers ever paid any significant attention to the further emotional trauma suffered by these medical

---

5. Scurfield and Tice, 1992, p. 90.
6. Ibid., p. 90.

casualties as part of the evacuation and stabilization process itself. This had been an almost completed ignored set of war-related trauma. By and large the casualty did not talk about it, the military establishment did not talk about it, the VA did not talk about it, and the family did not talk about it. It was as if the entire chain of distressing post-injury events never happened.

When the Persian Gulf War was imminent, there was nothing in place to help us do a better job concerning the mental health issues related to the medical evacuation process this time around. Although few people realize it, the VA is designated as the medical back-up system for the Department of Defense medical system. As such, the VA was responsible to gear up for the anticipated large number of combat casualties that might be incurred if and when full-scale hostilities erupted with Iraq. As part of this gearing-up process, I was one of the VA staff designated as national training faculty to provide training to both VA and DOD health care providers regarding assessment and intervention strategies to deal with the mental health aspects of anticipated casualties, including both physical wounds and psychological ones.

In preparing training materials for the VA/DOD national contingency preparedness program for the Persian Gulf War, I was amazed to discover that there was virtually no literature on specific psychosocial clinical strategies to assist direct-service medical, surgical, and mental health providers in addressing acute psychological reactions that accompany that accompany traumatic physical injury in a war zone. In fact, going back to the literature on all of the wars from World War I onward, only one document was located.[7] However, there were a number of personal accounts[8] that did poignantly describe various

---

7. Tice, S., R. Hinds, E. Bialobok, H. Carter, J. Cecil, D. Koverman, N. Makowski, R. Pierson and A.R. Batres, *Report of the Working Group on Physically Disabled Vietnam Veterans* (Washington, DC: Readjustment Counseling Service, Department of Veterans Affairs, April, 1988). This is a landmark monograph prepared almost entirely by physically disabled Vietnam veterans who were team leaders or counselors at various Vet Centers throughout the US. I served as the VA HQ liaison/consultant with this working group.

8. Dramatic personal accounts by veterans who had gone through the evacuation and rehabilitation process include: Blank, Joseph P., "The long return of Warrant Officer Meade. Drama in real life," *Reader's Digest* (December, 1970), 71-77; Cleland, Max, "Strong at the Broken Places" (Atlanta: *Cherokee Publishing Company*, 1986); Downs, Frederic, *Aftermath: A Soldier's Return from Vietnam* (New York: Norton, 1984); Eilert, Rick, *For Self and Country: A True Story by Rick Eilert* (New York: William Morrow Publishing, 1983); Kovic, Ron, *Born on the Fourth of July* (New York: McGraw-Hill, 1976); and Levine, S., *Healing Into Life and Death* (New York: Doubleday, 1987).

aspects of recovery dynamics from the viewpoints of the survivor and the health care provider.[9]

The literature did contain accounts of clinical strategies to treat the acute manifestations of psychiatric casualties while in the war zone,[10] and the chronic manifestations of traumatic stress years afterwards.[11] However, once again, there was almost no description of what the experience was for the medical casualty during the entire medical evacuation process, from the battlefield back to discharge from a stateside hospital. Since this entire process was not even described, it naturally followed that there also was an absence of descriptions of specific clinical intervention strategies that would enable medical care-givers to ease the patient's psychological distress during the various stages. Steve and I were appalled at what we did not find in the literature.

Steve is a fellow veteran, a front-line soldier who was seriously wounded by a rocket-propelled grenade in Vietnam. He was medically evacuated and, with the support of his wife Lisa and three sons, has gone through what has turned out to be a life-long recovery process. Steve has been very active in treating longer-term psychiatric casualties of war, both in the VA Vet Center program and with the American Lake VA PTSD program. Together, we set out to gather necessary information directly from veterans who had experienced a medical evacuation so that we could describe the process and the dynamics that occur, and on that basis draw up recommended interventions. We were adamant that

9. For example: Glasser, R.J.: *365 Days*. (New York: Braziller, 1971); May, G., Counseling considerations in working with disabled Vietnam veterans. In Williams, T. (ed.), *Post-Traumatic Stress Disorder: A Handbook for Clinicians*. (Cincinnati: Disabled American Veterans, 1987); Meshad, S., *Captain for Dark Mornings*. (Playa del Rey, CA: Creative Images Associates, 1982); Shea, F.T., Stress of caring for combat casualties. *US Navy Medicine*, January-February, 4-7, 1983; Thompson, J., Sandecki, R., Barajas-Gallegos, L. et al: *Report of a Working Group on Women Vietnam Veterans and the Operation Outreach Vietnam Vet Center Program*. VA Monograph. December 15, 1982; Van Devanter, L., *Home Before Morning: The Story of an Army Nurse in Vietnam*. (New York: Beaufort, 1983); Walker, K., *A Piece of My Heart: The Stories of Twenty-Six American Women Who Served in Vietnam*. (New York: Ballantine Books, 1985).

10. For example: Glass, A.J. Psychotherapy in the combat zone. *American Journal of Psychiatry*, 110, 725-731, 1954; Grinker, A.A., and J.P. Spiegel, *Men Under Stress*. (Philadelphia, Blakiston, 1945); Rahe, R.H. Acute versus chronic psychological reactions to combat. *Military Medicine*, 153, 365-372, 1988; Sokol, RJ. Early mental health intervention in combat situations: the USS Stark. *Military Medicine*, 154, 407-409, 1989; Solomon, Z., Benbenishty, R. The role of proximity, immediacy and expectancy in frontline treatment of combat stress reaction among Israelis in the Lebanon War. *American Journal of Psychiatry*, 143: 613-621, 1986. Stokes, J., *Information Paper. Management of Combat Stress and Battle Fatigue: Current Information on US Army Medical Department Doctrine*. HSHA-MB., FSHTX 78234, November, 1990.

Persian Gulf casualties would not be subject to the deafening silence their combat brethren from other wars had suffered.

I remember the moment very clearly. I lightly knocked on Steve Tice's office door at the American Lake VA PTS Treatment Program. I was depressed and agitated. We had just heard that the build up of US troops in Kuwait seemed to be reaching a peak and that armed combat appeared to be quite imminent. I leaned in and simply said, "They've started [the war]. We need to get to work." Steve replied, "It's terrible. Another war! Who knows how many casualties there are going to be? We can't just sit here and do business as usual."

We were busy enough already. Our program continued to be filled to capacity with Vietnam veterans from an 11-state catchment area who were psychiatric casualties. But we could not let this brewing catastrophe go unaddressed. We both sat there for a little while. It was hard to let go of the denial that we might be going to war again. We started discussing what we could do that might have some benefit; we needed to write something very specific for military and health care providers concerning what we knew about the do's and don'ts in working with medical casualties as they are being evacuated from the war zone. Steve's firsthand experiences as a severely wounded combat vet gave him an invaluable perspective and I could add my experiences as a medical service corps officer at the 8th Field Hospital in Nha Trang. (*Pax mentis* was the unofficial unit motto of our 98th Medical Detachment psychiatric team in Vietnam, and outside our mental hygiene clinic in Nha Trang a large sign portrayed Snoopy lying on a couch and a medical caduceus along with the words *pax mentis*. But the entire evacuation and subsequent treatment process gave our vets anything but peace of mind!) Also, we both had been providing therapeutic ser-

---

11. Some of the seminal writings include: Figley, CR (Ed.). *Stress Disorders Among Vietnam Veterans*. (New York, Brunner/Mazel, 1978); Figley, CR (Ed.). *Strangers at Home: Vietnam Veterans Since the War*. (New York: Praeger, 1980); Figley, CR (Ed.), *Trauma and Its Wake, Volume I. The Study and Treatment of Post-Traumatic Stress Disorder*. (New York: Brunner/Mazel, 1985); Kelly, WE (Ed.), *Post-Traumatic Stress Disorder and the War Veteran Patient*. (New York: Brunner/Mazel, 1985); Sonnenberg, S.M., A.S. Blank, J.A. Talbott (Eds.), *The Trauma of War: Stress and Recovery in Viet Nam Veterans*. (Washington, DC: American Psychiatric Press, 1985); Scurfield, RM. Treatment of PTSD among Vietnam veterans, in *The International Handbook of Traumatic Stress Syndromes*. Wilson, J.P. and B. Raphael (Eds.). (New York and London: Plenum Press, 1993); Williams, T. (Ed), *Post-Traumatic Stress Disorders of the Vietnam Veteran: Observations and Recommendations for the Psychological Treatment of the Veteran and His Family*. (Cincinnati: Disabled American Veterans, 1980); Williams, T. (Ed.), *PTSD: A Handbook for Clinicians*. (Cincinnati, Disabled American Veterans, 1987); and Wilson, JP. *Trauma, Transformation and Healing*. (New York: Brunner/Maze, 1989).

vices to war veterans for many years, including many psych casualties who had been medical or psychiatric evacuees from Vietnam and several from the Korean War.

I started to type an initial draft and Steve weighed in with insights of his own, translating my chicken-scratch into something readable and articulating what it was like to be severely wounded and then to go through a series of agonizing medical stages of recovery and relapse (including bitterness and cynicism), and to move along a healing journey of body, mind and spirit.

Military Medicine had given us a deadline. Steve hammered away with his skillful one-hand hunt-and-peck typing and produced the final draft while I was in Los Angeles. But *Military Medicine* wanted the veterans' firsthand narratives, which are interspersed throughout this chapter, to be deleted; this was not the kind of thing they include in their journal. No way. To Steve and me, this was the most powerful part of the article. We insisted: and the veterans' statements still stand.

To help the VA and DOD get ready for expected Gulf War casualties, I was asked to participate in the Office of Emergency Preparedness training of VA staff from 22 primary receiving hospitals in the Eastern United States as part of the VA/DOD contingency plan for Operation Desert Storm. Steve and I wanted to provide the most useful and specific information possible, and to give dramatic "life" from the veterans' experiences to our writing. Therefore, we decided to interview Vietnam veteran inpatients who had been medically evacuated out of the war zone and who were currently hospitalized in the American Lake VA Medical Center PTSD Treatment Program in December, 1990.

An important secondary benefit that came from soliciting this information from current inpatients was that the process helped to at least partly counter their growing negative reactions as hospital patients, for they were becoming increasingly agitated and conflicted as the war was brewing. On the one hand, they deeply wanted our country to be ready to help wounded military personnel with the most knowledgeable and responsive services. On the other hand, many of them were also very much afraid, and enraged, at the possibility — or probability — that once again they were going to be pushed aside as priority was given to the new Operation Desert Storm casualties. After all, that is what happens when a new war comes along: the veterans of previous wars are pushed to the back of the line, or forgotten. Their comments were poignant, and pointed.

A Telegram from Uncle Sam

Western Union telegram 1003A POT May 23 69 LA105 NSB190 NS WA070 EH XV GOV'T PDB

12 EXTRA FAX WASHINGTON DC 23 NFT

Mrs. Lorna Anton, report delivery, don't phone, check dly

442 Madera Sunnyvale Calif

The secretary of the army has asked me to express his deep regret that your son, Specialist Steven Tice, was wounded in action in Vietnam on 18 May 69 by fragments while on a combat operation when a hostile force was encountered. He received wounds to his abdomen with lacerations of the right kidney, the liver, and the diaphragm; wounds to his right arm necessitating surgical amputation of his right arm below the elbow; wounds to his face with facial fractures and lacerations; had wounds to his chest with right hemopneumothorax. He was hospitalized in Vietnam and subsequently evacuated to Japan. He has been placed on the very seriously ill list in Japan and in the judgment of the attending physician his condition is of such severity that the best medical facilities and doctors have been made available and that every measure is being taken to aid him. Address mail to him at the 106th General Hospital, Yokohama, Japan APO SF 96503. You will be notified progress reports and kept informed of any significant changes in his condition. Delay in notifying you of your son's wounds was due to non-receipt of this report in my office.

Kenneth G. Wickham Major General USA C-4150-1

Adjutant General Dep't of the Army Washington DC.

Telegrams reporting the wounds of young Americans were delivered to families throughout the US and "hammered home the stark reality of combat to several hundred thousand families during the Vietnam War."[12] The above was one of those actual telegrams, and it was about Steve. The legacy of Vietnam included 202,704 wounded Americans, of whom over half required serious hospitalizations. Vietnam created an unprecedented number of seriously disabled individuals (some 75,000) in America. Indeed, in previous wars, people with wounds like Steve's had not survived.

The same is true, and even more so, regarding Americans who are severely wounded in the Iraq war. And now, for the first time, the medical community faces the new problem of how to care for persons with severe traumatically-induced disabilities as they age. Few medical personnel have any idea how to provide optimal care for such veterans in their later years, and indeed, may never have seen before anyone with such severe and complicated physical disabilities

---

12. Tice, S.N. et al, 1988.

24

— at any age. The numbers of such casualties will be more than matched by other veterans who experienced less severe wounds but find that their condition is deteriorating through the natural aging process.[13]

Such a specter haunted us at the outbreak of the Persian Gulf War, and led the VA and the DOD to conduct a series of training sessions around the country to help prepare for the potential onslaught of casualties.

EMOTIONAL STATES COMMON TO RECENT EVACUEES FOR A WAR ZONE

Steve and I came up with a list of common features in the trauma experienced by a recently and seriously injured, wounded, or psychiatric casualty who has been evacuated out of a war zone. The impact extends well beyond the overt clinical symptoms (both physical and psychological) that are manifested and attended to as the primary treatment concern. Traumatic experiences regularly occurred immediately after they were wounded: experiences that have never been discussed, simply because the focus had been on the wounding itself and life- and organ-saving emergency procedures to stabilize the acute medical condition.

> "I was aware that not everyone got treatment in the initial triage area [those deemed too seriously injured to survive were by-passed so that more immediate treatment could be given to those judged to be more likely to survive]. And so, I fought to stay awake to make a case for myself to receive treatment. I was afraid that I was too badly wounded to receive treatment and would be left to die." — Steve Tice

The actual process of being evacuated by chopper out of the battlefield in and of itself may have been extraordinarily traumatic.

> "There were shots all around me as I was being put on the chopper; I was so scared, and when the chopper took off, it got hit and we crashed. I was even more terrified. We then got put on a second chopper, and I was so scared the whole time that we'd be shot down again."

The patient typically has received relatively rapid transport through several levels of medical triage, stabilization, and treatment. The abrupt transition from one stage to the next is fraught with anxiety and confusion. With each move comes a termination of any degree of comfort, security and familiarity that may have developed at a previous medical receiving site, as well as under-

---

13. This and the next quotes in this section are from: US Congress, House of Representatives, Vietnam Veterans Leadership Program, *Congressional Record* (October 1, 1982), E4641.

standable concern about the seriousness of the injury or a natural preoccupation with an as yet unstabilized condition and an uncertain prognosis.

The medical evacuation flights were another possibly traumatic event.

"The medevac flight back [from Japan to Stateside] was bizarre. We were placed on cots attached to the walls of the plane at least two rows high, one atop the other; the rest of the plane had seats. Because of safety [concerns], my mother wasn't allowed to visit with me, but had to remain strapped into her seat. The guy above me couldn't control his arm and it kept falling over the side of his cot, striking me and bleeding on me." — Steve Tice

Even for psychiatric casualties:

"One of my worst experiences as a psychiatric casualty was the med-evac flight back to the US, where I was with a whole plane full of severely wounded vets. It was a horrible ride. I have so much guilt out of that plane ride, and no one's ever asked me about it."[14]

And perhaps most of all, there was the fear of the unknown. How serious are my wounds? Will I recover, or die? If I do recover, will I be only half a man? Harried medical staff rarely have the presence of mind to attend to this crying need.

"No one ever explained to me what they were doing, or why. Doctors have a tendency to keep us in the dark. We have a right to know!"

"The hospital staff at Letterman in San Francisco was under orders as late as July (I had been wounded in May) to not tell me about the disfigurement of my face. I never even saw myself in a mirror for months. When I did, it was very upsetting. They also were under orders not to tell me my weight (90 pounds). Of course, someone eventually did tell me." — Steve Tice

The terror surrounding the wounding and med-evac oftentimes was not relieved by hospitalization. The soldier, although now removed from the battlefield and placed in the relative safety of the hospital, might experience a return of the initial terror because he was constantly exposed to his peers' cries as they struggled with their wounds, and indeed, sometimes, died.

"A guy next to me had a blown-up face. We lay there, next to each other, for days. I still haven't forgotten, and no one has ever asked me about this."

"I knew I shouldn't do it, but I let myself get close to a guy in the bed next to me in Japan. We both were going through so much pain and fear, and anger and grief, how could we not bond to some degree? And then he died, right there next to me. And I watched them trying to save him, but it was no use. And then they took his body

---

14. This and all subsequent quotes in this chapter are from Scurfield, RM and SN Tice, *Interventions with Medical and Psychiatric Casualties and Their Families: From Vietnam through the Gulf War* (1992).

away and his bed was empty. And then a few hours later a new guy was brought in to be next to me. And it started all over again."

It is not commonly understood that considerable stress may have been generated during early phases of evacuation, because there may have been a time when it was unclear whether or not the patient would go back to the war zone. This uncertainty and ambivalence are stressful in themselves, heightening the patient's fear, anxiety, and guilt.

It is not surprising that during these stages of evacuation and extending into the period of stateside hospitalization, the patient would typically experience a host of bewildering emotions, cognitions, and reactions. These include reality-based feelings of loss of control over physical body and emotions, cognitive abilities, and behaviors. The soldier may have experienced severe mood swings, helplessness, feelings of intimidation, powerlessness, confusion, depression, anger, and/or numbing of feelings.

"I was so angry, at everyone. Why me, Lord? Part of me wished that I had died rather than have to face a life as a cripple."

If the veteran had serious physical injuries or wounds, there was a natural tendency towards preoccupation by both the patient and the health care provider with treatment and recovery from the physical condition. There was also a very strong tendency, again for both patient and provider, to avoid the expression or discussion of emotional issues at this time. Common denial and avoidance mechanisms included simply denying having any significant feelings or emotional issues, excessive use of medications or alcohol, absorption in television, and exaggerated joking. Comparisons with others was used as a coping tool.

"Staff would collude with us to shame people who complained by saying things like, 'what are you whining about, Jones has no limbs at all!' That kept people from focusing on what may have seemed overwhelming, as someone else could always be found who had it worse." — Steve Tice

The patient may have become overly passive and remained silent in the face of inquiry by others or, conversely, may have excessively ruminated or exploded in anger.

"I got so damn angry, and I just couldn't take it anymore. I reached up and grabbed the IV bottle and threw the damn thing across the room. Then, I started throwing my meal all around. I was cursing and shouting. I really lost it, and I feel so guilty that I took it out on the nurses."

One veteran reported how he had become sensitized as to what behaviors to engage in to get what he wanted: more drugs.

"You know, we learned real quickly about what would happen if we argued with staff, complained too much, or came across as too "demanding." They would raise our meds! So we quickly learned the ropes: if we wanted more meds to numb out more, then just be disruptive and a pain in the ass, they'd pump us full. If we didn't want more meds, then just be quiet and not bother anyone."

The veterans reported that certain aspects of the way they were treated exacerbated their stress and frustration. For example, just a simple thing about how they would be repeatedly asked if they were OK would drive them up the wall.

"Don't ask, 'how are you doing,' or, 'Are you OK?' That's bull; of course we'll answer, 'I'm fine,' or 'I'm OK.' Do ask, 'What are you feeling?'"

"Have an attitude and approach that communicates 'I care,' and 'I know; I understand that you're going through all kinds of emotions right now,' or that "you're numbing out and don't want to talk — but it's really important that you do, now.'"

What came through loud and clear from the vets who had been hospitalized was that they wanted some positive attention, to have staff interact with them as if they were human beings who had feelings to be considered, not just bodies with physical wounds.

"We needed much more personal contact with the doctors and nurses than their standing around at the foot of the bed, reading a chart and making some notes in it. Pull up a chair, sit down, and at least look interested, for God's sake!"

Hospitalized veterans described a few typical hospital situations as being extremely dehumanizing and unnecessarily stressful. In addition to the demeaning way in which "grand rounds" were conducted (mentioned above),

"It's really intimidating as a confused, scared, suspicious vet, to be called into a treatment planning session and be cross-examined by a group of staff."

I'm not criticizing all Navy medical personnel, especially not our corpsmen, but when we were in the Navy hospitals there seemed to be a real condescending attitude towards us Jarheads [e.g., Marines]. We didn't need that.

Of course, medical stabilization and acutely needed interventions clearly had to be a priority in the early stages of the medical evacuation process. However, in the early phases of recovery and treatment, it also would have been critical for staff to be demonstratively supportive and caring, even when such attention was not easy for the patient to accept. Evacuees oftentimes would experience nightmares, flashbacks, and depression that might be accentuated by narcotic medications and/or fever. This in itself was terrifying, and patients should be advised that it is normal and expectable.

Hospitalized veterans remember vividly how they were treated by various hospital staff. A repeated plea was that staff who are working with seriously injured veterans behave appropriately and considerately with their patients.

> "Please be careful about having staff with the right attitudes and knowledge on the ward; don't assume that all the staff want to work with us, or with Middle East casualties. Please take volunteers only."

> "It may be very inappropriate to have "part-time" residents, interns, etc., to work with war casualties. They won't know anything about the military, veterans or war. It's not fair for them to be learning on us."

And the veterans' concerns about the hospital staff were not confined to the doctors and nurses. Paraprofessional staff have much more contact with patients than do most of the professional staff, and can have an inordinate influence on the hospital experience of the patient, both good and bad.

> "Support staff on the wards are really important on the night shifts, the maintenance staff, administrative people, etc. Please make sure that they are sensitive to us and have the right attitude. Some of them have a lot more contact with us than the professionals. They could be really helpful, and some were very cruel and had a lot of power over us after hours."

A common misconception was that once the acute medical treatment had been accomplished, the veteran was not going to face significant further physical and emotional trauma. Wrong. For a number of veterans, their hospital stays were characterized by a seemingly never-ending series of very serious medical concerns and procedures. Additional physical trauma may well have occurred at various later stages; for example, one or more amputations.

> "It went on for months, trying to save my arm from being amputated. But then, it had to be amputated. And that was a really terrible time, after months of keeping my hopes up that my arm could be saved. And then it was taken."

As the veterans' hospital stay began drawing to a close, several reported that they were not given very much (or accurate) information about their benefits or what they were entitled to.

> "I felt very uninformed about my benefits. Could I get an early medical discharge, what kind of medical disability benefits was I entitled to? This information seemed to be kept a secret from me."

Another common complaint was that once they left the hospital, absolutely no one ever followed up to contact them and check up on how they were doing. This lack of follow-up reinforced feelings of being abandoned and forgotten.

"There was absolutely no follow-up when I left the hospital. Now, I may not have been very receptive to such contact at the time, but absolutely no contact did not help my negative attitude about the military and the government using and then discarding me when I was broken and of no further use."

FAMILIES OF MEDICALLY EVACUATED AND HOSPITALIZED MILITARY PATIENTS

The relationship between the evacuated and hospitalized veterans and their families was also crucial, of course, and often rife with difficulties. First, there was a logistical problem; when personnel have been medically evacuated out of a war zone, they may be sent to a hospital quite distant from their family. Space availability, the need for specialized treatment, random chance, and other factors may dictate that the initial hospitalization, at least, may be far from the patient's home. This makes it difficult or impossible for either staff or patient to maintain accurate and sufficient communication with the family. It also strains the family's financial situation.

"Please evacuate vets close to their families. I was really angry to be evacuated to a hospital so far from home. It was financially disastrous to my family and many other families that we weren't in a nearby hospital."

Several vets gave some practical advice about the initial notification to the family that one's son or daughter had been medically evacuated to a specific hospital:

"Why not have service organizations (or the Red Cross) go out and notify families personally that a vet has been evacuated, not just a telephone call from someone at the hospital?"

Primary clinical needs concerning hospitalized patients and their families include the necessity of communicating accurate information about the patient and his/her condition and prognosis to the family, and facilitating interactions between patient and family to optimize the patient's recovery process. It is common for evacuated patients and/or their families to have strong mixed feelings about communicating with each other. One must not assume that the recently evacuated patient desires or is even willing to have family visit during the initial stages of recovery. Indeed, ambivalence about contact with family and friends may persist far into the recovery process.

And yet, a healthy stress recovery process dictates that expeditious communication and interaction is necessary and ultimately therapeutic for both the patient and the family; such interaction may well be awkward and will certainly benefit from professional staff guidance and preparation prior to the first face-to-face meeting and during the hospital course as well.

Vietnam veterans who had been medically or psychiatrically evacuated out of the war zone offered the following opinions about possible future interactions with the families of Persian Gulf medical evacuees. First, don't assume that they will want to see or contact their families. Give them the courtesy of discussing it with the veteran first.

"I was never asked for permission to have staff call my family."

"I was given money to call home; I didn't want to, and the staff was pushy."

"No one ever explained to me what they were doing, never asked how I felt, and so I never got to resolve issues with my family."

Formerly hospitalized veterans had very concrete advice regarding the hospital social worker's communications with the family. Perhaps the most poignant request concerned something that most families would have no way to understand: that their veteran might refuse to see family members, or feel extremely ambivalent about such a meeting:

"Please tell the family they should try to talk to the vet, even when we don't seem to want to!"

"Please talk to the family ahead of time, educate them regarding acute emotional shock and denial."

"Make absolutely sure that you prepare the family for what I actually look like, what my physical condition is, what they will see when they first walk into my hospital room. My family was absolutely unprepared for what they were going to see when they walked in and they were devastated; my father actually turned around and left the room! He couldn't tolerate seeing me in the condition I was in."

During the family's initial visit with the evacuated soldier, both the evacuee and the visitors often experience great anxiety. Family members may respond with feelings of repulsion in reaction to the veteran's wounds and/or deep sadness marked by uncontrollable crying.

Family members had trouble with eye contact and would physically distance themselves from us — as if they could catch an amputation like a cold.— Steve Tice

There is often much discomfort and awkwardness as well as physical and emotional distancing on the part of both the soldier and the family. This may include difficulty making eye contact or fear of making reference to the evacuee's wounds. Guilt or anger experienced by family members during the initial meeting or through subsequent reflection may lead to avoiding or minimizing further contact. Vets had specific suggestions about what to say to or ask their family.

- Please talk to the family and explain what you are doing and why, such as if I'm on medications and what they're for; if I'm depressed or suicidal and why, etc."

- Don't give them diagnostic labels; talk instead about what the symptoms are, what the vet needs."

- Inquire about the vet's military career status. Did he/she volunteer? If so, how does the family feel about it? Are they liable to think, "It's your fault, then?"

- Find out the vet's emotional history from the family; for example, any trauma in the vet's background?

The vets currently hospitalized for PTSD treatment made a fervent plea:

"Please involve us with any hospitalized vets who are medically evacuated here from the Persian Gulf. Many of us are unemployed and we have the time and want to be involved. It's important to us, and vet-to-vet support could be crucial to getting through to them."

The family of the evacuated veteran faces multiple challenges prior to reuniting with the veteran and following that reunion. Indeed, the family often experiences guilt and anger regarding the injury which may have resulted from the family's belief in their complicity in the veteran having gone to war, i.e., the family may actually have, or believe that they have, sent, encouraged, or "allowed" the veteran to go to war. And, the family may have projected anger towards the veteran for having been injured, and/or with the military and the government for their part in the event. In addition:

"Social workers needed to be on hand to assist family members, not only in the first contact, but also to assist in the loss and grief process... Everyone is experiencing loss in the family, not just the vet." — Steve Tice

For psychiatric evacuees, anger and confusion may arise as both the veteran and the family wonder why there was a "breakdown." There may have been a shamed sense that this breakdown reflected a weakness or inadequacy on the part of the evacuee or, indeed, on the part of the family. Shame and guilt may have emerged, and manifested as belief that blame must be attributed, i.e., "It's my fault" or "I did a poor job as a parent."

The family normally enters this new relationship with the injured evacuee with preconceived notions related to physical and psychiatric disabilities, the government, the military, and war. The family might have held strong opinions regarding the "rightness" of the particular war in which the injury took place as well as with the events leading to the soldier's entry into combat. Such views can seriously hinder communication while the vet is in the hospital and following his or her discharge. Finally, the family and the veteran may experience confusion and uncertainty regarding appropriate communication and interaction when the veteran has returned home.

Knowledgeable therapists have been able to assist, for example, by bringing the family and the veteran together at the hospital to practice specific likely courses of conversation and rehearse interventions associated with probable uncomfortable situations. Many therapists (social workers, counselors, psychologists) have little understanding of the military world and culture, and specifically of the trials that await a wounded soldier returning stateside. They may overlook the many related issues, as may the family — and even the recovering veteran.[15]

"Of course, a minority of vets actually had any visitors. Some never did. My family was there EVERY day after the first week (when they didn't know I was wounded). I awoke from multiple surgeries to ALWAYS see a family member or more likely members. They also supported the other family-less vets...there were usually two to three families on the ward at all times. I'm still friends with some of them. I KNEW I was loved and credit that for my survival. God's messengers. I bring this up because there needs to be a balance, to show what healthy families being present can do for their vets. Of course, some are not geographically close enough. Where there is a will...my sister moved into nurses' quarters at Letterman and then got an apartment nearby. Both parents flew to Japan when I was evacuated there from Vietnam. The Red Cross paid my Mom's airfare. My Dad took out a loan." — Steve Tice

---

15. Fortunately, other assistance also may be available. The military equivalent of family service centers — also known as Fleet and Family Service Centers (Navy), Army Community Service and Family Support Centers (Air Force) — are very important in providing support, counseling and practical assistance to the family while the spouse is deployed overseas and upon return. Ombudspersons play an invaluable role; they are spouses of active duty personnel designated to intercede on behalf of the various families within in a military unit, and typically are coordinated or led by the spouse of the base command or spouse of larger military units within the command. Also, the Red Cross historically has served as an important link between servicepersons and their families, providing arrangements for emergency leave and travel from overseas in response to family deaths and other crises that require the presence of the spouse. Veterans Service Organizations or VSOs, such as the American Legion, Disabled American Veterans, AMVETS, Veterans of Foreign Wars and Paralyzed Veterans of America, have a vast network of service officers and chapters nationwide to serve both hospitalized and other veterans and their families. Military and civilian hospitals, to include the VA, also have social work services that serve as a primary connection and support link between the hospitalized patient and the family.

In conclusion, to hear Vietnam veterans so eloquently describe their experiences throughout the entire medical evacuation process, from battlefield to stateside hospital, was a sobering experience. Unfortunately, it confirmed the fear that many aspects of this experience added to the trauma of the injury; they were (often) unspoken sources of great pain, confusion and anger; and many health care providers, family members and the community were oftentimes quite unaware of them.

No wonder, Steve and I thought, so many wounded and disabled war veterans had not recovered as well from their psychological wounds as they had from their physical wounds. And our country was now entering the Persian Gulf War and anticipating many new casualties. Thankfully, there were not, in fact, large numbers of casualties on the US side that time. Unfortunately, since President Bush declared war on Iraq in 2003, we don't yet have a good idea as to the numbers and extent of the medical evacuation and rehabilitation problems that are now being visited upon the many thousands of Americans wounded in the Iraq War. Have we, the military and civilian health and mental health providers, learned all we could from the veterans evacuated from Vietnam, and are we in a position to advise the families and friends of the untold numbers of new American war casualties?

THE IRAQ WAR AND MEDICAL EVACUEES

Survival rates of soldiers injured in Iraq are far higher than for any other war in US history. In fact, as of November 16, 2004, only 10% of the total US wounded in Iraq and Afghanistan have died. This is more than two times better than the rate for the Vietnam War (24%) and about three times better than the World War II rate of 30%. However, a large proportion of the injuries among surviving combatants are devastating in their severity and will have a profound life-long impact on the combatants and their families.[16] The lessons we could have been taught by the Vietnam War must be learned fast, now, and used to help the current wave of casualties and their families.

Indeed, extraordinary life-saving services are now available to combat units in the war zone. A remarkable 98% of wounded combatants who are still alive by the time medical personnel arrive now survive their injuries. However, such life-

---

16. Homans, Charles, "Analysis: More soldiers surviving combat injuries." *SunHerald*, Biloxi, MS. December 9, 2004, p. B-1.

saving success at the battlefield is predicted to swell the number of psycho-logical casualties among wounded soldiers as they ultimately "must come to terms not only with emotional scars but the literal scars of amputated limbs and disfiguring injuries."[17]

The symptoms of PTSD may not emerge until months or years after dis-charge from the military. Hence, any psychiatric casualty rates being reported by the military during wartime inevitably underreport the eventual longer-term casualty rate.[18] And so, besides the obvious lessons revealed by the veterans we interviewed, there are additional lessons that need to be applied as we relate to Iraq war veterans.

DO'S AND DON'TS CONCERNING HOSPITALIZED AND PHYSICALLY DISABLED VETERAN PATIENTS[19]

Along with attention to physical injuries and disabilities, it is essential that health care providers systematically and proactively reach out to hospitalized veterans and to their families while the veteran is in the earlier phases of treatment. Clinical experiences and recent studies all indicate quite clearly that physically disabled veterans are among the highest risk groups of war veterans to develop PTSD. The prevalence of PTSD among wounded Vietnam veterans is over 30%[20]; in contrast, the prevalence rate among all Vietnam veterans is almost half that, 15.2%[21] to 16.8%.[22]

There is a cardinal rule in working with veterans who have been seriously wounded and/or disabled. Don't accept at face value their assertions that the injury/illness and med-evac/triage/treatment process had no impact on them or

---

17. Shane, Scott, "A flood of troubled soldiers is in the offing, experts predict." *New York Times*, December 16, 2004, p. 2.
18. Ibid.
19. Much of the following information is excerpted from Scurfield and Tice, 1992.
20. Buydens-Branchey, L., D. Noumair and J. Branachey. Duration and intensity of combat exposure and posttraumatic stress disorder in Vietnam veterans. *Journal of Nervous and Mental Disorders, 178,* 1990: 582-587; Kulka, R.A., W.E. Schlenger, JA Fairbank et al: *Trauma and the Vietnam War Generation: Report of Findings from the National Vietnam Veterans Readjustment Study.* (New York: Brunner/Mazel, 1990); Pitman, RK, B Altman, ML Maclin: Prevalence of posttraumatic stress disorder in wounded Vietnam veterans. *American Journal of Psychiatry, 146:* 667-669, 1989.
21. Kulka et al, 1990.
22. Goldberg, J., W.R. True, S.A. Eisen, et al: A twin study of the effects of the Vietnam War on post-traumatic stress disorder. *Journal of the American Medical Association, 263:* 1990, 1227-1232.

was "uneventful." Indeed, the entire evacuation process must be carefully assessed as a routine part of any psycho-social inquiry. For example, there is a high probability that deaths or traumatic and unexpected additional radical medical procedures may have occurred to others in the immediate vicinity of the veteran. Always inquire: had the veteran gotten close to anyone who died or suffered a terrible deterioration in his condition while in the hospital? How did this affect the veteran's feelings about himself and about his condition?

Compared to their able-bodied veteran cohorts, physically disabled veterans are apparently reluctant to utilize specialized PTSD programs; this in itself suggests that there is a need for a proactive approach to address psycho-social issues early in their hospitalization. Health care providers are strongly encouraged to consider a proactive screening of all patients medically evacuated out of a war zone for possible adverse psychological reactions. The Mississippi Scale for Combat-Related PTSD[23] has been one of the best psychometric instruments available as a general screen for war-related PTSD, as reported by the researchers who conducted the National Vietnam Veterans Readjustment Study.[24] Considerable additional work has been accomplished by the VA National Center for PTSD, Boston Division, on screening instruments specifically designed for armed forces personnel who have been deployed and their families.[25]

Further, it is important to provide psycho-educational information regarding traumatic stress and typical reactions to physical and emotional trauma. This information can be provided on the wards in both group and individual modalities.

> "Please start groups quickly in the hospital, educating us about why we feel the way we do, and what you're doing. And the vets will definitely resist such debriefings, but please be insistent. And maybe a fellow or sister vet on the staff will be able to get through to us when other staff can't."[26]

The emotional state of most recent evacuees who were rapidly transported from a war zone is frequently confused, disoriented, and preoccupied. This is to be expected, and it is strongly encouraged that patient and family be advised

23. Keane, T., J. Cadel, K. Taylor: Mississippi scale for combat-related PTSD: three studies in reliability and validity. *Journal of Consulting and Clinical Psychology* 56, 1988: 85-90.
24. Marmar, C., personal communication, 1991.
25. See King, D.W., L.A. King and D.S. Vogt, *Manual for the Deployment Risk and Resilience Inventory* (DRR) A Collection of Measures for Studying Deployment-Related Experiences of Military Veterans. (Boston, MA: National Center for PTSD, 2004).
26. Scurfield and Tice, 1992, p. 90.

about this, at least in some part, in written hand-outs that they can refer to later, when they may be better able to digest the information.

During hospitalization, it is critical for health care providers to facilitate, at minimum, an initial discussion with both the veteran and the family focusing on the range of guilt, loss, and adjustment issues which will be faced upon the soldier's return to peacetime military service or to civilian life. The depth of the inquiry will clearly depend on the status of the soldier's physical wounds as well as his emotional receptivity to such issues.

However, at minimum, such exploration may open a door to later examination of feelings associated with the wounding and disability and may be the foundation for important grief work undertaken at a later juncture.

> "How are you feeling about having become a casualty and having been evacuated (in terms of what you believe your unit thought of you as well as what you thought of them; feelings about yourself; what your family might think, before and after actually seeing you)?"

> "How has your disability or condition affected your relationship with your family (parents, siblings, spouse, children, extended family) and friends, including issues of physical intimacy? What are your future expectations?"

Attribution issues will always be present concerning how and why you were wounded/injured/psychiatrically impaired.

> "Do you feel you were totally or partly at fault, was it "bad luck," are you a victim of fate, are you enraged and do you blame your commanding officer, another military person(s), or the military?"

Denial and minimizing are common: This is the "comparison" coping attempt. "My wounds (or condition) don't mean that much: look at how much worse others are." "I shouldn't be having these feelings, I'm much better off than so many others are."

Soldiers learn in collusion with staff to minimize the severity of their injuries. Stoical ones are rewarded compared to "whiners." Stoicism can, initially, be a useful tool, but eventually the soldier must have permission to grieve his/her losses.

> "Do you want and will you be allowed to remain on active duty? What are your (and your family's) feelings about this?"

> "Do you wish you could return to a war zone? Is that realistic? Is it that you have 'unfinished business' to complete there? If so, what is your unfinished business?"

> "What were the veteran's reactions to the differences between overseas and stateside military hospitals; between military hospitals and VA hospitals?"[27]

The months and years spent in stateside hospitals can be extremely stressful and these experiences are generally not addressed in treatment. Again, in the American Lake PTSD Program we considered the entire period from the time of the wounding or injury through discharge from a stateside hospital as a "second tour of duty" to be assessed and thoroughly debriefed utilizing clinical strategies similar to those used in working through war-zone trauma. Framing it in this way also gives a powerful message to the wounded/disabled veteran: we recognize what you went through and you have the right (and need) to talk about it.

All that has been discussed in this chapter is pertinent to medical evacuees from the Iraq War, in which American soldiers are being wounded at the highest rate since the Vietnam War. These are the so-called "hidden casualties." Sara Corbett, in spending considerable time with severely injured members of the 101st Airborne Division, remarked:

> "It was dawning on the soldiers that they were expendable. As they saw it, the war was going on without them. The Army was going on without them. The nation was going on without them. What they're going through is so profound to them, yet so little attention is paid to it. And they may have to deal with it for the rest of their lives."[28]

Yes, they will have to deal with it for the rest of their lives. That is a given. You don't lose body parts and functions and not have it impact you from then on. And, as soldiers are surviving explosions and gunfire in greater numbers than in previous wars (due to advances in body armor and battlefield medicine), once the immediate life-saving and stabilization interventions have been completed and physical, vocational and emotional rehabilitation are underway, care providers are encouraged to pursue not only the issues described herein, but also issues of sacrifice and loss as well as concerns surrounding self image, as part of the longer-term recovery of the veteran.

Finally, spirituality issues are of great importance for many veterans and assessment and appropriate referral are essential to the healing process.[29]

> "Eventually, recovery is cloaked in the value of sacrifice. What meaning can be found in the losses incurred and how do they measure up with the life being led? This is ultimately a spiritual process and therapists would do well to have an awareness of the survivor's spiritual or religious background. Loss must be grieved.

---

27. Ibid.
28. Corbett, Sara, "The Permanent Scars of Iraq." *The New York Times Magazine*, February 15, 2004, p. 4.

The survivor ultimately wishes to be put back together spiritually, emotionally and physically as he or she was before the injury. This is not possible.

"I have referred to my own intransigence as a young man in this area as my humpty-dumpty theory. That is, "the government broke me; they have to put me back together again." By adopting this attitude, I allowed myself to become dependent on the government for the outcome of my life. When I began taking responsibility for my recovery, I truly began healing. Joseph Campbell, the late mythologist, said: where one stumbles, there lies his treasure. Our wounding is where our gift lies.

"To utilize the compassion gained in the healing process to assist others in a like process is one avenue to accessing a survivor's journey. That is, if I were told shortly after my wounding that I would find meaning in that wounding at some point — I would and did reject such blasphemy — for what meaning could come from having one's body shredded by a rocket-propelled grenade! Yet, once the grief of such loss is digested and a meaningful reconnection with community afforded, doors open to the heart. The survivor is freed to return home with the gifts to society only the witness can bring." — Steve Tice

---

29. Scurfield and Tice, 1992. For a discussion of spirituality issues, see for example two writings by Vietnam veterans: Tice, Steven N., *From Trauma to Enlightenment. The Survivor's Journey*, Gig Harbor, WA, unpublished manuscript; and Mahedy, William, *Out of the Night: The Spiritual Journey of Vietnam Veterans* (New York: Ballantine Books, 1986). Also see Campbell, Joseph, *The Hero With a Thousand Faces*; Kuenning, Delores, *Life After Vietnam: How Veterans and Their Loved Ones Can Heal the Psychological Wounds of War*; and Wilson, John P., *Trauma, Transformation and Healing: An Integrative Approach to Theory, Research and Post-Traumatic Therapy* (New York: Brunner/Mazel, 1989).

CHAPTER 3. COLLUSION: SANITIZING AND SILENCING THE TRUTH ABOUT THE IMPACT OF WAR

As Operation Desert Storm and the Persian Gulf War unfolded in the early 1990s, with massive television coverage, naturally there was a concern about forecasts of major casualties when we invaded Iraq. At the same time, the US military and governmental strategy, and media coverage, markedly downplayed the extent of Iraqi civilian casualties. This reflects the historic and continuing legacy of our country's tendency to sanitize and impose silence about the full impact of war and the totality of the human costs. Readers may judge for themselves how similar the following description of the Persian Gulf War is to the circumstances of the American military occupation of Iraq.

There also was a major and controversial VA program evaluation outcome study of the specialized PTSD programs that VA national officials used to justify the implementation of radical, centrally-directed reductions and changes in PTSD programs nationwide. Then, several groups of Soviet Afghantsi veterans visited our PTSD program in American Lake, Tacoma, WA. This series of interchanges between US Vietnam veterans and Soviet Afghantsi veterans kindled long-held issues about Russian involvement in Vietnam, and resurrected issues about how the governments had been less than forthcoming with their nations about the progress and human costs of the wars. The resulting interchanges promoted a remarkable cross-cultural interchange and discovery of common bonds between soldiers of two countries long at odds with each other — and laid further groundwork for the rationale of returning to Vietnam to face old enemies

.

A DECADES-LONG HISTORY OF SELECTIVE AMNESIA AND DENIAL

Our country has had a long history of a collusion of silence about the full human impact of war. I am not going to give a detailed accounting of this history, as much of it has been eloquently described elsewhere.[30] Most of us — the medical professions, the military, society and even many veterans themselves — have perpetuated a remarkable pattern of collective amnesia by which we deny the full social and psychological impact of war on its participants. This collusion of denial has been characterized by a convergence of military, medical and political forces that are responsible to maintain a fighting force: ready and able to engage in a war, to continue and finish the war successfully, and then afterwards to marshal sufficient human and fiscal resources to respond to the next threat to our country. It happened about Vietnam; and it's happening in Iraq.

Both during and immediately following a war, you will notice that when talking about acute psychiatric casualties, military and military psychiatry officials tend to claim that acute psychiatric interventions have been highly effective.[31] At best, this is a disingenuous practice that highlights what was done to "conserve the fighting strength during war-time." At the same time it avoids any conscientious effort to evaluate the longer-term post-war impact of war on its veterans. After all, the long-term problems have historically been considered to be something for the Department of Veterans Affairs to address and not the Department of Defense.

I can only say that this consistent pattern of avoidance of investigating the longer-term impact of war has been short-sighted and/or purposeful. Would not an awareness of, or an emphasis on, the longer-term impact of war and the

---

30. See, for example: Kutchins, H., and S.A. Kirk, *Making Us Crazy. DSM: The Psychiatric Bible and the Creation of Mental Disorders* (New York: The Free Press, 1997); Boulanger, G., "Post-traumatic stress disorder: An old problem with a new name," in Sonnenberg, S.M., A.S. Blank and J.A. Talbott (Eds), *Stress and Recovery in Vietnam Veterans* (Washington, DC: American Psychiatric Association, 1985), 13-29; Goodwin, J., "The etiology of combat-related post-traumatic stress disorders," in Williams, T., (Ed.), *Post-Traumatic Stress Disorders: A Handbook for Clinicians* (Cincinnati, OH: Disabled American Veterans, 1987), 1-15; Figley, CR, "Introduction" (xiii-xvi) and Kormos, H., "The nature of combat stress" (3-22) in Figley, CR (Ed.), *Stress Disorders Among Vietnam Veterans* (New York: Brunner/Mazel, 1978); Solomon, Z., *Combat Stress Reaction. The Enduring Toll of War* (New York: Plenum Press, 1993): and Wiest, A., LP Root and RM Scurfield, "Post-traumatic stress disorder: The legacy of war. In Jensen, G., and A. Wiest (Eds.), *War in the Age of Technology* (New York: New York University Press, 2001), 295-232.
31. Camp, NH and CH Carney, "US Army psychiatry in Vietnam: From confidence to dismay," *California Biofeedback*, 7(3), (Summer, 1991), 11-12, 15-17.

extent of the sacrifices it entails severely hamper efforts to recruit military personnel for future wars?

COLLUSION TO SANITIZE AND DENY THE IMPACT OF WAR: MYTHS AND REALITY

On an individual level, active duty military personnel who have served in a war zone contribute to the collusion of sanitization and silence about the personal impact war has had on themselves. It is essential to remember that, upon return from any war zone, nearly all veterans tend to downplay both to themselves and to others the presence of any serious issues that might be related to their war experiences. Most other veterans do, too. A typical response seems to be, "I need to put the war behind me and move on." On the face of it, this is an appropriate attitude, and a majority of veterans are able to actualize this attitude; but a sizable minority are not.

The inability to move on is complicated by several myths about military war veterans. [32]Individuals and society as a whole tend to believe that "Heroes don't [or should not] have any problems."

This myth was shared by many Gulf War veterans, family members and others, and has been applied to US veterans of military actions in Panama, Grenada, Korea, and both World Wars. [33]

Some readers may not be aware of the frequency and duration of the military conflicts and wars just since World War I in which the United States had a major — or *the* major — military combat role. These include: World War II (1941-45); the Korean War (1950-53); the Vietnam War (officially from 1964-75); the invasion of Grenada (1983); Operation Just Cause in Panama (1989); the Persian Gulf War (1991); Afghanistan and Iraq (2003-current). In addition there have been numerous "peace-keeping" deployments of US military forces (Bosnia, Somalia et al), and innumerable covert operations by elite special military units

---

32. A much more extensive discussion of myths and realities about the impact of war, which extend beyond sanitization and silence, is found in Volume III of *A Vietnam Trilogy*. This includes the myth that talking about one's trauma experience will necessarily lead to re-immersion in the trauma memories and provoke a loss of control, or reduce one's ability to function.
33. Scurfield, R.M., "Needs of returning Gulf War veterans and their families: A Department of Veterans Affairs perspective." Presentation on the national satellite teleconference: *The VA/DoD Continuing Response to Our Returning Veterans* (Salt Lake City Utah: Regional Learning Resources Services (142), Salt Lake VA Medical Center, September 16, 1991).

and the Central Intelligence Agency in Latin America, Africa, the Middle and the Far East that were never labeled officially as wars. Indeed, in many cases, the very presence of US military and CIA forces was minimized, not acknowledged, or denied.

These myths send an extremely negative message to any veterans of *any* war who might be experiencing post-war symptoms or problems:

> "You must be weak of character or psychiatrically troubled if you have any war-related problems."

Family and friends also may actively practice a second myth that they will repeat directly to the veteran, or will whisper among themselves:

> "The war is over; you should just forget about it and move on with your life."

By believing and reinforcing this myth, the family and friends of the war-trauma survivor give a profound double message. First, if you don't move on with your life, you alone are the cause of your problems; the war was inconsequential enough that you certainly ought to be able to just put it aside. And second, this message persuades the veteran him- or herself, not to mention the family and friends, to avoid having any meaningful discussion of his/her war experiences. This contributes to the collusion of avoidance and ignorance in American society, preventing many from achieving a realistic comprehension of what war is all about.

The consequences of this double message can be severe. Essentially getting the message that their war experience was insignificant, veterans are likely to distance themselves from others and to feel alienated, angry, marginalized, not understood or accepted. Yes, a number of veterans are able to "move on with their lives." However, when the war-related issues and reactive detachment and denial mechanisms are severe enough, a troubled or disordered post-trauma process occurs.[34]

The National Vietnam Veterans Readjustment Study (NVVRS) showed that 30.9% of all male Vietnam veterans and 26.9% of all women Vietnam veterans developed full-blown PTSD at some time in their post-war lives, and an additional 22.5% of male and 21.2% of female Vietnam veterans developed "partial" PTSD.[35]

---

34. Hammond, K.W, R.M. Scurfield and S.C. Risse, "Post-traumatic stress disorder," in D.L. Dunner (Ed.), *Current Psychiatric Therapy* (Philadelphia: W.B. Saunders Company, 1993), 288-295.
35. Kulka et al, 1990.

Another related powerful myth seems to be entrenched in our culture:

"Time heals all wounds."

First of all, this is patently not true. About one-fourth of Vietnam War veterans continued to have significant "partial" or full-blown PTSD at the time the sophisticated and extensive national study of Vietnam veterans was conducted in the mid-late 1980s, well over a decade since they served.[36]

Second, this myth supports the false notion that war zone returnees who continue to manifest "re-adjustment problems" for a prolonged time must have been unstable to begin with, or must have had significant problems prior to military service, which would explain their current war or post-war difficulties. This is a line of thinking that far too many mental health providers share. How easy to say that any post-war problems are not due to being in a war but to "pre-morbid" or "pre-existing" personality problems. Of course, this may well be a factor; no doubt some veterans were unstable to begin with. But it is fanciful and insulting to suggest that war was not a legitimate stressful if not traumatic experience in their lives.[37]

A very disturbing fact is downplayed by critics of PTSD statistics and governmental agencies who emphasize that vets with post-war problems "probably already had problems before they entered the military." The Selective Service was called that for a very good reason; the Selective Service was, indeed, very selective. The poor, the working class, the less educated, and minorities all are disproportionately likely to be selected for regular military service, and are dramatically under-represented among the ranks of officers; the more wealthy and better educated, the whites, and those with "connections," were much less likely to be selected or if they were, they were much more likely to be able to get a non-combat role or become an officer. In other words, those with less resources to begin with, and less access to resources, are the ones most likely to end up serving in the enlisted ranks in the military. This also is true to a substantial degree of recruits in the all-volunteer military. And, of course, it is the foot soldiers, the Army and Marines, who bear the brunt of the casualties in war.

Further, the myth that "time heals all wounds" reinforces the attitude among the military and the government that routine debriefings of returning sol-

---

36. Ibid.
37. Scurfield, R.M., "Where do we go from here?" Presentation on the national satellite teleconference: *The VA/DoD Continuing Response to Our Returning Veterans* (Salt Lake City, Utah: Regional Learning Resources Services (142), Salt Lake VA Medical Center, September 16, 1991).

diers are unnecessary, and are not the responsibility of the military or any governmental resource, in any case. But if we place any value at all on the welfare of returned soldiers, it is essential to provide opportunities to address their exposure to war-related stressors. This is not to be confused with operational debriefings for noting lessons learned regarding tactics and the efficacy of various military actions that were taken; that kind of debriefing, the military does provide, for its own benefit. But for the benefit of those who served, some kind of "critical incident debriefings" must be provided on a systematic basis to address emotions and reactions to what happened.

As one veteran said to me:

> "We spent two months in boot camp becoming trained in how to respond instinctively to danger, to not question orders, and to dehumanize the enemy. Then we were conditioned time and again and again while in the war how to kill and be numb to what we were seeing and doing, day after day after day. And then we returned stateside, were discharged and just expected to do okay in the civilian world and unlearn everything we had been taught to do and did do in war. Well, it just does not work like that."

THE PERSIAN GULF WAR: A RESURGENCE OF ACTIVE SANITIZATION AND DENIAL ABOUT THE IMPACT OF WAR

On a societal and institutional level, there are powerful military, governmental and community forces that come into play to help a nation heal from a war experience. Such forces have both positive consequences and quite negative ones that contribute to the collusion of silence about the impact of war on its combatants.

The Persian Gulf War exemplified many of these tendencies, and we are doing the same with the Iraq War. "Operation Desert Storm" (ODS) illustrated the persistent way in which many institutions and persons in the United States continue to cast the horrors of war in more palatable terms, and to "confuse the warrior with the war."[38] The surge of relief, euphoria, and rekindled feelings of pride and patriotism over the cease-fire and Iraqi troop withdrawals from Kuwait had a chilling counterpoint. There was a marked denial or minimization of the degree of pain and loss suffered by all those involved in the war, military and civilian, on both sides of the conflict.[39]

---

38. Scurfield, R.M., "The collusion of sanitization and silence about war: One aftermath of Operation Desert Storm," *Journal of Traumatic Stress*, 5 (3), (1992), 505-512. Much of the content of this section is derived from this article.

This denial concerning the casualties, especially among the Iraqi civilian populace, is a replay of how the US downplayed the toll on the Vietnamese people during the Vietnam War. This was reinforced by our government's policy of "punishing" Vietnam after the war by isolating the country diplomatically and economically. Almost all contact was cut off with post-war Vietnam for many years, reinforcing an avoidance and denial of the full impact of the war on not only American veterans and their families but also on millions of Vietnamese people. This was further complicated when Vietnam's Communist government failed to offer the other cheek by being as helpful as they could regarding US attempts to account for missing-in-action US military personnel. (Not that anyone was helping the Vietnamese account for their own missing and dead.)

The US-enforced diplomatic and economic isolation of Vietnam had a profound impact, especially on our Vietnam veterans.

The isolation of Vietnam entrenched memories and feelings that were frozen in time for a considerable number of veterans who were plagued with guilt and anguish over "what the US had done to the Vietnamese people and their country" during the war.

On the other hand, there are many Vietnam veterans who have little or no such guilt feelings about the death and destruction inflicted on the Vietnamese people and land during the war. This viewpoint may be expressed in terms like, "we were in a war, and in war casualties are inevitable. What is there to feel guilty about?"

The collusion of sanitization and silence about the impact of the Persian Gulf War was manifested on several levels. For example, following the Gulf War, many persons in the military, health care officials, political leaders and the public basically thought along these lines:

"The war is over, and we won; and when you win a war, there are few psychiatric casualties."

"There were very few [physical] casualties for the US and its Allies. And when you have few physical casualties, you don't have to devote resources and attention to helping veterans, their families and the country to heal from the war."

"We should be very proud of what our troops and our country have accomplished. Let's provide huge celebratory parades and ceremonies to welcome our troops home; that will help to prevent mental health problems among all Gulf War vets."

---

39. Ibid.

"The military can take care of its own. If any Gulf War veterans do happen to have war-related problems, our military medical services can and will give them proper treatment."

"We did not have another Vietnam; finally, we can put Vietnam behind us. We don't have to give more resources or attention to Vietnam vets, and there won't be much need to fund social and family programs for Persian Gulf War vets."

Some of these attitudes and activities can be very helpful and healing, and are to be encouraged. On the other hand, such attitudes and reactions, by which our society and its institutions collude in perpetuating the sanitization and silence about the horrific costs of war on our soldiers, our society, and yes, even on "the enemy," and on the civilian populations of the country in which the war was waged, distort our thinking about the full human impact of war and military service and prevent us from providing the necessary resources for the care that veterans deserve and need.

In addition, we are kept from understanding the full scale of the death and injury to the civilian populace and the enemy. For example, the United States government and military almost never have reported on the estimates of 900,000 North Vietnamese Army and Viet Cong personnel killed or missing, 500,000 North Vietnam civilians killed by Allied bombings, one million South Vietnam Army personnel killed or missing, 1 million to 2.5 million South Vietnamese civilians killed or missing, and 200,000 Vietnamese affected by Agent Orange. And there are estimates of up to 100,000 "excess" deaths of Iraqis since the war started in 2003.

MILITARY AND MEDIA REPORTING THAT SANITIZED AND DENIED THE IMPACT OF THE PERSIAN GULF WAR

The reliance during the Vietnam War on the "body count" (e.g., number of confirmed enemy dead) versus terrain objectives as the yardstick to measure battlefield success was resolved in the Persian Gulf War and to a large extent in Iraq today by a refusal to give any cumulative body count estimates for enemy combatants or civilian casualties. Instead, the Persian Gulf War coverage focused on a term with a much blander and more impersonal connotation — "ordnance." It seemed that a scorecard was kept showing tanks, planes, and other military equipment that had been destroyed; there was no suggestion that any people might have been inside of them or near them.

The almost unimaginable extent of bombings in the tens of thousands of US military sorties was repeatedly pictured and described in dramatic television shots as "surgically-precise air strikes, of which about 80% were estimated to have been on target." We were reminded repeatedly of this very high accuracy rate, a testimony to US technological advances and superiority and the justifiable expenditure of multi-millions of dollars on such sophisticated and expensive weaponry. The fact that some of the targets were later proven to have been mis-identified, and were civilian rather than military installations, for instance, goes overlooked.

At the same time, there was an almost complete avoidance of any real examination of the extent of the unspeakable suffering imposed on innocent Iraqi civilians who happened to be hit with the "ordnance" of the 20% of the tens of thousands of sorties that were not on target. If the US objective in the Persian Gulf War was to free Kuwait, were the deaths of 100,000 to perhaps over 200,000 Iraqis justified?

The dehumanization, and thus the devaluation of the loss of life among the enemy, whether military or civilian, is a replay of a too-familiar refrain that we all utilize to mask the intolerable realities of the human costs of war. Pejorative generalizations about Arabs and Islam were heard, and racist behaviors towards Arab-Americans occurred here in the US. These all were disturbingly reminiscent of descriptions of that "dirty little war the US fought in Southeast Asia against gooks, dinks, and slopes." Many Americans know very well that over 58,000 US service personnel were killed in the Vietnam War. However, far fewer of us know that reportedly more than fifty times that number, an estimated 3,000,000, Vietnamese were killed on both sides of the war and some 300,000 Vietnamese are still unaccounted for.

But to deny or play down the cost of war, to all who were directly or indirectly involved, seems to be inevitable; if we did not dehumanize and devalue the lives of the enemy and of civilian casualties, how could we overcome our inhibitions against killing? If we admitted how much short- and long-term suffering our own side would incur, even in victory, how could we sign up ourselves, or send our family members off to war? And so, it is happening again, now, in regard to the Iraq War; notice how seldom any estimates of civilian casualties have been reported. The numbers are hard to come by, but some researchers give an estimate of well over 100,000 Iraqi deaths between the time of the invasion of Iraq and October, 2004.[40]

In fact, a recent political cartoon illustrated this issue. Two US soldiers stand next to a pole on which the first soldier is writing "War dead total, 1,500." The second soldier asks, "What are you doing?" He replies, "Counting the dead.

We Americans always count the dead." The second soldier then asks, "And the Iraqis?" The reply: "I dunno. Do the Iraqis count?" And the last picture shows a sea of gravestones, unmarked except for "civilian deaths" and the caption, "Apparently not."[41]

Another example of sanitization during the Gulf War was the constant description by many Westerners of the Iraqi chemical and biological weapons as horrible and inhumane, or barbaric, indeed beyond the scope of any "civilized" nation to even consider using. There was a direct implication that more traditional weaponry, i.e., guns, rockets, bombs, anti-tank and anti-personnel weapons and "surgically precise" air strikes somehow are more humane and civilized methods of killing. These more "humane" methods include delivering death and injury via napalm burns over 80% of one's body, or multiple fragmentary wounds and dismembered limbs via a cluster bomb. No one has satisfactorily explained why that is more civilized or humane than a nerve agent or mustard gas. The process of dying is presumably just as painful and final. The resultant physical injuries and psychological pain, and the loss, grief and suffering of the families, are no less.

In the same vein, Western countries continue to justify conventional warfare (that we, of course, consider to be for a just cause) as being much more defensible than the enemy's guerilla warfare or terrorist acts. Of course, anyone who is a vilified terrorist in the eyes of one side is almost always seen as a heroic resistance fighter by the other. In Vietnam, we vilified the Viet Cong for their notorious and widespread terror tactics. On the other hand, US forces at times resorted to the razing of villages and killing of Vietnamese who might well have been, but were not confirmed as being, VC; we did whatever we had to, in an attempt to eliminate guerrilla forces and weaken their support among the civilian population and thus minimize US military casualties. All of this is logical; and it is part of the full and inevitable human cost of war.

And yet, who is to say which is more civilized or reprehensible: or are both equally inhumane and senseless? Czech civilian uprisings decades ago using rocks against foreign tanks were portrayed as heroic in the Western press; Pales-

---

40. As reported by researchers from the John Hopkins' Bloomberg School of Public Health: "Making conservative assumptions, we think that about 100,000 excess deaths or more have happened since the 2003 invasion of Iraq. As cited from a report published on-line by *The Lancet* medical journal on October 28, 2004, in Aljazeera.Net, News Arab World, retrieved from the web on 3.30.2005.

41. Thompson, Mike, *Detroit Free Press* for *USA Today*. March 7, 2005, p. 12A.

tinians throwing rocks at occupying Israeli Army soldiers have been branded by many American media accounts as "angry Arab mobs." Yes, it seems as if all sides brand the enemy's violence as horrible and unjustified, and their own as not so very terrible and by definition as being for a good cause.

In the aftermath of the Gulf War, there were many optimistic proclamations that any negative social and psychological impact on our troops and on their families had been short lived and relatively mild. And, of course, the public relations picture promoted for years repeatedly denied the validity of the mysterious "Persian Gulf Syndrome" that a substantial number of returning veterans eventually reported. Somehow, we were supposed to believe, these problems are not as bad as they seemed or that they had nothing to do with having served in the Persian Gulf War.

Why would veterans distrust such proclamations by the government and military authorities? Look how long they denied that any Vietnam veterans might be suffering any negative consequences from their exposure to the chemical defoliant Agent Orange, and the similar lengthy denial after the Gulf War of the negative health consequences of requiring our active duty military to be forcibly inoculated with a vaccine that had not been fully tested for long-term negative side-effects. The military health officials insisted these inoculations were necessary in case of exposure to chemical/biological agents; in the event, as it turned out, apparently no such agents were used against US troops but a number of active duty personnel claim to have suffered ill health effects from the inoculations themselves.

Government and military officials have repeatedly asserted that PTSD is far less prevalent among World War II and Korean War US veterans than among Vietnam veterans. There is little basis for this assertion; but it has been accepted by much of our society and the mental health community. There has never been a national prevalence study of the impact of war on US veterans of any war other than Vietnam. Of course, "heroes" and "victors" — such as World War I and II veterans — are not supposed to have problems. Was this myth resurrected and maintained among most of us for yet another era of "victorious" veterans: of the Gulf War? And will it be revived again for veterans of the Iraq War, especially if there eventually is a "successful" outcome?

At least, the military today has been willing to conduct mental health surveys in the war-zone (Iraq) and among returning military personnel.[42]

THE REALITY OF THE FULL HUMAN COST OF WAR

Even as the US is scrambling to deploy more and more men and women to fight in the ongoing Iraq War, most of our society seems to be shockingly blind to the horror that war will bring to the troops, their families, and our society, now and for decades to come. In the age of "technologically smart" weapons, it is easier than ever to pretend that we can get away with waging destruction from afar, while scarcely putting our own personnel at risk — it seems like a video game where the enemy is destroyed and you get to walk home afterwards and forget about it.

But Iraq has turned into a very nasty up-close and personal war being fought primarily on the ground by Army and Marine foot soldiers — very similar to the Vietnam War, in many ways.[43]

War is unforgettable and has an indelible, enduring impact on us all.

No one predicted that the psychiatric impact of the Gulf War would approach the magnitude of the impact of Vietnam; and, at first, it didn't appear to. Similar optimistic predictions about casualties of the Iraq War were constantly being made, early on, by military and governmental officials. Certainly, the initial reports concerning the minimal number of psychiatric casualties among US troops who served in the Gulf War were encouraging. However, a low acute psychiatric casualty during war doesn't necessarily have any relationship to longer term, chronic, or delayed psychiatric casualty rates.[44]

Still, the seemingly minimal acute and longer-term impact of the Gulf War on American forces, combined with the massive national recognition and welcome-home events, reinforced our collective denial and selective amnesia about the longer-term impact of war on its participants. Like Vietnam, with Persian Gulf military and veterans we once again "confused the warrior with the war," e.g., feelings that many people had against the war were projected onto returning US veterans.

And with Gulf War veterans, there was a twist. In contrast to returning Vietnam veterans, most Gulf War veterans were given a warm welcome home, if not a hero's welcome. Ironically, in our fervor not to scapegoat Gulf vets the way

---

42. See *A Vietnam Trilogy*, Volume III, for discussion of the mental health findings among current and recently deployed Iraq and Afghanistan war veterans, and the implications for not only the veterans but also for their families, communities and our nation.
43. Which are discussed in Volume III.
44. Scurfield, R.M. "Needs of Gulf War veterans and their families."

so many Americans did Vietnam veterans, and not to ignore Gulf War vets like so many Korean War and many Vietnam War veterans, we seem to have ended up promoting the worthiness of both the warrior and the war. And so, it would appear that a powerful new catch-22 has emerged. In order to support our troops and not undermine their efforts, we are told that we must avoid expressing opposition or reservations concerning a particular war, or war in general, or about peacekeeping military operations and pro-war policies of our government.

There is a strong parallel today. In regard to the Iraq War, many of our national leaders have repeatedly asserted that we have to support the war in order to support our troops.

THE IMPACT OF THE PERSIAN GULF WAR ON OTHER VETERANS

The cumulative and interactive "serial impact" of several different wars on veterans of all eras was demonstrated during the Persian Gulf War. For example, a number of war veterans who had not received a welcome home when they returned from Vietnam or Korea had profoundly bittersweet reactions to the outpouring of relief and joy in the receptions and parades for Gulf War returnees. Such veterans vigorously supported proper recognition of the troops, because they know firsthand the terrible impact of a hostile homecoming or absence of any recognition at all. And yet, they had their own longstanding war-related psychological wounds torn open again.

> "I was glued to the television, watching the hero's welcome and ceremonies for our troops returning from the Persian Gulf War, tears streaming down my face, as I thought, "Yeah, this is the welcome home that Nam vets never got. I felt so good for our Gulf War vets — but at the same time my old hurt and rage at our unwelcome home resurfaced."

Even among the enemy:

> "War has been their whole world. So many lives, so many fates. The end of the fighting was like the deflation of an entire landscape, with fields, mountains and rivers collapsing in on themselves. Suddenly, he felt terribly alone; he sensed he would be lonely forever.

> "In later years, when he heard stories of V-Day or watched the scenes of the fall of Saigon on film, with cheering, flags, flowers, triumphant soldiers and joyful people, his heart would ache with sadness and envy."[45]

And now, in the midst of the Iraq War, there is the inevitable recurrence of war-related problems and issues for combat veterans of prior wars.

The longstanding issues of many hospitalized US veterans were further exacerbated by national contingency planning during Operation Desert Storm. Preparations were made to relocate veterans out of various VA medical facilities to make room to admit possible Persian Gulf War casualties. Once again, veterans of Vietnam and earlier wars were angry at being pushed aside as the nation focused on the new era of war veterans.

America is by far the wealthiest nation the world has ever known. Those men and women who served in earlier conflicts earned our care and support for as long as they need it. It would seem to be possible and, indeed, it is ethically imperative that we continue to fulfill our duty to provide medical and social services to them even as we focus on current active duty personnel and the "new" veterans.

The Inevitable Result of Continuing to Deny the Full Human Cost

I was distressed to realize, in 1992, that unlike the outpouring of emotion during and immediately following the Gulf War , there obviously were not and would not be many yellow ribbons commemorating our Persian Gulf War troops attached to lapels, telephone poles, vehicle antennas and houses five, ten, twenty, or forty years after this or indeed any war had ended.

How deep is this impulsive outpouring of "support," anyway? What patterns can we observe in the actual spending to support the troops, much less the veterans? With every round of national debate over budget priorities, services for the families of active duty military service personnel and all services for veterans seem to come in last. The initial euphoria and the call to "support our troops" seems to be empty; they have definitely not been translated into long-term sensitivity, understanding, and the resources necessary to help veterans and their families survive after "giving their all."

The initial enthusiastic support for our troops and their families, and our memories of them, inevitably fade as time goes on. Kyle Gilbert, an Army Private First Class stationed in Iraq in 2004, made a plea to his mother just before the last satellite phone call between them disconnected. These were the last words he spoke to her; he was killed in action three weeks later:

---

45. Bao Ninh, *The Sorrow of War*, p. 43. Many of Bao Ninh's poetic observations as a North Vietnam Army veteran are presented in *A Vietnam Trilogy* to show the parallels between his experiences and those of American soldiers.

"Just don't forget me."[46]

The individual who loses a family member in a war will never forget. However, as a nation we must fight to stop this recurring amnesia and denial of the impact of war, and commit the necessary resources to address the impact. We must be willing to speak out, time and again, about the full human costs of war on all of us and on both sides of any war: before the government commits our troops to go in harm's way anywhere in the world, during any such wars, and long after any war is over. Otherwise, the collusion of sanitization and silence about the true and full impact of war will continue.[47]

I am reminded of the State Department's and the VA's refusal to support our return trip with a group of eight combat veterans with PTSD to a peacetime Vietnam in 1989. It would seem that the government and our society should not only tolerate but support any of our nation's veterans to return to former battle-grounds in distant foreign countries, if they so wish, to face their perpetual demons of war and to help eradicate their lingering pain. But this would require a recognition that war is devastating, and goes on being devastating, for decades, for great numbers of our war veterans and their families.

THE BUREAUCRATIC RESPONSE TO A CONTROVERSIAL AND FLAWED VA NATIONAL OUTCOME STUDY OF PTSD PROGRAMS

In the early 1990s, the VA conducted a massive national study of the hospital-based inpatient PTSD programs across the country,[48] and a second study on the VA's hospital-based outpatient PTSD programs.[49] Many VA health care professionals voiced serious criticism about the methodology, limitations and conclusions drawn by the Northeast Program Evaluation Center (NEPEC) that

---

46. Hampson, Rick, "Divisions over Iraq war delay a soldier's tribute." USA Today, December 13, 2004, p. 8A.
47. Scurfield, R.M., Collusion of Sanitization and Silence, p. 511.
48. Fontana, A. and R. Rosenheck (1996). *An evaluation of the inpatient treatment of posttraumatic stress disorder in Department of Veterans Affairs specialized PTSD programs.* West Haven, CT: Department of Veterans Affairs, Northeast Program E valuation Center (NEPEC), VA Connecticut Health Care System — West Haven Campus. Fontana, A. and Rosenheck, R. Effectiveness and cost of the inpatient treatment of posttraumatic stress disorder: Comparison of three models of treatment. *American Journal of Psychiatry*, 154 (6) (1997, June) 758-765.
49. Fontana, A. and R. Rosenheck (1996). Improving the efficiency of outpatient treatment for posttraumatic stress disorder. *Administration and Policy in Mental Health*, 23 (3), 197-210.

had designed, conducted and interpreted these studies. In fact, I was one of several "national PTSD experts" who had been invited by the VA to submit written critiques of the NEPEC study. Each of us wrote a position paper outlining shortcomings and inadequacies in the NEPEC study, and their sweeping conclusions. However, once submitted, these written critiques disappeared in VA Central Office, and to my knowledge they never have been publicized, distributed or openly discussed.[50] The results of the studies therefore stand, on the public record, their flaws remaining hidden from view.

The VA did not officially disseminate or seriously consider the sharp criticisms of this study — despite having invited nationally-recognized PTSD experts to assess its validity. The findings of the NEPEC study were disseminated nationwide, and NEPEC's sweeping conclusion recommended to dismantle the VA's specialized inpatient PTSD programs. VA national officials accepted the findings and conclusions uncritically, and used them to justify a radical reduction of the specialized inpatient units. The specialized PTSD units did have their share of responsibility, as they themselves had not conducted the necessary research to justify to critics the continuing substantial cost of operating such programs.

The NEPEC study findings also were used as a rationale to go one step further: to proclaim that the NEPEC study "proved" that PTSD programs really should not be focusing clinical attention on war-related trauma and its impact. Rather, NEPEC concluded that PTSD programs should re-focus their clinical attention on current dysfunction and quality of life factors. And this conclusion was promulgated through the findings of a study that did not even conduct a valid examination of whether the various specialized inpatient PTSD programs adequately utilized exposure-therapy in treating PTSD.[51]

And so, a federal government agency supported a one-sided "in-house" program evaluation that reported extremely questionable findings about specialized inpatient PTSD programs, obtained expert critiques of the study and then suppressed them, subsequently used the findings to justify dismantling inpatient PTSD programs, and then redefined the mission of PTSD programs to minimize a clinical focus on war-trauma symptoms and issues. Many such programs became "PTSD programs" more in name than in substance.

---

50. Scurfield, R.M. *Critique of report by Drs. Fontana and Rosenheck.* Memorandum submitted by Director, Pacific Islands Division, VA National Center for PTSD, Honolulu, HI, to Director, Mental Health and Behavioral Sciences Service (111C), DVA, Central Office, Washington, DC). Unpublished manuscript.

The VA also "strongly encouraged" its outpatient PTSD programs (except for the Vet Center Program, which is not under the line of authority of VA Mental Health) to move towards a more traditional mental health model of managed care, short-term interventions and a focus on current life functioning. Simultaneously, they took the position that "since chronic war-related PTSD symptoms have remained quite resistant to improvement over time," they should be avoided and given very little trauma-specific treatment attention.[52]

Admittedly, this is an extremely challenging and complex issue, and the few outcome studies conducted on the longer-term specialized programs were unimpressive in terms of reducing PTSD. Two studies involving the American Lake PTSD Program (which I directed from 1985 to 1992) did show improvement in functioning in other very important areas, such as enhanced self-esteem and increased ability to live with enduring PTSD symptoms more peacefully.[53] But throwing out or minimizing PTSD-specific treatment for veterans who continue to have serious PTSD symptoms cannot possibly be a solution.

One disturbing implication is that a number of VA mental health treatment programs that serve veterans with war-related PTSD may have, in one critical respect, reverted to the VA's traditional mental health position in the 1970s and

---

51. For a comprehensive analysis and critique of both NEPEC studies, see: Ask not for whom the bell tolls. Controversy in post-traumatic stress disorder treatment outcome findings for war veterans. *Journal of Trauma, Violence and Abuse, Vol.* 4 (2) (2003, April), 112-126; also see Rogers, S. (1998). An alternative interpretation of "intensive" PTSD treatment failures. *Journal of Traumatic Stress,* 11 (4), 769-775. I also wrote and presented summaries of the major concerns about the NEPEC study, such as, "Controversy in PTSD Treatment Outcome Studies," Regional Conference, Department of Veterans Affairs (Chicago, IL, September 25, 1998). In my many presentations and discussions with various VA providers throughout the country, I talked to VA research scientists and clinicians who also had major concerns about the NEPEC study methodology and interpretations and conclusions. They continued to be very reticent to write anything or speak out nationally about their concerns because (1) they feared negative repercussions from higher-ups in the VA, such as having their programs targeted for great scrutiny, and/or (2) they believed that nothing would be accomplished by voicing such concerns.

52. Fontana and Rosenheck, Administration and Policy in Mental Health. (1996, January.)

53. Scurfield, R.M., S. Kenderdine and R. Pollard, "Inpatient treatment for war-related PTSD: Initial findings on a longer-term outcome study." *Journal of Traumatic* Stress, 3 (2) (1990), 115-202. and Hyer, L., R. Scurfield, S. Boyd, D. Smith and J. Burke, "Effects of Outward Bound experience as an adjunct to inpatient PTSD treatment of war veterans. *Journal of Clinical Psychology, Vol.* 52 (3) (1996), 263-278. [While the latter study focused on the impact of Outward Bound, it also revealed important treatment outcomes of the American Lake PTSD Program in comparison to the Atlanta VA PTSD Program.]

earlier. And that is to "treat" war veterans with PTSD by focusing on life skills and problems other than the lingering direct impact of trauma experienced in war, and to minimize or avoid adequate attention to trauma-focus therapy. This is very troubling in the face of the evidence that war-related PTSD symptoms are very enduring among a substantial number of veterans, and that there are trauma-focus therapy technologies available with impressive treatment outcome data that could be applied, e.g., EMDR (Eye-Movement Desensitization and Reprocessing).[54]

THE IRAQ AND AFGHANISTAN WARS: THE FULL HUMAN COST IS STILL DENIED

One might hope that the collusion of sanitization and silence about the full human cost of wars ended with the Persian Gulf War, and that with all the real-time media coverage, and with the Internet and cell phones enabling service personnel to communicate with their families back home, American citizens are now fully and adequately informed about what goes on in the war zone and what the full human costs of war are in Iraq and Afghanistan. Unfortunately, this does not appear to be the case, as illustrated by just a few relatively recent examples. The credibility of national officials is undermined by inaccuracies that have been uncovered in official statements and pronouncements, and the selective sharing of information that is obviously being carefully managed so as to avoid giving the impression that the war may be going worse than had been predicted or hoped for. Such inaccuracies and distortions of information make it difficult to understand or believe the information that is presented.

Jessica Lynch. In Iraq, Pfc. Jessica Lynch's capture following an ambush, the fact that she was a woman, and her subsequent rescue, were highly publicized in a story that captured the nation's attention. Media reports based on information released by military officials initially described the heroic actions of Pfc. Lynch in emptying her rifle magazine and being captured only after valiantly fighting against overwhelming enemy forces. Equally glowing information was provided concerning the extremely dangerous circumstances surrounding the brave actions of the rescue team that plucked her from the enemy's grasp. Only later was it revealed that Pfc. Lynch had not even fired a single shot during the ambush (something that she readily admitted when she had recovered sufficiently from her injuries to talk in detail about what had happened), and that the

---

54. EMDR is discussed and referenced in a later chapter.

conditions at the time she was rescued were quite different than had been initially reported. Pfc Lynch, like others, was heroic; this is not intended to disparage her courage and strength, or to belittle the unknown dangers that the rescue team had to be prepared to encounter; rather, the issue is the credibility of the official information that was publicized and maintained for quite some time.

Pat Tillman. Pat Tillman, National Football League defensive back for the Arizona Cardinals, who left a $3.6 million contract to join the Army Rangers, was killed in Afghanistan during an engagement with enemy forces. Military officials provided information suggesting courageous actions by Tillman at the time of his death, putting his life on the line to protect his fellow soldiers when he was killed by enemy fire. Only later was it revealed, following an extensive investigation by the *Washington Post,* that the Army "embellished" the circumstances surrounding Pat Tillman's death. He was not killed by enemy fire but tragically was killed by "friendly fire" from other American soldiers who mistook Tillman and his unit for the enemy.[55]

Such obfuscation, prevarication and lack of immediate and open analysis of the facts as they actually happened deny our armed forces, stationed in harm's way, the opportunity to learn the lessons that need to be learned about small unit maneuvers and communications in hostile terrain. For example, an immediate analysis should have been done to identify how it happened that communications broke down between two US forces and resulted in friendly fire deaths. This could and should have been immediately reported to other forces in Afghanistan to prevent further possible friendly fire casualties. Was such an analysis blocked by the public-relations need to promote a false report that Tillman's death was from enemy — and not friendly — fire?

Also, the Tillman family — and the public — were denied an honest accounting of his death until an outside investigation forced authorities to recant. And this in no way denies the tremendous courage and patriotism evidenced by Tillman and his unit.[56] Death by friendly fire and by accidents are part of what is inevitable in a war. And both are equally permanent.

Is it too much for military officials to be accurate in reporting on these various causes of death and injury that are part of what happens in war?

Flag-Draped Coffins. Considerable national attention and controversy were unleashed following the release on April 9, 2004, of a "contraband" snapshot

---

55. McFeatterr, Dale, "Pat Tillman is still a hero." *SunHerald,* Biloxi, MS. December 7, 2004, B1.
56. Ibid.

taken of flag-draped coffins of American military personnel arriving on an air-plane from Iraq. The publication of this picture set off a firestorm of debate. It was argued that this picture violated a government policy against showing images of the remains of military personnel and that it violated the privacy rights of the deceased and their families. These reasons also were given to justify the policy of returning such remains on planes that would land in the US in the middle of the night and out of sight of the media. Others argued that this was a further attempt by the government to downplay the full human cost of this war, and that, indeed, the flag-draped, clean and orderly array of coffins in the bay of the airplanes actually was very respectful of the deceased.

Humvees and Armor. It also was discovered that the military did not acknowledge how poorly the war was progressing in terms of the unexpectedly fierce and deadly targeting of unarmored US military vehicles, especially the Humvee. In spite of numerous complaints by US troops in Iraq over many months that they were being unnecessarily placed at risk because they were riding in non-armored vehicles, in spite of numerous stories in the press about how US personnel in Iraq were scrounging for scrap materials to jerry-rig their own make-shift armor plating for some of their vehicles, and in spite of con-tractors clearly stating that they had the capacity to step up the production of armored vehicles (if they were authorized to do), such authorization was delayed for many months — many months.[57] And how many US casualties could have been prevented? One such preventable casualty is disgraceful, and you can bet there were many more than one.

Critics have stated that the reluctance by the military to authorize an increase in production of such armored vehicles appeared to be based primarily (if not solely) on political concerns over possible weakening of support for the war effort; that such an authorization would be tantamount to an admission that there had been a serious error in judgment as to how deadly and sustained the insurgent resistance would be, and an admission that the war was not going as well as had been predicted. It was beyond dispute that increased production of armored humvees was delayed for many months — apparently not because of any shortcomings on the part of the suppliers but because of political concerns.

"My son called me the week before he was killed," says Brian Hart of Bedford, MA. "He said they were getting shot at all the time. They were in unarmored Humvees

---

57. Squitieri, Tom. "Army late with orders for armored Humvees." *USA Today*, 3.27.05, Cover Story, A1-A2.

and were out there exposed to fire. He was concerned they were going to get hit. He was whispering this into the phone to me. He was right. That's how he died."[58]

Two days after Secretary of Defense Rumsfeld was publicly asked (while visiting the troops in Iraq) why the Army didn't have armored humvees in Iraq, and he suggested that it "was beyond the Pentagon's control," the Army somehow reworked its contract and asked the sole company producing factory-armored humvees to boost its production by more than 20%.[59] Doesn't seem to be that difficult. How would you feel if it were your son or daughter, or spouse, or sibling, who was riding in one of the many unarmored humvees during all those months of unnecessary delay, and was seriously wounded or killed?

Med-Evacs Arrive Only At Night. And then there is the policy of having the planes carrying the remains of those killed in Iraq and also the wounded personnel who have been evacuated from Iraq land back in the US at night, away from exposure to media coverage. Critics see this as yet another tactic to shield from the American public the full human cost of the Iraq War. Wounded soldiers are also prevented from having a proper welcome home and are deprived of the recognition that is provided to those who are uninjured. The irony of this was described by a wheel-chair bound 100%-disabled Iraq combat veteran:

> "There are celebrations when the troops come home, the troops who are walking and physically OK. But when he was flown home on a C-17 with 100 injured, no one but his wife was there to greet him."[60]

And so, perhaps those returning troops who are most in need of recognition for their service and sacrifice are denied proper recognition — for political reasons.

Casualty Figures. Finally, CBS 60 Minutes reported on an investigation that showed the casualty figures routinely released by the military concerning US forces in Iraq and Afghanistan were dramatically under-reporting the actual number of casualties in the war zone that have occurred from all causes; and military officials then admitted that the much higher figures were accurate.[61] This is on top of the military's policy not to provide regular estimates of Iraqi civilians who are killed or injured as a by-product of military operations. And, of course,

---

58. Ibid.
59. Ibid.
60. Nelson, Karen. "Disabled veteran coming back. He wants to celebrate NMCB 7's return." *SunHerald*, Biloxi, MS, March 30, 2005, pp. A1, A4.
61. 60 Minutes, CBS, November 21, 2004.

the vast majority of psychiatric casualties from war are not identified during war time, but only in the months and years following their return from the war zone.

The cumulative impact of all of the above is that there is increasing doubt (if not disbelief) that the official US data, information and pronouncements are credible, accurate and complete. This raises great concern that US citizens continue to be misinformed about the true cost of war. Concern also is heightened when it is seen that there are government officials and agencies who cannot be trusted to provide credible information about such matters — and especially during a time of war.

Furthermore, this lack of credibility has enormous implications for the post-war struggles of many veterans; they feel betrayed and misinformed by the government. Such perceptions and feelings of being betrayed have a strong impact on the ultimate post-war psychological healing of many combat veterans; this is described in the forthcoming third book of *A Vietnam Trilogy*.

Emotionally charged meetings between Vietnam veterans and Soviet Afghantsi veterans in the late 1980s and early 1990s revealed that such dynamics were not confined to the picture of war painted by some American government officials during the Vietnam War. Furthermore, such actions by governmental leaders have a devastating impact on combatants, as do the attitudes and behaviors of a country's citizenry in their treatment of veterans following a war, be they American or Soviet.

THE RUSSIANS ARE COMING: FORMER ADVERSARIES MEET

During the late 1980s and early 1990s, there were a number of exchange visits between Vietnam veterans and US mental health professionals and our counterparts in the Soviet Union concerning the post-war problems of Soviet veterans of the Afghanistan War ("Afghantsi"). Our program was visited in 1990 and 1991 by Afghantsi veterans and their doctor, Dr. Valera Mikhailovsky. He was the courageous and gifted director of a rehabilitation program at the Moscow Regional Hospital for Veterans of the Great Patriotic War, located at Krukovo.

We also were visited in 1990 by Dr. Alexandr I. Kitaysky, Chief Doctor, Sanatorium Baikal, Listvianitchnoe, Irkutsk Region, in Siberia. These trips were coordinated by Diana Glasgow, Earthstewards Network, Bainbridge Island, WA. On the 1991 trip, Dr. Mikhailovsky was accompanied by three Afghantsi veterans and a translator. On his second trip, he brought about five Afghantsi veterans. George Sapegin, who had emigrated to the US from the Soviet Union before serving in the Vietnam War, served as our volunteer translator.

Many of our vets initially were very resistant to meeting with the Soviets. After all, it was the Soviet Union that had provided the North Vietnamese with much of their military weaponry. Indeed, many of our veterans or their buddies had been killed or disabled by Russian-made weapons in the Vietnam War. We found out that many of the Afghantsi veterans were equally resistant, at first, to meeting with veterans from the very country that had supplied substantial amounts of weapons and munitions to the people whom the Russians were fighting in Afghanistan.

Recognizing the strong negative feelings of a number of our veteran patients, we made the first meeting with Dr. Mikhailovsky and the Afghantsi vets optional; any of our veteran patients who wished to attend were welcome to do so. Ten (out of 30) chose to participate. It was a remarkably emotional meeting. Dr. Mikhailovsky, through our translator, even demonstrated several of his therapy techniques in a joint workshop with the visiting Soviet veterans; this was a moving, in fact heart-stopping experience to share such a cross-cultural healing experience with soldiers from our former enemy country. They could not even speak our language, nor we theirs.

Both the American and Soviet veterans, and our staff, were struck by the remarkable similarities in the veteran experience across two countries and different generations. They had fought in two different parts of the world, in different decades, yet "their" wars were eerily alike in several ways. Both were guerilla wars. Both wars were not called wars by our governments; it was the Vietnam "conflict" and the Afghanistan "affair." Both governments gave less than truthful information to their citizens about the wars, and how the wars were progressing. In both cases, especially during the latter stages, veterans themselves increasingly questioned why they were there, in far-off lands, in the first place. This questioning was exacerbated when they returned home and discovered that the government didn't care, and that many people were indifferent or just could not understand the experiences that they had gone through.

The following perceptions and experiences relayed by several of the Russian veterans illustrate the remarkable parallels with the perceptions and experiences of many Vietnam veterans.

"When people [vets] came back from there [Afghanistan], these negative influences jumped right out at them: for instance, the indifference that hides behind documents and paperwork," Sokolov said. "Sometimes you just feel mean, you want to grab them and kill them. It is hard to explain. And in the end, there is a kind of intense feeling, an unpleasant taste in your mouth: for the sake of what did I go through this? Why can't people understand? Then you understand...that for them it is difficult to understand."[62]

"The wars were not very popular back home, and there was a lot of confusion and opposition to having military personnel there: and prejudice against them after their return."

"My tour of duty was an experience that affected my soul. When I returned home, nobody needed me. I wanted to kill all those people who didn't understand."[63]

One veteran recalled the derisive reaction he encountered when he wore his Afghanistan service medal in public for the first time. He said that older people would upbraid him with questions like, "Hey, kid, what are you wearing your daddy's medal for?"[64]

"The people of Saki remember," Turshatov says, "an evening when a local young man, tipsy with drink, sighted a disabled [veteran] patient and called out, 'Hey, cripple.' The soldier hobbled to where the offender stood and struck him with his crutch."[65]

Isolation is not uncommon for many veterans returning from the war.

"I didn't have anything in common with the people around me," said one veteran. "I didn't have anyone to confide in." His pain and isolation led him to drinking and drug abuse.[66]

The credibility of government statements about the conduct and progress of the war effort, and the post-war impact on veterans, was highly suspect. In both cases, the foes were extremely resilient and skillful. There were gruesome numbers of casualties, both severely physically disabled and psychiatric casualties, who returned home to much less than a hero's welcome. There was a denial by the governments that returning veterans had any significant war-related problems and an avoidance of real discussion. Both groups of vets discovered the universality of the horror and longer-term impact of war on warriors: an indelible mark that cuts across different cultures.

---

62. Bohlen, Celestine. "Soviet veterans open up about their doubts. Many disillusioned about progress of war in Afghanistan," *The Washington Post* (January 30, 1988). A1, A13.

63. Grogan, David. "A tale of two wars: Vietnam vet Charles Figley helps to heal Russia's traumatized Afghantsy," *People Weekly* (October 24, 1988), 19-20.

64. Dobbs, Michael. "Soviets say 13,310- soldiers died in Afghan war," *Washington Post* (May 26, 1988), A1, A14.

65. Tuohy, William. "Soviet War Wounded Find Little Joy in Homecoming," *Los Angeles Times* (December 12, 1987), 1, 12.

66. Bule, James. "Vets share agony of war in visit to the USSR," *The APA (American Psychological Association) Monitor*, 20 (8) (August, 1989), 1, 22.

"Unfortunately, there was not enough understanding towards Afghantsi when we returned to the Soviet Union," Vladislav Tamarov said. "Many people think, 'Well, you came back from Afghanistan so, good for you, rest a month and get back into the swing of things quickly. Get back to work! Get moving!' But war is not a clip from a film. You can't tear it out of your memory. The war will always live with us.[67]

"I had lost my leg, and I thought my life was over. I drank and drank, and then the drugs they had given me in the hospital, I began to find and take on my own."[68]

"You feel you have stepped into a room where the only way out is death, and you don't want that," Kalandarishvili said. "So, somehow you arrive: you fight, you hide, you yourself kill, and you survive. But it changes you, it changes your soul, and afterward you are not the same, never what you were before, never what you might have been, never what people still expect you to be."[69]

The Soviet people, like the Americans, did not really want to know the details of what the troops were going through. Especially when the enemy was well-known for using torture and terror tactics that are intrinsic in guerilla warfare.

At a crowded public meeting sponsored by his magazine, Borovik says he recounted the torture of a Russian soldier by the (Afghanistan) rebels: they allegedly made an incision around the soldier's waist and pulled his skin up over his head like an undershirt. Afterward, one horrified woman whose nephew was fighting in Afghanistan came up to Borovik and implored him not to write about such things. "Before, it was easy waiting for our boys to return."[70]

Both Vietnam and Soviet Afghantsi veterans who came back wounded psychologically from the war found that medical treatment in and of itself was not sufficient to help them to heal from the many wounds of war.

"Many of our patients suffer from shattered nerves in addition to serious physical afflictions. They need more than good medical treatment. They need friendly attention, support and love from the people around them. But unfortunately, most remain indifferent. Worse, some prompt the guys to drink."[71]

Both groups of veterans found plenty to complain about and were bitter concerning their respective governments.

---

67. Kashismba, David. "Afghantsi: a Soviet veteran tells his story," *The Carrier, Naval Air Station* Alameda, CA. 47 (8) (February 23, 1990), 1, 6-7.
68. Fein, Esther B. "Veterans from 2 Armies and 2 Wars Finding Shared Wounds in Moscow," *NY Times* (October 3, 1988), 1-A.
69. Parks, Michael. "Vietnam vets go 'soul to soul' with Soviets," *St. Petersburg Times*, (Oct. 19, 1988), 1-A, 8-A.
70. Keller, Bill. "Russia's divisive war. Home from Afghanistan," *The New York Times Magazine* (Feb. 14, 1988), 85.
71. Tuohy, William. 1, 12.

"Turshatov said that disabled veterans are often treated shabbily by the bureau-
cracy. He said that only the cheapest, underpowered models of the tiny autos used
by disabled people are fobbed off on wounded veterans, that prosthetic appliances
are hard to come by, as are jobs, and that disability pensions are not enough to make
ends meet."[72]

"Veterans' self-help groups and organizations spontaneously started in both countries: a reaction to mistrust of the government and the lack of adequate government
programs that war veterans required. Both Vietnam and Afghantsi veterans realized
that they had to start their own organizations to combat official government
neglect of those who had served in the war — and even to press for monuments
honoring those who died there."[73]

The experience of meeting and sharing with Soviet Afghantsi went a long
way toward helping Vietnam veterans to break through strongly held stereotypes about "the enemy" and to have a positive and healing interchange.

"The pain of veterans and their families and friends 'is so pure and so universal.' The
experience of camaraderie between citizens of two countries that have for so many
years been such ardent adversaries gave Shea a deeper sense of a common humanity,
he said, and of the chances for peace. 'If the men who actually do the fighting for
each country begin to see each other as human beings, as people not so different
from themselves, they will inevitably have more reservations about war as a means
of solving conflict.'"[74]

However, other Vietnam vets refused to be exposed to any such interactions and considered this to be "consorting with the enemy." The parallel issues,
and benefits, of interchanges with Afghantsi veterans and with former enemy
veterans in Vietnam in 1989 were remarkable, as illustrated by two of the vets
comments during our 1989 trip:

"Some of my friends told me before we left home that our group was being made a
pawn of the Vietnamese government, which desperately wants to regain diplomatic
relations with the United States. 'This is going to come back to haunt us. That was
strictly propaganda, that's all it was, propaganda [e.g., the meeting with former
NVA veterans at a veterans factory today]. And you guys enjoyed the hell out of getting it done to you.'"

"We came here, and the purpose for this was to heal within oneself. Now, if healing
within myself means I'll go to a former enemy and shake his hand, and admit that
the war was over and I don't have to have hard feelings.... That's the whole thing of
my PTSD, all this anger and hatred that I have built up, and I got to let it out. And I
gotta stop it."[75]

72. Ibid., 1, 12.
73. Keller, Bill. "Soviet veterans of Afghan war lobby for their rights," *St. Petersburg (FL)
Times* (November 22, 1987), 1-A, 7-A.
74. Bule, James. 1, 22.
75. Smith, Stevan, *Two Decades and a Wake-Up*, PBS Documentary, 1990.

I must admit, even though I had just recently returned from dramatically emotional meetings with former enemy soldiers in Vietnam, prior to the several delegations of Soviet Afghantsi veterans and professionals visiting our American Lake program, I had been quite skeptical of the number of American Vietnam veterans who had gone to the Soviet Union in the late 1980s to meet with the Afghantsi. Sure, I intellectually understood the value in going. However, uppermost in my mind was the question (and judgment!), "How is it that Vietnam veterans can somehow find the time and resources to go traveling off to Russia, but not to return to Vietnam! Is this not yet another avoidance of their own Vietnam issues?"

And then, after getting to know a number of Soviet professionals and Afghantsi veterans and their stories, I finally understood. Yes, I had opened my eyes — and my heart:

Vietnam veterans are willing to visit with former enemies in Vietnam — who had been provided weapons by the Soviet Union.

Russian Afghantsi veterans are willing to visit with US Vietnam veterans — whose country supplied Soviet enemies in Afghanistan with weapons.

And all were casualties of government policies and society's indifference that got them into these wars in the first place — and then colluded to deny the full extent of the negative impact of the war on these veterans following their return.

Two different journeys, one of American veterans, going thousands of miles to Vietnam, to meet with former enemy Vietnamese veterans. And another journey, one of Soviet veterans, coming thousands of miles to America, to meet with former enemy American veterans. Yes, American veterans and Soviet veterans, finally coming face to face, only this time in peace time — and completing an on-going circle of healing.

Chapter 4. Racism and War

As the build up to the Persian Gulf War was escalating, the media reported a surge of race-related prejudiced attitudes and behaviors towards people who were — or looked like they were — of Middle Eastern heritage. There was controversy generated over FBI interviews of Arab-American leaders in the US that were conducted "in the national interest." Racist comments reportedly became common in some military units, with typical references to "A-rabs" or "towel-heads." There were pejorative generalizations about the Islamic faith, lack of knowledge or appreciation or interest concerning the diversity among various Moslem, Arabic and non-Arabic cultures and traditions. Yes, most Iranians are Moslem; no, Iranians are not Arabs.[76]

As a Syrian-American (my maternal grandparents had emigrated from Syria), I of course was particularly sensitive to actual or perceived prejudices towards people of Middle Eastern descent that were being triggered as the war-drums were beating louder and louder during Operation Desert Storm. However, my reaction went well beyond my personal ethnic and cultural heritage. What was resurging in my memory and sensory circuits was a nasty after-taste from basic training and the Vietnam War that had never completely dissipated.

I was familiar with how racism had been infused in the Vietnam War. In basic training I was exposed to blatant racism towards the Vietnamese throughout the training provided to us. I then personally observed many US military personnel in Vietnam directing blatant racist attitudes and behaviors

---

76. Scurfield, R.M. and S. Tice, 1992.

towards not just the enemy military personnel — but towards all Vietnamese people.

In my subsequent two decades of working with Vietnam veterans in mental health programs, through the stories of hundreds of veterans, I became painfully aware of the virulence of this racism and how it had permeated relationships among US military personnel in Vietnam and afterwards — and continued to be directed, even decades later, by many veterans towards the former enemy and towards any Vietnamese people.

And then, in the aftermath of the Gulf War and later, with the terrorist acts of 9/11, our country's predilection for dehumanizing the designated enemy, especially through racist generalizations, blossomed once again. Never mind that we were led to direct much of that hatred to Iraq (and now Iran), which even President George W. Bush admits had not been involved in the 9/11 attacks, despite his earlier efforts to suggest that they had been.

All of this exposed decades-old race-related hurts engendered during and following the Vietnam War; they had never been fully recognized by me, let alone resolved. Hence, the critical importance of understanding this extremely important issue — it is resurrected time and again when our country goes to war. And the cycle must be stopped.

In the aftermath of the Persian Gulf War, I discovered just how strong the impact of having experienced racism during and following the Vietnam War still was in the 1990s. I relocated to Hawaii in 1992 to plan and lead the implementation of the new $3 million Pacific Center for PTSD, an education, research and treatment center based in Honolulu. Then I established and directed the Pacific Islands Division of the VA's National Center for PTSD in Honolulu. Our massive catchment area, the entire Pacific region, included Hawaii, American Samoa and Guam.

As part of my job as a National Center Division Director, I regularly flew to the "Big Island" of Hawaii to co-lead trauma-focus therapy sessions with the veterans who were in our PTSD Residential Rehabilitation Program, the PRRP. Through these intense therapy sessions, I became quite familiar with something that I had heard about over the years but had not seen firsthand. Now I was hearing from veterans of Asian-American and Pacific Islander (AA/PI) ethnocultural backgrounds how prevalent and destructive racist-related attitudes and behaviors towards them had been, in basic training and in Vietnam. Such negative race-related experiences were much more likely to be expressed in our trauma-focus groups at the PRRP in Hilo since a majority of the veterans in residence tended to be of AA/PI ethnicity.

I strongly supported precedent-setting research as a co-investigator on a major VA research grant. Chalsa Loo was the Principal Investigator, and John Fairbank (Durham, NC) and Dan King (Boston) were co-investigators on this study of how exposure to race-related experiences such as racist abuse was associated with the war-related PTSD among Asian American Vietnam veterans.[77] I then became even more familiar with how this legacy of racism had affected Vietnam veterans of Asian and Pacific Islander heritage.

Most of this chapter discusses traumatic racist incidents that occurred both in basic training and in the Vietnam War. However, there is another, positive aspect to race and the military. There is no doubt that for many active duty personnel, the experience of being in the military is a positive eye-opening experience. When men and women of different backgrounds find themselves working together for a common cause for the first time, it can give them a very favorable new perspective on diversity. This is true for Yankees and Southerners, rural mid-Westerners and hip West-Coast types, residents of small towns and big cities, a remarkable panoply of cultural groups, and last but certainly not least, folks of different skin color and heritage. And brothers- (and sisters-) in-arms find themselves sometimes bonding with comrades of different races, because race no longer seemed to matter, and especially not in the middle of combat. In the end, we all bleed the same color — red.

Indeed, over the decades the military typically has been at the forefront of providing equal opportunity for people of all colors, shapes and persuasion. If you could do the job, and do it well, and could work well with others of diverse

---

77. Loo, C., J. Fairbank, R.M. Scurfield and D. King. *Asian American Vietnam Veteran Race-Related Study* (Honolulu, HI: VA Merit Review, Department of Veterans Affairs, 1996-99). This was the first VA-funded study to specifically investigate "race-related PTSD" among veterans of any era, in this case Asian American Vietnam veterans. See also: Loo, C., J. Fairbank, R.M. Scurfield, L. Rusch, D. King, L. Adams and Y. C. Chemtob. "Measuring exposure to racism: Development and validation of a Race-Related Stressor Scale (RRSS) for Asian American Vietnam Veterans," *Psychological Assessment, Vol. 13* (4) (2001): 503-520; Loo, C., K. Singh, R.M. Scurfield and B. Kilauano, "Race-related stress among Asian American veterans: A model to enhance diagnosis and treatment," *Cultural Diversity and Mental Health, 4* (1998): 75-90; C. Loo, "Race-related trauma and PTSD: The Asian-American Vietnam veteran," *Journal of Traumatic Stress, 7* (1994), 1-20; C. Loo, "Race-related posttraumatic stress disorder," in *A Report on Asian Pacific Islander Veterans by the Vet Center Asian Pacific Islander Veterans Working Group* (Washington, DC: Readjustment Counseling Service, Department of Veterans Affairs), (1998, Spring): 40-50.

background and demographics, you could reasonably expect to be recognized and rewarded. And the military is to be highly commended for that. Even so, all is certainly not rosy in the military concerning race relations, as was documented in a major study of race relations among active-duty personnel conducted by the DOD in 1999.[78] However, while what is discussed in the remainder of this chapter was not the experience of all, nor perhaps even a large majority, of the members of the Armed Forces, it is important to emphasize that it certainly was the experience of far too many of them, and of more in the later years of the war.

Institutional or structural racism that is characteristic of America greatly influenced who ended up serving in the military during the Vietnam era and what roles they performed. The working class, the poor and the less educated were much more likely to be drafted or enlisted in the first place, and racial minorities are over-represented among these socio-economic groups. Hence, minorities were very visibly over-represented (in comparison to their proportion of the general population), especially in the combat arms of the Army and Marines — the two military branches that constituted almost the entire ranks of the foot soldiers, by far the highest risk category. The foot soldier or infantry have historically been referred to as "cannon fodder," and for good reason: the vast preponderance of combat casualties come from their ranks.

Blacks accounted for about 10% of the US general population between 1964 and 1967, but 16-17% of all combat troops were Black, and 22% of all US troops killed in action during this period were Black.

The over-representation of minority troops among foot soldiers was plain to see. As one American Indian veteran said:

> "The white dudes stayed in school, you know, and we [Indians, blacks and other racial minorities] fought the war. They don't know nothing about anything except what they get out of a book. But they get the jobs."[79]

> "American Indian veterans easily noticed how institutional racism in the military was expressed by calling Indian soldiers 'chief,' 'Tonto' or 'Scout.'"[80]

---

78. Scarville, J., S.B. Button, J.E., Edwards, A.R. Lancaster, and T.W. Elig. *Armed Forces Equal Opportunity Survey.* (Arlington, VA: US Department of Defense, Defense Manpower Data Center, 1999). This survey reported that exposure to and negative impact from negative race-related experiences (i.e., racist-oriented attitudes and behaviors) is a significant current problem among members of the US Armed Forces. While this was particularly true for ethnic/racial minority personnel, it also was true to a lesser extent for white personnel.
79. Holm, Tom, "The National Survey of Indian Vietnam veterans," in Barse, H. et al., *Report of the Working Group on American Indian Vietnam Era Veterans* (Washington, DC: Readjustment Counseling Service, Department of Veterans Affairs, May, 1992), 25-34.

By many accounts, Vietnam was a war saturated with racism, and it had a profound impact in two critical areas before, during and following the Vietnam War. First, it affected relationships between US military personnel. And second, it affected relationships between US military personnel of all colors and the Vietnamese people.

It started on two basic levels. One was in the attitudes and behaviors of US troops towards the Vietnamese; the other was in the attitudes and behaviors of Americans of different color towards each other. Minority troops were very frequently exposed to negative race-related actions and attitudes; however, some white troops also were so victimized by minority soldiers.

Basic training taught active duty personnel to dehumanize the enemy; this was reinforced in the war zone. Obviously, then, military personnel of all colors tended to take a racist attitude towards the Vietnamese. And it is reasonable to conjecture that the encouragement of racism directed toward the Vietnamese contributed to racial tensions amongst American personnel.

Racism, of course, was not and is not confined to the military experience. America, like most multiracial nations, has a substantial history of racist attitudes and behaviors. Over the years the military forces have been quite progressive, relative to the civilian sector, in terms of promoting positive race relations and opportunities for advancement to members of all races.

RACISM IN BASIC TRAINING

In order for the reader to appreciate the extent and pathology of the racism infused in basic training, I borrow from R. Wayne Eisenhart a brief description of the brutal and pervasive context.

Racism in Boot Camp Towards Vietnamese

The milieu of basic training was blatantly racist. The overall purpose of basic training is to produce soldiers who are superbly conditioned physically, and who are disciplined (e.g., conditioned) to obey unquestioningly and immediately the orders of their superiors. Traditionally, the intent has been to form a cohesive fighting unit filled with (selfless) men of confidence, full of masculinity,

---

80. Johnson, D., and R. LaDue, "A Cultural and Community Process," in Barse, H. et al, Report *of the Working Group on American Indian Vietnam Era Veterans*, 39-42.

instilled with a personal and unit pride steeped in the glorious tradition of the military branch to which they belonged.[81]

New inductees are subjected to daily conditioning and structuring of *all* activities in order to both attain a state of "resigned routinization" and to reshape individual self-image and self-esteem. This is to insure that one not only totally accepts military authority instantaneously and unquestioningly, but that one also remained utterly passive in the face of verbal and physical abuse, physical exhaustion and being physically assaulted.

It also is made very clear that the primary lesson toward which all boot camp training is directed is aggression, to seek dominance, to "close with the enemy and destroy him." Indeed, aggression and seeking dominance are equated with masculinity, and it is only by expressing the depths of violence that the recruits could get the drill instructor to cease the endless barrage of insults, like "you dirty faggot" and "can't hack it, little girls?"[82]

And racism was adroitly incorporated into the above.

"The linking of the military function with sexual identity, the stimulation and promotion of violence and aggression, and the repeatedly hammered ideal of seeking dominance at all cost, produced in the recruits a well-honed emotional edge. We were out to 'kill them gooks,' as many and as soon as possible.

The terms 'gook' and 'slope' were continually used by training personnel as well as in written material and movies. Although the racism instilled in boot camp was directed towards Asians, it also increased black-white tensions. A black marine cannot help but be reminded of the racism inherent in the structure when he hears a white marine say, 'We're gonna kill the yellow bastards.' We did not question or challenge this racism as it made it considerably more comfortable to denigrate our potential enemies while learning how to kill."[83]

Denigrating racist terms that were widely and repeatedly used to describe the enemy in Vietnam included chinks, slant-eyes, dinks, slopes, Charlie. And there was certainly no serious attempt to train us in cultural sensitivity or an appreciation for the people of Vietnam. There was a constant denigration of the culture of Vietnam as something alien, weird and unimportant. This all became more powerful as part of the extremely tense conditioning of mind and body that occurred in boot camp.

---

81. Eisenhart, R. Wayne, "You can't hack it little girl: A discussion of the covert psychological agenda of modern combat training," *Journal of Social Issues*, 31 (4), (1975): 13-23. See also: Shatan, Chaim, *Bogus Manhood, Bogus Honor: Surrender and Transfiguration in the United States Marine Corps*. Paper presented at the annual meeting of the American Orthopsychiatric Association (San Francisco, CA: April, 1974).
82. Ibid. 16.
83. Ibid, 17-18.

However, much of the military mission in Vietnam amounted to guerrilla war, and a guerilla war requires "winning the hearts and minds" of the civilian populace, unlike the conquering of territory that occurs in a traditional war. And in Vietnam enemy and ally, and those innocent civilians caught in between, often were indistinguishable! Thus, many in the American military could not help but apply the inculcated racism to all Vietnamese, no matter who they were.

Racism in Boot Camp Towards Minority Troops

"You didn't have white friends. White people were aliens to me. This is 1963. You don't have integration in the South. You expected them to treat you bad. But somehow in the Marine Corps, you hoping all that's gonna change. Of course, I found out this was not true, because the Marine Corps was the last service to integrate. We had a Southerner from Arkansas that liked to call you chocolate bunny and Brillo head. That kind of shit. A white lieutenant called me a nigger."[84]

The racist stereotyping and abuse were not confined to lower-ranking enlisted persons.

"General Larsen was something else. He was the commanding general of Camp Lejeune. One day he came over to speak to us. I'll never forget when he walked in. It was the first general we had ever seen. Here I am, a hard charger, thinking I want to be a general. I want to be like him. Well, he started talking about the war.

"He said, 'I just came back from Guadalcanal. I've been fighting through the jungles. Fighting day and night. But I didn't realize there was a war going on until I came back to the United States. And especially tonight. When I came back and I find out that we've now got women Marines, we've got dog Marines, and when I see you people wearing our uniforms, then I know there's a war going on.'

"Goddamn. You never saw so many Coke bottles fly. Knocked him down. And there was a riot that night. The first black riot in Marine Corps history."[85]

RACISM IN THE VIETNAM WAR TOWARDS THE VIETNAMESE PEOPLE

The racism directed towards the Vietnamese people was of epidemic proportions.

[Asian-American Vietnam veteran] "They always talk about the Vietnamese people and stuff like that. They say, 'Oh, but we're not talking about you. We're just talking about the rest of the slant-eyes.' That's how they ridicule the people. But I can't say anything or they'll think I'm on their [the Vietnamese] side."[86]

---

84. Edwards, Reginald, "Private First Class Reginald "Malik" Edwards, Phoenix, Louisiana," in Terry, W., *Bloods. An Oral History of the Vietnam War by Black Veterans* (New York: Ballantine Books, 1984), p. 5.
85. Huff, Edgar A., "Sergeant Major Edgar A. Huff, Gadsden, Alabama," in Terry, W., 147-148.

"When we were going on convoys, going through the villages, the kids on the sides are trying to sell you something, and the white Americans would show them [middle] fingers, yell at them, swear at them, call them names, and throw things at them. And here I am, sitting on the truck with these groups, and in my mind, you know what [voice cracks], those kids or those people can be my family [weeps]. You guys have no respect for these people! Totally! [weeps]."[87]

Some vets didn't even realize that this derogatory treatment of the Vietnamese was racist, until after they had returned home.

"I would hear the word 'gooks' all the time. Not so much 'slant-eyes' and 'slopes,' but 'gooks' or 'chinks.' That was everyday language for the men that I worked with. The way I dealt with all these words, it never really dawned on me till I came home that these words were actually derogatory. It's like calling a black guy, 'nigger.' It's the same thing."[88]

Such racist attitudes were not only directed towards enemy Vietnamese. For many American soldiers, such attitudes and behaviors became generalized towards all Vietnamese.

"Like all GIs, I just killed everyone. They were all gooks to us. But when I came back and looked at the faces of my friends and family, they looked like the people I killed. I felt very strange and very bad."[89]

"The only good gook is a dead gook."

"Most GIs couldn't stand the sight or smell of Vietnamese. White GIs couldn't understand for the life of them why I would associate with South Vietnamese, which made me, in their eyes, lower than South Vietnamese."[90]

RACISM IN THE VIETNAM WAR AMONG AMERICAN MILITARY PERSONNEL

This attitude helped GIs get over any inhibitions at killing the Vietnamese, and was therefore "useful" for the war effort. But, more remarkably, and damaging to the war effort, racist attitudes and behaviors were also prevalent between US soldiers who needed to bond together rather than exaggerate their

---

86. Loo, C.M. *Report on the Asian American Vietnam Veterans Race-Related Study (AVRS)*, (Honolulu, HI. National Center for PTDS, Pacific Islands Division, VA National Center for PTSD, VA Medical and Regional Office Center, 2000) p. 64.
87. Ibid, p. 14.
88. Ibid, p. 14.
89. Yokota, S., Alcaras, D., Loo, C., Adams, L and Kimoto, E. Clinical Issues: A Report on Asian Pacific Islander Vietnam Veterans, by the Vet Center Asian Pacific Islander Veterans Working Group, 1998. (p. 43). Washington, DC: Readjustment Counseling Service, US Department of Veteran Affairs.
90. Loo, 2000, p. 70.

differences. US minority vets say that there wasn't much racism out in the bush, but that there sure was back in base camp:

> "The racial incidents didn't happen in the field. Just when we went back to the base."[91]

Part of the racial discord was due to a clash of cultures, a clash between groups that for the most part had little prior contact, and especially little in the way of positive experiences with each other.

> "In the rear we saw a bunch of rebel flags. They didn't mean nothing by the rebel flag. It was just saying 'we for the South.' It didn't mean that they hated blacks. But after you're in the field, you took the flags very personally."[92]

The fact that minority solders were more likely than whites to be assigned to combat duty only aggravated the situation. A higher proportion of minority soldiers saw front-line combat than whites, and this means that a staggeringly disproportionate percentage of minority troops were killed in Vietnam.

Blacks were being killed at such an alarming rate that Marvin Gaye voiced the deep sentiments of the Black community in his hit song, "What's Going On?"

> *Mother, Mother, there are far too many of you crying.*
> *Brother, Brother, Brother, there are too far many of you dying.*
> *You know, we have to find a way*
> *To bring some loving here today*
> *What's going on? What's going on? What's going on?*[93]

Many soldiers of background found themselves wondering what they were doing in Vietnam, "fighting a white man's war against a third world country." This was especially difficult when they knew full well that race relations back home had not improved. At the height of the civil rights movement in the US, it was hard for people of color not to identify to some (or a considerable) degree with the Vietnamese as an oppressed people who were common targets of racist attitudes and behaviors by American troops.

> "Veterans come in and tell just what it was like killing a person of color," [Erwin] Parson says, noting that it provided a special trauma....Killing a Vietnamese was tantamount to killing a part of one's self — the guilt that the brothers talk about

---

91. Ford, Richard J., "Specialist 4 Richard J. Ford III, Washington, DC," in Terry, p. 38.
92. Ibid, p. 38.
93. Parson, R.P., H. Doughty, A. Woods, R. Henry, L. Porter, G. Johnson, L. Jones and R. Armstead. *The Struggle Continues. Report of the Working Group on Black Vietnam Veterans* (Washington, DC: Readjustment Counseling Service, Department of Veterans Affairs, 1986).

even today. Some Black soldiers felt a commonality with the Vietnamese, identifying with "the poverty of that downtrodden, Third World people."[94]

"But I think blacks got along better with the Vietnamese people, because they knew the hardships the Vietnamese went through. The majority of the people [US troops] who came over there looked down on the Vietnamese. They considered them ragged, poor, stupid. They just didn't respect them. I could understand poverty."[95]

Race relations among American personnel in Vietnam became increasingly tense and violent during the latter phase of significant American troop involvement in the war (1969-72). During this phase there was a severe deterioration in troop morale. Factors reflecting, and contributing to, this deterioration included: the perception that the war was not going to end positively anytime in the foreseeable future; continuing anti-war protests at home; a large increase in the use of drugs in a number of units in Vietnam; and escalation of violent acts between American soldiers, such as fraggings or attempted fraggings of NCOs and officers by disgruntled lower-grade enlisted personnel.[96]

THE MURDER OF MARTIN LUTHER KING: IGNITING A TINDERBOX IN VIETNAM

No small contributor, indeed perhaps the igniting factor, to the deterioration in race relations between and amongst various US military personnel was the assassination of Martin Luther King, Jr. The reverberations were felt throughout Vietnam. Understandably, the murder of Dr. King aroused rage, resentment, and an *angst* amongst Black soldiers who were laying their lives on the line for their "fellow Americans" while one of their leaders was killed back home.

Many African-American troops became very bitter. And, there was a concomitantly heightened "black power" movement that certainly surfaced in Vietnam.

"When I heard that Martin Luther King was assassinated, my first inclination was to run out and punch the first white guy I saw. I was very hurt. All I wanted to do was to go home. I even wrote Lyndon Johnson a letter. I said that I didn't understand how I could be trying to protect foreigners in their country with the possibil-

---

94. Ransom, Lou, "Black vets, study stays, suffer more...70 percent face stress," In *National Leader*, 2 (16) (August 25, 1983), 1, 8-9, 11.
95. Holloman, Emmanuel, "Specialist 5 Emmanuel J. Holloman, Baltimore, Maryland," in Terry, 83, 37.
96. "Fragging" is when one military person attempts to kill another US military person, typically of a higher rank.

ity of losing my life, while in my own country people who are my heroes, like Martin Luther King, can't even walk the streets in a safe manner....

"A few days after the assassination, some of the white guys got a little sick and tired of seeing Dr. King's picture on the TV screen. Like a memorial. It really got to one guy. He said, 'I wish they'd take that nigger's picture off.' And we commenced to give him a lesson...a physical lesson."[97]

VICTIMS OF RACE-RELATED ACTS CAN BE WHITE, TOO

It is understood that the vast majority of race-related acts are perpetrated by persons of the majority race and are inflicted against persons of a minority race. However, the opposite also happens. There is recent empirical evidence to indicate that whites are subjected to negative and damaging race-related behaviors in the Armed Forces today, although not to the extent of minorities.[98] And there are hurtful individual accounts to indicate that such also happened during the Vietnam War.

In the midst of the increasing racial tensions in America and in Vietnam, there were severe frustrations about how the war was going. It was almost inevitable that there would be a backlash of militancy by some white troops against blacks and the Black Power movement. And there were white soldiers (and African-American and other minority troops) who were caught in the middle.

One white veteran describes a series of escalating incidents of harsh words and threats between black and white soldiers in his unit.[99] Then, there was a reported episode of two white soldiers beating up a black soldier. Tensions escalated yet further, leading to several fights between whites and blacks. In the midst of this rapidly rising racial tension, he was threatened by three black soldiers, and one held a knife to his throat. But then, they let him go.

"More black vets started arriving in our unit, and I was just trying to stay out of trouble. But many white soldiers left the barracks area, not willing to sleep there any longer because of the racial tensions and threats; this left a handful of us behind. "And then there was a mass gathering of blacks; it seemed like there were perhaps a

---

97. Browne, Don F., "Staff Sergeant Don F. Browne, Washington, DC," in Terry, 167.
98. Scarville, J., S.B. Button, J.E. Edwards, A.R. Lancaster and T.W. Elig, *Armed Forces Equal Opportunity Survey* (Arlington, VA: US Department of Defense, Defense Manpower Data, 1999).
99. Personal communication, Steve Ryan, Carlsbad, California, August 14, 2001. I am indebted to (a) Steve for calling me to consult regarding a case of a white veteran who was suffering from exposure to race-related trauma in Vietnam, and (b) to the veteran who has given his permission for me to describe this abridged and paraphrased description of his traumatic war experience.

100 or so. They came charging up to our barracks door; and we were inside, having blockaded the door. It was really scary; we feared for our lives. Finally, we knew we couldn't hold them out much longer, and so we ran down the hall and jumped off the second floor and just ran as fast as we could. We ran to where the weapons were, and grabbed some. I didn't want to hurt or kill anybody, but I was really terrified for my safety. I fired over the heads of the advancing group of blacks...and they dispersed. We were safe, at least for awhile.

"Us white guys who were left were sticking together, we were determined not to be chased away. But they came back at us a few days later. Again, I didn't want to kill any fellow Americans, but we were surrounded. And then, miraculously, a leader of the black group called a truce, and had his black soldiers back off. And then, a few days later, tensions and threats had gotten so bad that we knew that we couldn't continue to stay in the barracks. And so we started staying at our duty station, and sleeping there as well. And then, my reaction was that I had had it; I wasn't willing to take this anymore and I left, going into town and renting a room with my own money. It was just too dangerous to stay there at the base after duty.

"And finally, we got a new commander, who took action. The most militant blacks were dispersed to other units, and order was eventually restored. But the damage had been done to me."

And this white veteran continues to be traumatically impacted (2002) by his exposure to this terrifying series of race-related encounters in his unit.

THREE DIMENSIONS OF EXPOSURE TO RACISM

Race-related stressors both experienced and perpetrated by American military forces can be considered in three dimensions or categories.[100]

1. *Direct Exposure.*

First, there was direct exposure to racism, e.g., racism directed personally at the veteran. One Japanese-American Vietnam veteran described derogatory race-related comments directed at him:

He was often singled out critically because of his race by officers and by fellow GIs who called him "gook." Once, an officer asked him if he spoke English.[101]

A Filipino-American Vietnam veteran reported being identified as a gook in his basic training:

---

100. Loo et al, 1996-99, 1998, 2001; Loo, 1994.
101. Hamada, R., C. Chemtob, R. Sautner and R. Sato, "Ethnic identity and Vietnam: A Japanese-American Vietnam veteran with PTSD," *Hawaii Medical Journal*, 47 (3) (1992): 102.

"You go to class and they say you'll be fighting the VC [Viet Cong] or the NVA [North Vietnamese Army] and the class instructor singled me out in a room and told everyone that I looked like them [VC or NVA]. After that class, everybody kept calling me a gook and stayed away from me."[102]

2. Racist Environment

Second, there was exposure to race-related attitudes and behaviors simply by being in a racist environment. While such stressors were not directed at the individual minority veteran, they clearly had an impact.

"You know, when you kept hearing about "gooks," "chinks," "slopes" all the time, it didn't take too much imagination to think that these are the very same kind of white Americans who would say "'nigger" and "'spics."

3. Bi-Cultural Conflict

Third, there was bi-cultural conflict, where the minority veteran felt internal conflict between his "American" and "minority race" dual heritage. For example, when an Asian-American Vietnam veteran was asked, later, if he felt a connection to the Vietnamese people because they were of a related race, he answered,

"[They were] human beings. How can I do this to them? [They're] also Asian. Reminding me, like I shot my own. My own kind, you know. I killed my own kind."[103]

A Black veteran described his inner turmoil at killing Vietnamese:

"It was the war...that made us question just what it was Black men were fighting for; just what it was our men were dying for; just why it was that Black men were fighting people of color halfway around the world who had never called them nigger."[104]

An American Indian Vietnam veteran found extremely painful reminders of parallels with the history of how his own people had been treated by Whites in America.

"We went into their country and killed them and took land that wasn't ours. Just like the whites did to us. I helped load up ville [village] after ville and pack it off to the resettlement area. Just like when they moved us to the rez' [reservation]. We shouldn't have done that. Browns against browns. That screwed me up, you know."[105]

---

102. Yokato et al, 1998, p. 33.
103. Loo, C (2000), p. 70.
104. Witherspoon, Roger, "Black Vietnam vets: No peace yet," *Essence* (December, 1981), 139.
105. Holm, The National Survey of Indian Vietnam Veterans, p. 31.

One American Indian soldier became painfully aware of the difference between his own tribal warrior culture and the war in Vietnam:

"We went into a ville one day after an air strike. The first body I saw in Nam was a little kid. He was burnt up — napalm — and his arms were kind of curled up. He was on his back but his arms were curled and sticking up in the air. Made me sick. It turned me around. See, in our way we're not supposed to kill women and children in battle. The old people say it's bad medicine and killing women and children doesn't prove that you're brave. It's just the opposite."[106]

A Japanese-American soldier was with his unit,

"...clearing vegetation and came under intense small-arms fire. As they returned fire, he saw an old Vietnamese woman firing a weapon at them with a child beside her holding ammunition. He and other soldiers fired at them, killing the woman and child. The full impact of this incident only struck him some days later, after he had returned to the rear. He was in an NCO club, drinking, and thinking of the woman and child. "I just kept on drinking and drinking, that's where I got started....I looked at the old lady and I was thinking of my mother. And I was looking at the kid and I was thinking of all my sisters. It was like killing your own kind. My own mother and sisters....it got to a point where it was like fighting your own people....You were put in an impossible situation. It's like you were asked to fight against yourself."[107]

Some soldiers from ethnic minorities were not consciously aware of this conflict until some time after they left the war zone.

Asian-American: "I guess because the way I was being treated by the Americans, my self-esteem, you know, I felt worthless. I just felt like I was a nobody. It got to the point where I was just a nobody. And it just got worse and worse 'till I didn't give a rip about anything afterwards."[108]

"They were all gooks to us...But when I came back [to Hawaii] and looked at all the faces in the shopping center, they looked just like all the people I killed. I felt very strange and very bad."[109]

The Persian Gulf War, too, was rife with racist incidents, as described briefly in the previous chapter. And in the upcoming chapter, a decorated African-American combat veteran who was part of our return trip to Vietnam describes a number of tragic and poignant race-related stressors that he was exposed to before, during and following his Vietnam tour of duty.

---

106. Ibid, p. 31.
107. Hamada et al, 1988, p. 102.
108. Loo, 2000, p. 72.
109. Hamada et al, 100-102, 105-109.

THE CONTINUING IMPACT OF RACISM ON THE RECOVERY OF VETERANS

Racism in the military and during wartime has received very little coverage, in spite of the long history of racism in the US (and elsewhere). While our society works to avoid, undo, and rectify expressions of racism at home, it still thrives in the military, through the very nature of basic training and the tendency to dehumanize the enemy (often based partly on race).

Four large-scale studies consistently showed elevated rates of PTSD and other psychiatric and social dysfunction symptoms among Black, Hispanic, American Indian and Hawaiian-American Vietnam veterans.[110] And not just because of simple exposure to combat stressors (in other words, not just because as minorities these troops were far more likely to have seen front-line action, making them far more exposed to combat stressors). However, only one study, in which I was a co-investigator, specifically investigated exposure to race-related stressors and their impact on PTSD. It focused on a sample of Asian-American Vietnam veterans in Honolulu. We found that exposure to race-

---

110.   Egendorf, A, C. Kadushin, R. Laufer, G. Rothbart and L. Sloan, *Legacies of Vietnam: Comparative Adjustment of Veterans and their Peers*. A Study Prepared by the Center for Policy Research for the Veterans Administration (Washington, DC: Superintendent of Documents, US Government Printing Office, 1981). See also Kulka, R.A., W.E. Schlenger, J.A. Fairbank, R.L. Hough, B.K. Jordan, C.R. Marmar and D.S. Weiss, *Trauma and the Vietnam war generation: Report of findings from the National Vietnam Veterans Readjustment Study* (NVVRS), a national psychiatric epidemiologic survey that was described in more detail in an earlier chapter. Also: Friedman, M., "The Matsunaga Vietnam Veterans Project," *PTSD Research Quarterly*, 9 (7) (Fall, 1998), 7. This project found markedly high rates of PTSD and other psychiatric symptoms among American Indian and Native Hawaiian (but not among Japanese-American) Vietnam veterans.
    In the study by Loo et al., 1969, Let et al., 2001, I was a co-investigator on this precedent-setting research study of the role of exposure to racism among Asian American Vietnam veterans. This study validated a Race-Related Stressor Scale (RRSS) and found that exposure to racism was by far the most significant variable associated with PTSD and other psychiatric symptoms. This finding raises the question that exposure to racism, a factor that was basically not measured in either the NVVRS or Matsunaga studies, may at least partially explain the elevated rates among minorities in those studies.
    Finally, the study by Egendorf et al, *Legacies of Vietnam*, offered considerable analysis of the post-war readjustment of minority veterans and the socio-economic factors impinging on their recovery from war duty. However, their insights have largely been ignored by subsequent researchers. *Legacies* was an important study but ahead of its time; it preceded modern PTSD measurement technologies and does not get nearly the credit it deserves for being the first national level study to highlight the extent of the war-related problems facing (1) Vietnam veterans in general, and (2) minority Vietnam veterans in particular.

related stressors was the *most significant* factor associated with PTSD and other psychiatric symptoms — even more so than exposure to combat stressors.[111]

And so, there has been a convergence of narrative and personal accounts of racism in the military and in the war zone, along with strongly consistent empirical research findings. Together, this combination of subjective and research data can be interpreted to suggest that racism was alive and well both before and during the Vietnam War, and that it continues to have a negative effect on veterans over three decades later. This corroborates my own extensive clinical experience with many Vietnam veterans.

The complete absence of any systematic inquiry about racism in any war and its impact on veterans is remarkable. Racism practically has not been recognized by researchers or funding sources as an important component of war-related stress to consider in clinical assessments and/or in research studies.[112]

At the same time, there is an even greater silence regarding possible *positive* aspects of being an ethnic minority on active duty and in a war zone. For example, some minority veterans have stated that their ethnicity helped them adapt to Vietnam. Is the absence of any inquiry into this topic another example of a collusion of silence and sanitization about the impact of war — in this case, about racism in war? No, not just about racism in war, but racism on the part of some US active duty personnel in basic training and then in the war zone, directed against the enemy and against the civilian population, too, and even against their own comrades. And how much of this is going on in the Iraq War today?[113]

The veterans' return trip to Vietnam in 1989 offered individual vets the opportunity to come face to face with the very people (combatants and the civilian population, as well) whom we had dehumanized during the war, and recognize them and greet them as the humans they are. It was a very liberating and healing experience. A similar opportunity existed in the meetings with Soviet Afghantsi veterans, veterans who had served in the army of a longstanding

111. Loo et al., 2001.
112. For a more detailed discussion of the concept of both negative and positive considerations regarding race-related trauma as it applies to persons of various racial heritages, see Scurfield, R.M. and D.W. Mackey, "Racism, trauma and positive aspects of exposure to race-related experiences: Assessment and treatment implications," *Journal of Ethnic and Cultural Diversity in Social Work*, 10 (2) (2002), 23-47; and R.M. Scurfield, Exposure to racism trauma and other race-related experiences: A guide to issues, assessment and treatment. Educational Credits. www.educationalcredits.com
113. See further discussion concerning the Iraq War and racism in *A Vietnam Trilogy* Volume III.

"enemy" of our country. And isn't that what racism is, too — a way to dehumanize others? Americans did it again after the terrorist acts of 9/11, as will be discussed in the third volume of *A Vietnam Trilogy*.

War is hard enough to heal from. Add to that the wound caused by racism, towards yourself or those around you, and between your own military team members. Returning to Vietnam offered some vets an unexpected opportunity to mitigate if not eradicate the effects of past racism and dehumanization, at least as it was projected against the Vietnamese people and country. Some veterans were aware of these effects before and during the war, some only later.

IMPLICATIONS OF RACISM FOR US FORCES

A multi-cultural and heterogeneous population lives in the US and serves in our armed forces. Our international policies have supported very active involvement of US armed forces in trouble-spots around the globe. Thus, it is inevitable that there will be some proportion of US troops who, deployed to any given country, will be of the same or similar ethno-cultural or racial heritage as the populace of that country, and of the currently designated enemy forces. It is reasonable to assume that such personnel are at increased risk for psychological conflict and stress. Conversely, they also may have unique strengths and insights due to their common heritage. This is a subject that needs to be studied.

It is not clear that the US military has even considered the effects of race-related conflict on our troops in war zones, basic training or elsewhere. The potential harm caused by racist incidents among uniformed personnel merits recognition, assessment, and attention, but it is an area that seems to be ignored by mental health professionals, by researchers, by the country as a whole.

THE POSITIVE SIDE OF RACE AND ETHNICITY IN WAR

Race and ethnicity were not only sources of stress among active duty personnel. Through my clinical contacts over two decades with hundreds of minority veterans, both on the mainland and in Hawaii, it has become clear that there is a very positive element to race and ethnicity. Minority vets have consistently said that their racial identity was a source of pride and gave them an invaluable perspective for relating to others who might have been discriminated against for various reasons. Indeed, in the war zone, minority vets consistently stated that they were able to be very empathetic towards the local civilian population and felt that it was easier for them to establish a rapport with the local population.

Also, because of the military's longstanding progressive stance concerning equal opportunity, minority veterans and immigrants come from families and/or from cultures with longstanding family traditions of having served their country. There is a strong sense of pride among soldiers who come from families or cultures with military histories. This seems to be especially so for veterans who are themselves or whose families are relatively recent immigrants to the United States, for veterans whose families are from such areas of the country as the Southern and Midwestern Unites States where there is a sustained and proud tradition of serving in the military, and for those American Indian and Asian/ Pacific Islander veterans such as Samoans and Native Hawaiians who come from historically "warrior" cultures.

FROM HAWAII TO MISSISSIPPI: VIETNAM BECKONS AGAIN

While my family and I loved Hawaii, by 1996 we were missing our kin on the mainland. When my wife Margaret was offered a position at the Naval Construction Battalion in Gulfport, Mississippi, we relocated some 4,500 miles to the Mississippi Gulf Coast, near Margaret's family.

I continued to work for the National Center for PTSD; I was off-stationed at the Gulfport Division of the Biloxi VA Hospital. During the year there, I did some clinical work with the PTSD Clinical Team (Leslie Root, PhD, Wayne Krepsky, PhD and John Liberto, MD). I co-led a Vietnam trauma focus group with Leslie. Through this group and other contacts with veterans living in surrounding communities, I learned firsthand that the lingering war-related issues of veterans from Mississippi were very much like those of veterans from throughout the US with whom I have worked over the decades. One difference, however, was that many of these veterans had never been involved in trauma-focus therapy groups before, in the two decades since their own traumatic war experiences.

In this position, I became connected to other PTSD treatment folks on the Gulf Coast, including Harry Becnel, PhD, Team Leader, and the great staff at the Biloxi Vet Center. What I didn't know at the time was that a major change in my employment status was waiting around the corner, one that would lead to my returning again to the one place that I had adamantly vowed in 1989 I would never, ever go back to — Vietnam.

Yes, I keep having to remind myself to never say "never."

CHAPTER 5. BACK TO VIETNAM: WITH STUDENTS

From 25 years in the VA to college professor: I retired from the VA on August 3, 1998, to accept an appointment as a graduate school social work faculty member at the University of Southern Mississippi (USM). I plunged into my new career in academia; however, I sorely missed my clinical contact with veterans and felt that loss tremendously. Knowing as a veteran how to use tunnel vision and task-orientation to keep my emotions away, I became immersed in learning how to be a college professor — and devoted myself to spending quality time with my family of three growing teenagers and Margaret. I also was still working (long distance) with our research group on the race-related experiences study of Asian American Vietnam veterans.[114]

I started settling in at the university. And then, out of the blue, it happened. A unique opportunity beckoned.

Leslie Root, clinical psychologist and director of the VA Gulfport PTSD Clinical Team (PCT), had been involved in getting PCT veterans to attend a Vietnam History class at USM. Dr. Andrew Wiest was the history professor, and as a military history specialist, he had invited veterans to participate in his classes to "help bring the history of the Vietnam War alive." Now, Andy was starting to plan to establish the first Vietnam History Study Abroad course at the university and involved Leslie in the planning. As I was one of the few professionals who had ever taken *anybody* to Vietnam (in 1989), I was invited to help out.

---

114. Loo, C., J. Fairbank, R.M. Scurfield and D. King, Asian American Vietnam Veteran Race-Related Study (Honolulu, HI: National Center for PTSD, Department of Veterans Affairs, 1996-2000). This was a VA Merit Funded research study.

I was very clear in emphasizing that while I would be happy to offer whatever consultation I could to the planning process, I had no interest in actually participating in the course. My memories of the painful aftermath of our 1989 return trip were still fresh; I had vowed that I had spent my last day in Vietnam, ever. I never even went back to read or transcribe the journal that I had kept during that trip.[115]

The course was open to undergraduate and graduate history students. The plan was unique: to integrate military history and mental health subject matter, and take several Vietnam veterans along as "guests" of the study abroad course and as resource persons who would talk to the history students about their war experiences and what it was like to return to their former battlefield locations.

Of course, during the planning process I found myself drawn into the project. Indeed, I became so drawn in that I found myself veering toward the unthinkable: making a second return trip to Vietnam. The university approved the Vietnam History Study Abroad course for the intercession period between the spring and summer 2000 sessions. Andy Wiest was the director of the project; Leslie Root and I were designated as Professors of Record.

This was a precedent-setting project: a fully-accredited undergraduate and graduate study-abroad history course in Vietnam History with a dual history/ mental health curriculum, and sixteen history students and a history professor, integrated with the inclusion of three Vietnam veterans and two mental health faculty. In addition, two other history professors joined the group as participants.[116]

LOGISTICAL PLANNING FOR THE VIETNAM HISTORY STUDY ABROAD COURSE

All pre-trip, transit and in-Vietnam travel arrangements were provided through Vietnam-Indochina Tours, Olympia, Washington. The tour company is owned by Courtney Frobenius, a Vietnam veteran who also taught English in Vietnam from 1995-1998, and is operated by his Vietnamese wife, Trang My Frobenius, who moved to the United States in 1999. Ms. Trang accompanied us

---

115. Scurfield, R.M. *A Vietnam Trilogy. Veterans and Post-Traumatic Stress, 1968, 1989 and 2000* (New York: Algora Publishing, (2004).
116. For a more in-depth description of this project, see: Scurfield, R.M., L. Root, and A. Wiest. "History lived and learned: Students and Vietnam veterans in an integrative study abroad course." *Frontiers: The Interdisciplinary Journal of Study Abroad* (Fall, 2003): 111-138.

on the trip, as did an in-country travel guide (Mr. Tran Quoc Cong from Danang, Vietnam). Their pre-planning and in-country knowledge and supervision, and many on-the-spot adjustments that were required during the trip, were absolutely vital to the success of this course.

DUAL PURPOSE OF THE COURSE

The course purpose was to supplement a standard Vietnam History curriculum with the "personal history" of three Vietnam veterans; the veterans were returning to former battle sites in Vietnam where they had significant combat experiences during the war. In addition to the three veterans' personal military histories, selected didactic presentations were provided in Vietnam on the mental health aspects of serving in a war zone, and in the post-war readjustment and treatment of Vietnam veterans with war-related PTSD.

Of course, besides being able to add my perspectives as a Vietnam veteran, I was able to offer a retrospective view of my 1989 trip. On that journey, we took veterans who represented the range of war-related PTSD, from the most severe to relatively moderate in the expectation that returning to the former war zone might have a therapeutic effect. Even though all the veterans did obtain unique and positive benefits from returning to Vietnam (i.e., meeting with a former enemy and feeling positive about that meeting), it appears that the veterans with the most severe PTSD did not fare nearly as well as those with more moderate PTSD. Also, only one-half of the group members had had a therapeutic relationship with either of the two co-facilitators prior to the project being organized, and this seems to have made a difference in the results obtained.[117]

Andy, Leslie and I agreed that we would be very careful in selecting veterans for this trip and would *not* select veterans with a wide range of severity of PTSD. Two of the veterans selected (John and Roy) were well known clinically to Leslie Root. Although they had substantial symptoms of chronic PTSD, these had been relatively stabilized through their extensive and on-going clinical involvement in PTSD treatment for several years, and they had progressed to the point that Leslie was convinced that this return trip would be beneficial. She had an excellent clinical relationship with them.

---

117. Again, this precedent-setting and very controversial trip is described in detail in Scurfield (2004), *A Vietnam Trilogy*.

Interviews were conducted with each of the vets as part of the screening process. Furthermore, the two vets with PTSD had several additional pre-trip counseling sessions with Leslie to explore their goals, fears, expectations and the potential positive and negative impact of returning to Vietnam. Leslie worked with them to identify the most likely and potent triggers for symptoms and negative emotional reactions, and identified coping strategies they could use. Both vets also were active in peer group therapy at the VA PTSD Clinical Team, Gulfport, MS, and had the opportunity to explore issues with fellow veteran support and reactions.

The third veteran, Charles Brown, was a well-known veteran advocate in the community and had an exemplary employment record with the State employment office as a Disabled Outreach Program counselor. He had never been in PTSD treatment, and thus was one of a large population of veterans who might have Vietnam-related issues but who had been able to move on with their lives without seeking mental health treatment. Charles also was an African-American; he was born and raised in Mississippi, was very active in civil rights and race-related issues, and thus offered that unique perspective to our group. A fourth veteran, who also seemed not to had any war-related PTSD, was selected but had to withdraw at the last minute due to health problems.

Finally, each of the three vets also had been a guest speaker at various history classes with Dr. Wiest. In fact, John had been participating in classes weekly for several semesters, and he and Dr. Wiest had formed a very close relationship. John also had established a very positive bond with several of the students who were enrolling for this course.

We decided to restrict the number of veterans to these three, partly in recognition of the logistical challenges of integrating visits to their former duty stations into the less than three-week travel itinerary for the history course. Also, by keeping the group small, and three-fourths students, the ambience would be dramatically less intense than if we had taken along a higher percentage of veterans. The fact that the students were all history majors, and Andy a history professor, also added a quite different dimension to the group composition. We hoped and anticipated that the history orientation of so many of the group members would be a nice complement to the mental health orientation of myself and Leslie, and vice versa.

This trip was different from the 1989 trip in one more extremely important way. The University of Southern Mississippi, including the History Department, the School of Social Work and the International Studies Department, all were enthusiastically supportive of our project. We were going as an official university educational program, not as a free-lancing group of individuals without the support or sanction of any institution.

There was strong local support from the Biloxi VA Psychology Service Chief, Dr. Gustave Sison, for Leslie's participation in this project. However, the VA as a federal institution was not willing to approve Leslie's request for an authorized absence. She was not to be considered an official representative of the VA or to function on this trip in her capacity as a VA psychologist. Rather, she had to take personal leave, and was not permitted to function as the therapist for the two veterans with whom she had a current clinical relationship. (I agreed to assume that role, in recognition of the VA's concerns that Leslie not be in a "dual relationship" with the two veterans).[118] Thankfully, USM was willing to give Leslie a Professor of Record affiliation with the project; thus she, too, was under the auspices of the University and not entirely on her own.

Will a large governmental agency like the VA ever change? They were extremely concerned about the potential for adverse publicity to the VA when I went in 1989. The VA would not recognize that participating in war veterans' innovative healing journeys of return to their former battlefields could be construed to be a direct part of one's official duties as a PTSD therapist with veterans; they were also preoccupied with concerns of legal and financial liability, in case anything went wrong. And in the end, the VA made the same decision in 2000 as it had in 1989, and refused to sanction the trip in any way.

The participants in the course included three faculty: Andy Wiest, PhD, History Department, USM; Leslie Root, PhD, Psychologist, Gulfport Division, VA Gulf Coast Health Care System; and Ray Scurfield, DSW, School of Social Work, USM. Two other faculty enrolled as course participants: Paul Harris, PhD, History, Visiting Professor from Great Britain; and John Van Sandt, PhD, History, USM. There were three Vietnam veteran guests: Roy Ainsworth, from Biloxi; Charles Brown, from Hattiesburg; and John Young, from Picayune, Mississippi. The sixteen undergraduate and graduate history students were Alice Archer, Danielle Bishop, Cheri Bolton, Patricia Buzard, Scott Catino, Trista

---

118. The various mental health professions all have strict ethical guidelines concerning therapists not engaging in "dual relationships" with their clients. In other words, it is viewed as very problematic for a mental health professional to be both a therapist and a friend or relative, for example, with a client. Such a "dual" relationship complicates or puts at risk the ability to have an unbiased, objective, professional therapeutic relationship with a client.

Dickerson, Janet Graham, Shane Jones, Richard Jordan, Yaron Kaplan (who did double duty as a second cameraman), John Littlejohn, Lana Lehrer, Martin Locaine, Erin McNeely, Adam Ray and Terry Whittington. Finally, there was a cameraman (John Csaszar), and the aforementioned tour facilitator originally from Vietnam, Trang My Frobenius, who accompanied us in Vietnam along with the local Vietnamese tour guide Tran Quoc Cong, from DaNang.

We held two pre-trip meetings at USM in the two weeks immediately prior to the trip so that everyone could meet each other and go over logistical preparations. We also provided a very brief overview of the structure and expectations for the trip. We discussed the purposes of visiting both tourist places and the former duty sites of the three veterans, and the fact that several educational presentations were also scheduled. Each participant was asked to briefly share his or her particular reasons for participating. Finally, we administered a pre-trip questionnaire to use as a baseline for comparison with a planned follow-up questionnaire, in order to be able to record and evaluate what participants might have gained through their experiences.

MAY 2, 2000. THE FIRST PRE-TRIP MEETING

At our "get-acquainted" meeting,[119] each participant spoke for a few minutes about his or her personal background, and the decision to participate in this course. As we had expected, several of the participants had very personal ties to Vietnam or to war veterans. Three students had Vietnam veteran fathers, one had an uncle who was killed in Vietnam, and a fifth had a grandfather who was a World War II veteran.

Several students expressed personal interest derived from their understanding of the major influence that Vietnam has played in the lives of so many Americans. Martin was involved in the history of immigration to the US and of Vietnamese immigrants in particular; he planned to do a one-year mission in Vietnam. The remaining students, history majors, and two adjunct history professors saw this as a unique opportunity to enhance their understanding of an important era in US history and gain some understanding of life in a different

---

119. The account of the 2000 study abroad course, from this point forward, is transcribed directly from the daily journal entries that I began two weeks before we left for Vietnam and continued throughout the trip. In some cases the tense has been changed from present to past for stylistic purposes.

94

part of the world. While most of the students had participated in other study abroad courses, only two had traveled to a third-world country.

A number of the students also expressed their desire to be in Vietnam to give their support to one of the three veterans participating, John Young. They had become very connected to John through his regular participation in Dr. Wiest's Vietnam History classes for the past several years. His participation had involved his sharing about his Vietnam experiences and his considerable knowledge of Vietnam military history.

Leslie Root has been treating war veterans with PTSD for many years, including two of the veterans in this course. Leslie was a very dedicated clinician, expertly familiar with war-related PTSD, who had established close therapeutic bonds with many Vietnam veterans. Naturally, she was delighted to have this opportunity to experience, firsthand, "the Nam" that she had been experiencing through so many veterans over the years.

And I was going for several reasons. I should emphasize that my initial return trip to peacetime Vietnam in 1989 had been very stressful on me personally and on the entire group who went. I never even looked back at my journal of that trip for eleven years. However, the ways things came together it was an unimaginable opportunity. Hokey as it may sound, to some, I really felt as if I were destined to be a part of this experience. I had visited my former duty station at Nha Trang in 1989 and confronted some of the many emotions that arose at that time; I thought that on this trip I might be able to concentrate more on the students and the veterans, rather than having to deal with my own Vietnam experience (what a pie-in-the-sky fantasy!). Also, it was a relief to have an established tour company making all of the travel arrangements so that I would not be hit with the logistical nightmares of our 1989 visit. Andy Wiest carefully selected Vietnam-Indochina Tours to plan and implement our itinerary. And the added benefit of having Ms. Trang from the tour company accompany us offered an invaluable resource in-country when and if logistical problems should arise — which they inevitably do.

I was actually starting to feel as if my first return trip, finally, was — at least mostly! — under my belt. The passage of another decade that was rich with life experiences helped. And, I had belatedly taken the opportunity to reflect on that trip through the process of transcribing my 1989 diary — eleven years later, in the year 2000.

MAY 9. SECOND PRE-TRIP MEETING

With our departure set for the coming Saturday, all of us were getting really excited: we were leaving in four days. We went over some more logistical details, and then we handed out a questionnaire, what we call a psychological instrument, to everyone in order to provide a baseline of information about their psychological state. There were immediate signs of resistance from several of the participants: the first indication that some of the participants might be less than enthusiastic about anything "psychological" or related to mental health on this trip.

Veteran Roy Ainsworth asked if it would be OK to wear a cap with some military insignia on it. Veteran John Young doubted it would be a good idea. But, in our experience in 1989 it had been an extremely positive experience when Vietnamese people found out that we were war veterans. And so, I recommended that he wear such insignia — if that is what he wanted to do.

Flashback to 1989[120]

> This discussion about wearing military insignia on a baseball cap stimulated a memory from our 1989 trip, and it was the first one that I shared with the group. In the midst of a sea of Vietnamese on one a city street in Vietnam, I saw a young man coming towards us. He wore a black baseball cap with white lettering, with the bizarre statement: "I know Jack S — ."
>
> I was now struck by the thought that that could have been our motto (certainly, at least mine) during my Army tour in Vietnam in 1968-69. As a psychiatric social work officer on one of the Army's two psychiatric teams, I had a very rudimentary knowledge about PTSD and treating acute psychiatric casualties in a war zone — and an almost total lack of insight as to the possible longer-term psychiatric impacts of serving in a war zone.[121]

Student Yaron Kaplan and His Uncle Joel

> One of the students, Yaron Kaplan, had an uncle who had served in Vietnam as a psychiatrist: Dr. Joel Kaplan. And, Yaron had a reel-to-reel audio tape film from him, with emotionally dramatic footage of treatment interventions in Vietnam. Several

120. The account of the 2000 study abroad course, from this point forward, is transcribed directly from the daily journal entries that I began two weeks before we left for Vietnam. In some cases the tense has been changed from present to past for stylistic purposes.

121. The first volume of *A Vietnam Trilogy* (Scurfield, R.M., 2004), gives a more in-depth understanding about how military psychiatry operations in a war-zone and the attitudes of typical combat unit command personnel dramatically influenced the actions taken in regards to psychiatric casualties — and the relationship of such to many such veterans having longer-term psychiatric and social rehabilitation issues and problems.

military acute psychiatric casualties in Vietnam had been given sodium pentothal interviews and apparently had vivid emotional cathartic reactions. Yaron had mentioned that he had had numerous conversations with his uncle over the years, and that he understood that his uncle was one of the few psychiatrists in Vietnam at that time.

I talked a little more tonight with Yaron and about his uncle. Then I gave him my business card and noted on it the exact times and location of my tour in Vietnam. Conceivably, his uncle and I might have known some of the same people or shared some other points of contact. If so, I wanted to communicate with him at some point following the trip — especially since I have had substantive communications with just two other military psychiatrists who had been in Vietnam: my former commanding officer on the 98th Medical Detachment, Captain James Janecek; and Arthur S. Blank, Jr., my former supervisor during my three-year tenure in VA Central Office with the Vet Center Program, 1982-85.

The Politics of T-Shirts

Andy had prepared a very nice surprise: a white T-shirt for each of us with a picture of John Young in a Vietnam war-scene (several US soldiers walking in a field on patrol), with the caption "Vietnam 2000" on the front and our names on the back.

This was a generous effort on Andy's part, one that both "honored" the special role that John had played in his regular participation in the Vietnam history classes over the past several years and helped promote group cohesion. On the other hand, I thought there was a risk that this tee-shirt would reinforce the counter-therapeutic message that "Vietnam" was still a country at war, that it still looked the way it did in 1968 or that that was its "normal" state — because it still matched the mental images of Vietnam vets with PTSD. "Vietnam 2000" is not a nation at war, and there are no foreign military combatants there — but that was what the front of the tee-shirt immediately conveyed to me.

Many Vietnam veterans with PTSD are still troubled by mental pictures of Vietnam that are "frozen in time." That is part of the benefit of a trip like the one we were embarking on: to see and experience Vietnam today, as a healthy, growing nation (entirely different from what we all saw during the War), and to be able to conjure these new images of peacetime Vietnam to juxtapose with their longstanding war-era mental images. (Another technique we had used with veterans was to fly once again in a Huey helicopter[122] — to provide new and more positive mental images to compete with the decades-old mental images.)

After the meeting, I discussed my concerns about the T-shirt with Leslie, as we were walking out to our cars. Leslie said that she had the same reaction, and that she would bring it up with Andy tomorrow.

The three of us, Andy, Leslie and I, agreed that we needed to make sure to set aside adequate time to "debrief" with each other, preferably on a daily basis, and to insure

---

122. See *A Vietnam Trilogy* for a description of the experiences of Vietnam veterans going up in Huey helicopters as part of their PTS treatment at the American Lake VA PTST Program, Tacoma, Washington, that I directed from its inception in 1985 until 1992. See also: Scurfield, R.M., L.E. Wong and E.B. Zeerocah, "Helicopter Ride Therapy For Inpatient Vietnam Veterans With PTSD." *Military Medicine, 157* (1992), 67-73.

that the stresses of the responsibilities were not overwhelming any of us. The co-leader of the 1989 trip and I had become distant and had not communicated with each other enough during our time in Vietnam, and that left some unresolved tensions between us. I sure did not want that situation to be repeated.

I also shared my concerns with Andy about the picture on the tee-shirt. Besides renewing an outdated and harmful impression in the minds of our veterans, what would the Vietnamese make of it? There were two sides to that war, and not everyone came out a winner. How would they feel, seeing this photo? Here was an occasion where mental health professionals might add a dimension of understanding to a history course that might otherwise not be fully considered, i.e., the emotional and psychological implications of various events.

Now, we were just about ready to head off to the New Orleans airport, where we were supposed to meet at 5:00 AM. Wow. It seemed surreal that my third departure to Vietnam was imminent.

Chapter 6. Journal Entries—Experiences and Observations by (and for) Veterans and Students

May 13/14. Getting There: An Extremely Long Way to Go

Our flight itinerary had us departing New Orleans via Dallas, then Los Angeles, and Seoul (Korea), to Saigon.

As we are on the first leg of the flight, from New Orleans to Dallas, Yaron comes up to me. He had spoken with his uncle after the last meeting, and lo and behold! His uncle, Joel Kaplan, psychiatrist, immediately recognized my name. He and I had served together for several months in the 98th medical detachment in Nha Trang!

I knew that a "Joel Kaplan" had been on our psychiatric team. However, it is a fairly common name, and I just didn't think the world was that small. Imagine the series of coincidences that added up to this moment: everything that led to my relocation to Mississippi and my role in this study abroad program, and everything that led Yaron Kaplan, born and bred a New Yorker, to relocate to Mississippi, of all places, and to enroll in the same program. And he was particularly interested in Vietnam history precisely because he was very close with his father's brother, Joel, who had served as a psychiatrist in Vietnam.

Until that moment, I had only had contact with two other persons who had been with the 98th: my former Commanding Officer and the former chaplain. This coincidence makes me feel even more strongly that I was destined to be a part of this program.

Of course, I easily could have gotten together with others of the men and women I served with in Vietnam, if I had wanted to. The above journal entry illustrates my disinclination to do so, and this lack of interest (or is it resistance?) is common among many Vietnam veterans. At the same time, there are many vets who, for example, stay in touch by telephone or e-mail and may attend occasional or even yearly reunions of their units. For me, I felt that such contact might encourage me to continually re-live my war experiences; and besides, I was already saturated with Vietnam through my clinical contacts with 1000+ other war veterans over the years.

Crossing the International Dateline

On the plane, LA to Seoul: Wow, I had forgotten; this is one really longggg flight! Leslie mentions seeing a guy sitting on the plane, holding a bar of soap in his right hand, and some food in his left. She was curious and asked him why he was holding the bar of soap while he was eating. He replied, "obsessive compulsive disorder — cleanliness." (Great story to tell in my Social Work Assessment class when we cover the *DSM-IV* diagnosis of Obsessive-Compulsive Disorder.)[123]

Drinking

One of the problems on long flights is that people tend to get bored, and some tend to over-drink. One of our veterans was obviously in this category. Leslie and I both explained to him that it was important not to drink too much on this trip because he needed to allow feelings, memories and anxieties to come up — or he would miss the whole point of the journey. By numbing out, he would lose the opportunity to face those feelings and be healed. He took the point; still, it was clear we would need to keep an eye on him. In addition, it is common for some students to party too much, under any circumstances; and it is common for some travelers to "let their hair down" and enjoy a sense of freedom from the usual rules that they abide by at home. Given all the factors that were working against everyone's normal sense of self-control, there would almost surely be some serious drinking among the vets and students.

Furthermore, the vet who was "under the influence" told Leslie something very personal regarding his significant other, something that he had never told her during therapy. This was problematic. First, something revealed while under the influence of alcohol is a poor basis for therapeutic discussion. Second, this was a situation that could never happen in the context of a regular, office-based counseling relationship and thus it interjected a potentially conflicting element into a normal counseling relationship.

Now Leslie and I came to realize that we had not included the three veterans' significant others in the screening before deciding whether it was therapeutically indicated for the veterans to be included on this trip, although we had asked each veteran what his significant other felt about it. This now appeared to be a serious oversight. There is nothing good in reinforcing what already is a sore point with many Vietnam veterans' families — having been left out of the vet's Vietnam experience.

Flashback to 1968

Talking to Yaron has reminded me of an experience with our psychiatric team in Nha Trang. I had been assigned to the outpatient clinic, which was at a physically separate location away from the hospital; I did not have any duty with the inpatient psychiatric ward on our psychiatric team. Our outpatients came from relatively near-by units. In contrast, the inpatients came from all over I and II Corps; only the Army's two psychiatric teams had the capability and mission to keep psychiatric casualties up to 30 days to assess, treat and make an ultimate disposition.

---

123. American Psychiatric Association, *Diagnostic and Statistical Manual of Mental Disorders, Fourth Edition, Text Revision (DSM-IV-TR)* (Washington, DC: American Psychiatric Association, 2000), pp. 456-463.

I realized for the first time that, possibly, the inpatient unit could have been seeing a significantly higher percentage of front-line troops than we were seeing at our out-patient clinic. I didn't actually know. If so, I may have been erroneous in my long-standing belief that a higher proportion of rear-echelon versus front-line psychiatric casualties were treated by our total unit.

During the several-hour layover in the LA airport, one of the veterans told Leslie he was concerned that many of the students were "too jovial," seeing this primarily as an adventure, a chance to have fun. By contrast, of course, the trip was an extremely serious matter for him. I shared his sense that some of the students were perhaps too playful, and it jarred with my own sensibilities about the trip. At the same time, at least two of the vets and I also saw this playfulness as a positive counter-balance to what otherwise might have been an unremittingly tense trip.

Flashback to 1989

Of course: the same dynamic was present on our 1989 trip, where our therapy group had been combined with a Vietnam Veterans of America (VVA) tour. This turned out to be very problematic. Many members of the VVA tour group partied and drank heavily; in contrast, we had several veterans whose continued sobriety was critical to their successful stress recovery. There was considerable tension between those who wanted to drink and "have a good time" and our group that was focused on resolving those traumatic war experiences.

I suggest to Leslie that we needed to have a discussion at some point with everyone, to make it clear this was a "sacred" trip for the vets; and, for me, too.

I am becoming increasingly aware during this trip how much I have felt, over the years, what a privilege it has been to listen to the remarkably intimate tales of war experiences shared with me by so many veterans. I am more aware now that, as a long-time care-giver, I feel that I have been "carrying the load" as a proxy back to Vietnam for the many vets I have known.

In effect, I have been continuing to reprise my role as a psychiatric social worker with psychiatric casualties from the war, all the way up to 2000. This is not 1989 or 1968. And I do seem to be somewhat caught up in the significance of it all, which adds to my inclination to react very strongly and seriously to everything about the trip. I continue to find myself unable or unwilling to be more relaxed and playful — and am bothered more often than not by the playfulness of some of the students.

On the other hand, the students have paid a lot for this course. They have the right to do what they want to do, within reasonable limits. And it is normal at their age to want to have a good time, be spontaneous, loud, exuberant, and naturally very excited to be in a foreign country with a bunch of fellow students. Maybe I am turn-ing into a crotchety old man, at 57, who is used to living more in solitude rather than traveling in close quarters with a large group of students.

In any case, both the vets and the students need to recognize what is going on. And the tension may be heightened at certain times during the trip, such as close to or during the time of each veteran's return to his former battle area. At least, it seems important that everyone become aware of this dynamic, and know that it might be a problem for some of the group members (both veterans and students) to be exposed to any or to too much drinking.

Andy, Leslie and I again agree that we need to have our daily debriefs together. We need to insure that we have our mutual support going for and with each other. [Yet, as in 1989, this turned out to be one of those good intentions that fell by the wayside under the crush of daily events that unfolded during our time in Vietnam.]

Making Profits From the Spoils of War

We find out that two Vietnam veterans who are not part of our group are on the plane. One is a recently retired policeman. This is their sixth trip to Vietnam since the mid-1990s. They go around to various villages in Vietnam, finding or buying war memorabilia. They have a web site. They also have a restored Huey helicopter, mannequins dressed in US and Vietnamese uniforms, and other Vietnam War paraphernalia that they display during presentations at schools, parades, and other public events.

I get a rather negative feeling about this: These two vets are "making profit from the spoils of war." We have a ten-minute conversation, standing in a small group at the rear of the airplane.

Ray: "Have you ever been accused of profiting from the war?"

Vet: "No, I deal mostly with war memorabilia collectors — about 2 are vets and 2 are not...and so they are all interested in the same thing...Besides, we don't make much of a profit...just about enough to cover our expenses."

He seems to be sincere and a nice guy, genuinely interested in the journey back to Vietnam for the three veterans in our group. He even mentions, "When I first came back in the early 1990s, I remember that I 'froze' the first time I stepped back into the Delta [where he had been stationed]."

Am I just being sanctimonious? "I am on a noble mission" while these men are "making money off the misfortunes of others"? Guess I could check out their web site one day and see if I feel any differently.[124]

Maybe it's just that I'm taking everything terribly seriously now, as we land in Saigon. (The name has been changed officially to Ho Chi Minh City, but I'll probably go back and forth in referring to HCM City and to Saigon — because I find myself having trouble relating to the new name). No, that's not the whole of it: I just don't like the idea of some vets or even non-vets coming over here, scouring the countryside for war leftovers, taking them back and selling them; seems to me to cheapen and commercialize the sacrifices that so many vets and their families have made.[125] But then again, maybe that is just my issue.

Ten hours, LA to Seoul; five hours, Seoul to Ho Chi Minh City. This is a really long trip. Once again I am reminded of how distant Vietnam is from the US. Way back in

---

124. I never have checked out the web site.
125. Courtney Frobenius, the head of Vietnam-Indochina Tours, offered me a quite different viewpoint about these two veterans collecting and selling war memorabilia from Vietnam. "The souvenir traders on the airplane . . . they have found peace, be happy for that; they are able to see beyond the things which tormented their youth. What difference does it make that they buy trinkets from people who would much prefer to have the money than the trinkets?" My positive and rational side would agree wholeheartedly with this perspective, and yet my feelings do not.

the early 1960s, the vast majority of Americans didn't have the faintest idea where Vietnam was or why we would consider stationing massive numbers of troops there. And many of us still wonder why.

DAY ONE IN VIETNAM. MAY 15. HO CHI MINH CITY AND AN EMOTIONAL DEBRIEFING

Arrive Saigon just before midnight Clear customs and immigration, transfer to hotel. Morning: Orientation/Briefing by USM officials.

Afternoon: Saigon city tour.

The Dragon House, Ho Chi Minh Museum. The director of the museum is an old revolutionary and a very interesting person; the Dragon House is where Ho Chi Minh departed Vietnam in 1911 on a thirty-year exile which was to take him to the United States, England, France, Africa, Russia and China.

Evening: Banquet at 6:30PM at Dam Sen Park, hosted by Vietnam-Indochina Tours. Guests will include former English-language students of Courtney Frobenius.

Tan Son Nhat airport has been modernized: a brand new building, air conditioning. This is a great contrast to what we saw in 1989. As we walk outside, the humidity and heat of Vietnam greet us with a familiar embrace. Then we find our bus; in great contrast to the faded old yellow military bus that we used in 1989, this one is modern and air conditioned.

As we pull out from the airport, we see bright blue neon lettering (now, that's new!) atop the terminal, "Tan Son Nhat Airport." I have a very heavy, sad feeling; I notice with a mild curiosity the numerous dimly lit little outdoor "cafes" along the streets, still doing some business at 1:30 AM. And my initial thought is that I am feeling the sadness of the history of a city that has seen so much death.

We check in at the Hotel Equatorial, very fancy and modern. When I get to my room, I am flooded with the awareness of how many people died here in Vietnam: estimated by some accounts at some 800,000 South Vietnamese and 1.6 million North Vietnamese killed, and reportedly over 300,000 Missing-In-Action (MIA); not to mention the 58,000+ US military personnel killed and all our MIAs still unaccounted for.

And for what? The Communists took over the entire country anyway. And then the tragic fleeing from Vietnam by any means, so many "boat people" taking desperate risks, and the resulting fragmentation of families.

8:00 AM. After getting some sleep, I am in a *much* better mood.

Flashback to Post-Vietnam War

Yaron mentions the book *Heaven and Earth*, in which there is a description of a Vietnamese family dinner. I flash back to a memory of my first post-war Thanksgiving. I'm sitting down for our traditional and sumptuous family Thanksgiving dinner at my parents' house in Pasadena. Suddenly I find myself having an extremely adverse reaction as my memories propel me back to Thanksgiving in Vietnam: "Here we are, in the comfort and safety of our home. At the same time, hundreds of thousands of vets, forgotten to all but perhaps their families, are experiencing who knows what loneliness, deprivations and horrors at this very moment 10,000 miles away, in the Nam."

I was very uncomfortable with Thanksgiving dinners for several years afterwards, and then, that dissipated. Since the war, I also have remained very uncomfortable with Fourth of July firework displays; perhaps it is the lingering memory of the Tet Offensive that was launched under the cover of the massive fireworks during the Chinese New Years celebration in Vietnam in 1968.

Morning Orientation and Briefing by USM Faculty

Our first meeting in Vietnam will be followed by an afternoon city tour. Having checked in after 1:00 AM and not yet seen anything, the group is naturally eager to get out and explore the sights and sounds and smells of Vietnam. However, we have to go over a few things first. This competition between briefings (or debriefings) and reaching for new experiences became a recurring theme throughout the trip, and almost all of our meetings had to be considerably shortened.

One topic that we needed to discuss was how to relate to our vets, now that we were in Vietnam. We would have to expect that different people would be on an emotional roller coaster from one day to the next. The students had observed one vet, for example, very deep in thought and looking very serious, if not grim. What should they say, if anything?

John Young gave his thoughts on that. "Don't ask, 'How are you?' 'How's it going?' Say 'good morning,' or 'Hello.' Then, just take your cue from how I respond. It should be very easy to tell if I just want to be left alone and don't want to talk."

Cheri added: "Don't say, 'I understand,' or 'I know how you're feeling,' because you don't, and can't possibly."

I commented: "We can expect that as we get close to the day when each vet is scheduled to return to his former battlefield, he will very likely start to become very focused on his return and whatever issues may be associated with that battlefield. I myself was hardly aware of anyone else as we got close to Nha Trang. I was really anxious and preoccupied. I didn't want to have to talk to anyone, and I was impatient. And I wanted some alone time."

I find myself walking a constant tightrope on this trip. On the one hand, I believe that our experiences in 1989 can offer helpful tips for our group to consider. On the other hand, oftentimes I hold myself back from sharing things that happened in 1989; 1989 is not 2000, and these are two very different groups. This will surely be a different Vietnam and our experiences will be different. Also, I get the distinct feeling that many group members are not really interested in what happened in 1989; they just want to get on with experiencing Vietnam 2000. Is this another example of how much each of us seems to "claim" our own personal Vietnam experiences? On our first day touring Saigon, a Vietnamese man tells us some local sayings:

"In Saigon, you can get everything; in Hanoi, you can get almost everything; outside of Saigon and Hanoi, you can hardly get anything."

Saigon is the city of opportunity: the place to go if you want to "make it," or to escape, or to disappear.

"Hanoi is the Paris of Vietnam, and Saigon is the Los Angeles of Vietnam."

We arrive at the Dragon House Ho Chi Minh Museum. However, it's closed. We move on to the next stop, the Notre Dame, the largest cathedral in the country. The Cathedral also is closed, but we can still take pictures. It is a large, impressive building. However, it is not as well kept as one would hope. I am told that this is a reflection of the Communist government's policy for many years of not allowing the Vietnamese to put money into the repair and upkeep of Catholic churches. Until relatively recently, much of the Catholic Church's resources were directed to funding the repairs and building of other churches.

The Post Office across the street also recalls the days of French colonialism. It is a large and beautiful structure, very carefully preserved (quite a contrast to the outside of the Catholic Cathedral across the street); it also was very hot, with the front doors open and a few fans blowing ineffectually. This was pretty much the norm wherever we went.

We then drive to the former Presidential Palace, emblematic of both the grandeur and fall of Saigon and the American-backed regime. Our guide tells us, several times, about an NVA tank that had been crashed into the front gate of the Palace during the fall of Saigon in 1975. This repetition of the story grates on my nerves. The tank is displayed to the right of the grounds. The group heads over to takes pictures. I have no interest whatsoever in going over to the tank. Been there, done that, in 1989.

Flashback to 1989

The tank propels me back to my first return trip. Several damaged US tanks were on display, and some of us found that depressing. Other group members looked at them with curiosity and excitement.

So now, while everyone else goes over to the tank to snap pictures, I go off alone in the other direction. A sign saying "Natural Display," leads me to an exhibit about one of the highlands ethnic groups of Vietnam. And it brings back sad thoughts of the Montagnard (mountain) people who fought on the side of the Americans. To my knowledge, historically the dominant Vietnamese ethnic group has not been kind to the other peoples who lived in the region.

Our group then goes on a guided tour inside the main building. I remain outside, wanting to pause and reflect. I go and sit on a low wall, outside the entrance. As I look outward at the expansive grounds and take in the view of the city of Saigon, I ponder the fall of the Saigon regime and what it must have been like for both South and North Vietnam troops during the last tumultuous days of the War.

I am fairly certain that the employees at this former Presidential Palace are all former Communist sympathizers, whether NVA (North Vietnamese Army) or VC (Viet Cong, indigenous Vietnamese in "South" Vietnam who opposed the Saigon-based government). I seriously doubt that any former ARVNs (Army of the Republic of Vietnam, the Saigon-based government of "South" Vietnam whom the US tried to prop up) or their family members could get a position here. It had become clear, in 1989, that former ARVNs were generally not allowed to work in any place like this in Vietnam.

And, in contrast to 1989, I notice that the novelty of seeing an American or Westerner has worn off, to some extent. Also, motorbikes and taxis seem to have largely replaced the bicycle and cyclos that were omnipresent in 1989. [I later learn that the

105

motorbike is the major personal and family transportation vehicle. It is common to see one or two parents *and* one or two children all perched on a small motorbike; apparently, only the poor continue to use bicycles and pedal-powered cyclos, especially in Saigon.]

I'm finding myself *much* more interested in the stories of our three veterans, and several of the students who have their own personal stories connected to Vietnam: such as John Littlejohn, whose father spent considerable time in Vietnam as a courier; Cheri, whose uncle was a Vietnam vet; Janet, whose father was a Vietnam vet; Yaron, whose uncle served with me; and Patricia, who had shared with us at our first pre-trip meeting the emotional impact the Vietnam War had had on her. I am much more interested in taking pictures of them experiencing Vietnam than I am in taking pictures of edifices and war relics, as I tended to do in 1989.

The "American War"

Mr. Cong, our tour guide, repeatedly refers to what we call "The Vietnam War" as "The American War." At first, this is an extremely discordant phrase to hear, after three decades of thinking, remembering, feeling, talking, writing and reading about "The Vietnam War." But, as "The American War" is repeated over several days, it gradually becomes acceptable and even understandable to me. After all, all of their wars have been "Vietnam" wars, haven't they? Thus, for them, it was "the Cambodian War," "the French War," etc., over the decades and centuries.

Vinh Nghiem Pagoda

We arrive at the Pagoda and find the grounds bustling with activity. Buddha's birthday will be celebrated in a few days. This is the first time that we encounter beggars. The pagoda and grounds seem to be somewhat in disrepair, except within the actual temple itself. We leave our shoes at the entrance.

Flashback to 1989

In 1989, I had quite an adventure while trying to find a large Buddhist temple south of Saigon. I had gone there to fulfill a promise to a veteran, to return for him a Buddhist wood prayer block that he had stolen from a temple in that area during the war. He had felt increasingly haunted, over the past several years, and had recurrent and terrifying dreams.

Inter-Generational Links Between Students and Veterans

Yaron offers to go to Nha Trang with me, if I want to do so at some time during this trip. Nha Trang is not on the schedule, and is not anywhere near the other locations that we are scheduled to visit. Yaron obviously really wants to go, since his uncle Joel had served there with me. However, I did not find my return to Nha Trang in 1989 particularly uplifting. We had been unable to find *anyone* who remembered where the 8th Field Hospital had been located. That had been a disappointment for me. I had not planned on going there again.

But, maybe I should do it with and for Yaron and Joel Kaplan.

My budding relationship with Yaron seems to be somewhat parallel to the bonding taking place between one of the Vietnam veterans, Roy, for example, and several of the male students, two of whom are in ROTC, Shane and Adam. Roy's perspective and personal military history is sincerely appreciated by these students; in turn they kind of "look out for" Roy and make sure that he is doing OK.

The student-veteran connections and interactions provide a distinctive and important inter-generational link. Many Vietnam vets, especially those with PTSD, have few chances to interact with 20-something college students. Similarly, the visits by hospitalized veterans at our American Lake PTSD Program who talked at veteran-student forums at Puget Sound University were very successful.[126]

OUR FIRST DEBRIEFING IN VIETNAM: EMOTIONAL AND CONTROVERSIAL

Our debriefing on the first morning we arrived in Vietnam allowed several group members to share some pressing emotional reactions; but, at the same time, several students clearly did not think this was a good use of time. As history majors and not psychology or social work students, they are not comfortable with group discussions where emotional sharing is an expected part of the process. However, many meaningful incidents had already occurred, and if we did not go over the in-transit experiences from the US to Vietnam soon, they would be swept away by other impressions.

The First Debriefing.[127]

We have to avoid getting hung up on one long story, so that everyone who wants to talk will have a turn. To "model" how one might share in such a debriefing, I start off with a short comment about my mistrust of the two memorabilia collectors on the plane, and my initial impressions and feelings upon landing at the airport. Paul Harris, who is a visiting military history professor from Britain, goes next. Paul talks of the struggles of a former Saigon ARVN officer and his family who had immigrated to Great Britain.

Janet, daughter of a Vietnam veteran, shares about a moving experience she had on the plane between Dallas and Los Angeles. A male passenger was disturbed by the

---

126. The involvement of veterans from the PTSD Clinical Team, Gulfport Division of the Biloxi VA Hospital, with the history classes taught by Andy Wiest, offered a very positive experience for both the veterans and students, and of course was a direct precipitant of the Vietnam History Study Abroad course, as described in this chapter. Related to this activity, I directed the American Lake VA Medical Center (ALVA) PTSD Program in Tacoma, WA, from its inception in 1985 through 1991. Through the initiative in particular of Doc Gene Dewese, one of our program's Vietnam vet peer counselors, we became involved in a series of veteran-student forums at Puget Sound University. Small groups of vets from our program, as part of their PTSD recovery, would go to the university and participate in lively forums with university students. Both vets and students would share their personal viewpoints and feelings about the Vietnam War. These forums became a highly positive aspect of the stress recovery journeys of the participating vets, and the students routinely would state that the forums were a highlight of their education. For moving veteran narratives of their experiences in several other "beyond the office walls" innovative therapeutic activities at ALVA, to include helicopter ride therapy, Outward Bound river rafting and rappelling excursions, usage of American Indian sweat lodges, and grieving and acknowledgement visits to veteran memorials, see Scurfield (2004), *A Vietnam Trilogy.*

students' commotion and asked the hostess to move him to another seat. But none was available. Then he overheard the students talking about Vietnam, and it turned out that he was a Vietnam veteran. He and several students then became very engaged in conversation about Vietnam, looked with some students at their maps of Vietnam, and it was very emotional for everyone involved.

Charles Brown describes changes he's noticed between the Vietnam of today and the Vietnam of the 1960s. "During the war, a bus could have had grenades thrown into any open windows. Also, we would avoid going around in large groups; that was just an invitation to the guerillas."

Yaron observes that he is shy to share his experiences, since "they are not as heavy or traumatic as the three veterans'." I encourage him to recognize that his life experiences were meaningful to *him*, and important on that score.

John L., a large young man with a shaved head, who wears boots, a Confederate hat, and a goatee, says, "When I heard that Charles [who is African-American] was coming on this trip, I was afraid he would see me as just a Southern redneck. In fact, the organization he is in and the one I am in are on opposite sides of a lawsuit right now.....Yes, my ancestors fought in the Civil War, but none of them had slaves. I am very proud of my Southern heritage." It turns out that he is a very articulate and sensitive man, and someone who feels very strongly and sincerely about war veterans. There goes another stereotype of Southerners out the window. Then he says,

"I wanted to go up and hug each vet at different times, because that's my nature, and I feel so much for the vets and admire them so; but I held back. I didn't know if I should do that or not."

I ask if any of the veterans wants to reply to John. One or two of them suggest that, if that was what John wanted to do, it was OK with them. (Hey, it's happening! Vet-to-student-to vet connections. All right!)

When we were visiting the Ho Chi Minh Museum, John L. had pointed out that "The South Vietnamese had money, guns and the US behind them: all things that the Confederacy during the Civil War hadn't had, and still they lost. Must have been that their hearts weren't in it enough to want it badly enough to win."

Charles later told me and Leslie that he didn't want to offend John Y., but he did not share his experiences and perception of the war. We assured him that he didn't have to invalidate John Y. to validate his own experience: he could just frame it as

---

127. The debriefing we conducted was modeled very loosely on the Critical Incident Stress Debriefing (CISD) model to providing acute debriefing interventions with emergency medical and rescue personnel who are repeatedly exposed to life-threatening medical emergencies. Subsequently, the CISD model has been applied to acute interventions with survivors of such trauma as natural disasters, hostage situations, school shootings, etc. See, for example: Everly, G.S. and J.T. Mitchell, *Critical Incident Stress Management: CISM: A New Era and Standard of Care in Crisis Intervention (2nd Ed)* (Ellicott City, MD: Chevron Publishing Corporation, 1999); Rose, S. and J. Bisson, "Brief early psychological interventions following trauma: A systematic review of the literature," *Journal of Traumatic Stress*, 11 (1998), 697-710; and Stein, E. and B. Eisen, "Helping trauma survivors cope: Effects of immediate brief co-therapy and crisis intervention," *Crisis Intervention*, 3 (1996), 113-127.

his own experience; there were many different experiences of war in Vietnam, and his was one of them.

Negative Feedback

Several of the students let it be known that they did not like the way the debriefing was run. It was a constant challenge during this trip to strike a workable balance between what we might do in a formal "critical incident" debriefing, in order to help everybody manage the stress that would otherwise build up, and quick, factual, information sharing. No doubt about it, the expectations of the history students were very different from what I had become used to in my long career of counseling.

A Benefit of Multiple Trips to Vietnam

Events on this trip are already triggering a mixture of recollections of my return in 1989, in addition to painful memories from the war. Now, when I return to the US again, I can expect to have flashes back to Vietnam 1968, 1989 and 2000 as well. And this is one of the more important possible benefits of such return trips: to develop new, positive peacetime memories to juxtapose alongside war memories.

Flashback to 1989

In 1989 the group consisted of eight veterans; much of out time was spent arranging visits to specific former battle sites. Now, with only three vets, much more of our time is scheduled for "touring." At first this strikes me as trivializing the experience; I come to realize later that this isn't all bad. The touristy and cultural things, interspersed with visits to the former battle sites of the three veterans, dramatically reduces the intensity that characterized every day of the 1989 trip; this provides a welcome respite from the potentially overwhelming emotions.

DAY 2. MAY 16. VETERANS CEMETERIES AND A QUESTION OF RESPECT

At breakfast Veteran John Y shares that he was just informed that the expression that he and most GIs used during the war, "*Di Di Mau*," is the *rude* way to say "go away" or "get out of here." So many of us used that phrase without knowing that it was impolite....

His comment reminds me of a conversation between two soldiers during the war in Vietnam.

One says, "I go to Vietnamese/GI bars a lot, but I don't like the fact that the only Vietnamese and English spoken there is 'GI slang' and poor English: 'You number-one GI.' 'I got buku money.' 'You no go with me, I di di mau.' How can I learn proper Vietnamese?"

Answer: "Go talk with the Vietnamese somewhere besides (American) GI bars."

Breakfast Conversation

John and Charles, Yaron, Janet and I get into a discussion about PTSD. Charles and I mention not remembering names of people we served with.

109

Then, there is the military view of PTSD that often considers psychiatric casualties to be cowards or quitters. Janet's dad (a Vietnam veteran) would get incensed when hearing people talking about Vietnam vets having "PTSD." Charles tells us, "We were instructed to shoot anybody who was deserting or running away." John recalls his Battalion Sgt. Major in 1981. "After all my time in Vietnam and coming home, then deciding that I really needed to get out of the Army, I go and tell him that. And he says to me, 'you're just a quitter.' "

Yaron observes that his good friend was killed in Lebanon during the Israeli occu- pation.... "After that, I wanted to go serve in the Israeli Army in Lebanon."

I just had a thought connected to yesterday about people comparing trauma, and what I often say when a vet denigrates the value of what he did (in comparison to others "who had it much worse. "): "Just think: if everyone with your MOS (military occupational specialty) suddenly disappeared from the war: would that have any impact on the military's ability to fight the war or on the welfare of other US mili- tary personnel?"

Ho Chi Minh City Veterans Cemetery

Woe to the Losers: This morning we visit two Vietnamese veteran' cemeteries. At the Ho Chi Minh City Veterans Cemetery — one of many in every city and district throughout Vietnam — we see rows of tombstones with dates, names and units, some of which date back to the inception of Communist Party operations in Viet- nam in the 1920s. There is an aura of respect for the memory of those who fell. The tombstones are laid out in small circles, five tombstones in each circle, facing inwards. Mr. Cong explains the significance: "This is similar to sitting around a campfire, in a small group. In this way, the deceased are close to each other and won't be so lonely."

By contrast, the "former" National ARVN Veterans Cemetery we visit later pro- duces a forlorn feeling for those entombed here — while it is still technically a cem- etery, it is stripped and languishing, with pictures of dead soldiers on the tombstones.

Standing in the first cemetery, four of us come together spontaneously under some young trees. Tombstones stretch away in three directions, with the massive large stone memorial immediately behind us. Of course, emotions are running high. Roy shares about his continuing journey of recovery from the war. Yaron and John L. support him. It seems quite surreal that two American Vietnam veterans and two students should be standing here, 10,000 miles from home, amidst hundreds of care- fully manicured graves of former enemy soldiers.

Yaron discusses his life's journey; it has been full of challenges. Yaron doesn't mini- mize the extent of his past difficulties, or his responsibility. However, he goes on to deny that he has had any meaningful role in moving ahead with his life. We try to help him accept the responsibility, and credit, for being part of the solution as well as part of the cause.

Being Respectful in Vietnam and in Asia

To my dismay, the students all seem to be calling our guide *Cong*, and not *Mr. Cong*. He is clearly older than they are, and is in a position of authority. Isn't it just com- mon courtesy to call him "Mr."? When I raise this issue with the group, they tell me that they had asked another Vietnamese how to address Mr. Cong, and had been told that everyone understood that Americans tend to use first names, as part of our informal culture, and that it was not taken as a sign of disrespect.

This rubs me the wrong way. We are in Vietnam, and since hierarchy is very important in most Asian countries, and respect for elders, and for positions, shouldn't we follow their rules? I come to realize that I cannot tell whether I am over-reacting, because I do have an unresolved issue from the Vietnam War: I had been offended by the demeaning attitude of many American military personnel towards the Vietnamese people. Also, I am sure that the Vietnamese person was being very sensitive and careful not to say anything that might offend the students when they asked the question. I make this a point to discuss at our next meeting.

The Former National ARVN Veterans Cemetery. "ARVNs Don't Exist"

We had been told on our return trip to Vietnam in 1989 that the cemeteries for former ARVNs had been bulldozed over or otherwise destroyed, or left deserted. Thus, I was surprised to even have such a cemetery on our itinerary. Vietnam-Indochina Tours had gone to great lengths to arrange for government permission for this visit. It was a most important part of our trip.

I expect the ARVN cemetery to be unkempt. Even so, I am upset and very angry when I actually see it. It is in squalid condition. At the main entrance, broken steps lead up through high weeds to a damaged and graffiti-laden entry building. There are condoms and needles on the ground. Someone is curled up, sleeping there.

Across where the main cemetery had been, squatting right in the middle, is a relatively new-looking factory complex. It acts as a barrier and an industrial blemish between the desecrated entry area and the remnants of the main burial grounds. The contrast with the beautifully kept Ho Chi Minh City Veterans Cemetery is profound.

Later, Mr. Cong tells me that when the government officials reviewed our itinerary, he was asked why we would even want to visit this place. I feel like shouting, "Because they were human beings, and were our comrades who we fought alongside, that's why!"

The remains of our former Vietnamese allies have been discarded at this site. Apparently, there are few remaining and recognizable ARVN cemeteries. In a country in which ancestor worship is extremely important, this is particularly unsettling. One Vietnamese person does tell me that, when possible, family members have tried to locate and take such remains back to their homes so that they can give them a proper burial and be honored as one's ancestors should be.

My anger has risen again. We spend about half as long here as we spent at the official government-run cemetery. Most people seem in a hurry to get back to the hotel. No one but me seems to be having the very negative reaction that I am having.

Courtney Frobenius offered this comment in reviewing the above diary entry: "The ARVN Cemetery is a place for ghosts. Woe be to the losers, and so it has been throughout history. When I go to the ARVN cemetery I don't mourn those who died or their wilting memorial: I mourn the senseless death of all young men who die in war; I mourn for their mothers and for their families." — Amen.

I later ask someone why former ARVNs are not allowed to be buried in cemeteries (let alone in well-kept government cemeteries)? He replies, "That would be like meeting Bill and Hillary Clinton, and saying, 'Hello, President Clinton, Mrs. Clinton. How is Monica Lewinsky these days?" I am puzzled. He explains, "To ask means that you recognize their existence. The Communist government doesn't recognize that the former ARVNs ever existed....When the North won, their soldiers and the Russians pissed on the remains of the former ARVNs, before the bodies were bulldozed and scattered. And if you become familiar with the long history of Vietnam, you will understand that this is the way it has been throughout our history."

Treatment of the US Confederacy versus Saigon Government: A Lesson in Contrasts

I find myself contrasting what I have just heard with what I know about Confederate cemeteries and memorials in the United States today. Indeed, in the US today, Confederate and Union soldiers are buried and honored in some of the same cemeteries. Confederate history has been kept alive in various historical and privately-funded and operated archives and displays throughout the South. To my knowledge, nothing like that exists in Vietnam. Of course, it has only been some 30 years since the end of the War versus 140 years since the end of the Civil War. Yet even today many Southerners are bothered by the negativity directed towards the Rebel battle flag; they claim that this denigrates their heritage, and is an attempt to stop them from honoring the legacy of their Confederate ancestors and the culture that was destroyed. Conversely, many black and white Americans consider that flag to be a symbol of racism and oppression.

The US, of course, has not always been as willing to allow the South to preserve and honor its Confederate heritage as it is today.[128]

Here in Vietnam I find myself reacting very negatively to the fact that the Communist government is not so much discriminating against former ARVNs. Rather, it refuses to *admit that they existed*. Could there be a more insulting stance? When will division and hatred disappear: in Vietnam, or for that matter in America?

And I find myself grieving sorely over the fractured lineage of proper respect and burial denied to hundreds of thousands of former ARVNs and the continuing extremely negative impact on their surviving family members. I am stunned to see that the Communist government appears to be continuing to dehumanize even the remains of their former South Vietnamese enemy while by this time they are no longer demonizing Americans. And I am struck by a thought: is the hatred generated by war so pervasive that it can be sustained by some governments to override even minimal basic acceptance of former enemies as human beings? My awareness of the negative fall-out from war has just been expanded a little more — and it is depressing.

---

128. For a critical account, from a libertarian perspective, of the deleterious intent and impact of post-Civil War Reconstruction efforts in the South, see Chodes, John. *Destroying the Republic: Jabez Curry and the Re-Education of the Old South* (New York: Algora Publishing, 2005). He describes how a New England dominated ethos, values and beliefs were promulgated through a compulsory educational system that was intended to enforce conformity to Northern politics and values.

Attitudes Toward Vietnamese, in America and in Vietnam

Roy: "I have felt very negative towards Vietnamese immigrants in Biloxi; some of my neighbors are Vietnamese. But I am not having that same reaction here in Vietnam. Now I'm thinking, 'Hey, people here have the right to try and seek a better life and I'm going to help some of them (when I go back).'"

Ray: "That's great, Roy. But just remember how many of us made promises like that during the war, promising to keep in touch through letters, or to visit someone's family. Most of us didn't keep those promises. You may feel inspired right at this moment, but your good intentions might fade away once you get back home."

Roy: "But now I feel very differently towards Vietnamese people. I don't have that hatred, now."

Yaron: "Roy, if you had come here only with other members of your unit, would it have been different?"

Roy: "Yes. I don't think we would have come here to Saigon, but would have gone straight north [to our former battle sites]. We probably would have kept focused on our hate."

An Emotional Debriefing: Cultural Nuances, Race and Respect

At the next group meeting, I express quite strongly my anger about the former ARVN cemetery and the stark contrast with the government cemetery. Several group members are surprised. None of the other veterans indicate any such reaction, and only a few others say that they had a negative reaction. One such member was Paul Harris, who is close personal friends with several former ARVNs and their families in England.

Charles asks a very powerful question: "What about no cemeteries for African-Americans in our own country, for 200 years. Do you have any feelings about that?"

That really brought us home to the reality of where we all live.

DAY 3. MAY 17. JOHN'S RETURN TO THE CAN GIOUC BATTLEFIELD

John provided a very informative and emotional pre-briefing to the class the evening before we are to go to his former battle site.

"When that battle started, I was a 22 year old clear-eyed kid out of college. When that battle was over, I was an old man. . . . We were sure we were going to die this time. . . . there were people (VC) popping up from the bunkers all around us. . . . I left my youth out there. War is not a thing you just watch on T.V. and then the characters just get up and walk away afterwards. It is a really ugly thing. . . . And the killing is the worst part of it, the killing is the worst part of it."

All day journey to Long An Province to the Can Giouc battlefield, via mini-vans, ferry, motorbikes, on foot and by small boats to the delta region where John Y.'s battle site was located.

John Young. Two and one-half tours, 1967-69. 4th Battalion, 9th Infantry Division; Purple Heart, Bronze Star.

John's former battle site is near a small village with small bridges and narrow dirt roads, so we make the trip in four mini-vans. No tourists here! People all along the latter part of the route react as though we are the first foreigners they have ever seen, especially in the market place next to the ferry. The van drivers refuse to cross the final bridge to the village: they don't think it can hold the weight of the vehicles. And so we walk across a rather long and narrow bridge and enter the village.

Our guide sets off to find the village officials. Custom indicates that he let them know we are entering their village. There is an impromptu meeting in what appears to be the "town hall," a small building with a long narrow room and a table that can accommodate about 15 people. The other group members wait outside the open door, taking pictures of curious children and adults who gather around.

The two Communist officials sit at the head of the table. They each stand up and give speeches, translated by our guide. The second official, a woman, gives a lengthy account of the battle itself. Apparently, she says that it was a rousing victory for the VC, with 10 Americans killed for every VC soldier. She waxes eloquent, and goes on and on, letting us know how badly the Americans were defeated. Veteran John later told us that, while it had indeed been a terrible defeat for the Americans, and he did not dispute that, the casualty figures provided by the Communist official were dramatically inflated from the figures John had read about the size of the forces at this battle. So that one may reasonably ask, how trustworthy was either our government *or* their government in regard to casualties statistics?

A Motorbike Adventure For Us All

Ah, but now we have a major problem, because it is apparently another several miles to the road that is closest to where the battle took place. As usual, it is very hot and humid, and many members of the group would not be able to walk that far. But to our surprise, help is at hand. The Party officials get the word out and sure enough, in the course of the next 30 minutes, several Vietnamese men make themselves (and their motorbikes) available to take us there. They arrive singly or in groups of two or three. Each picks up one member of our group and takes off down the road.[129]

It is a remarkable experience: with no choice but to trust our erstwhile "enemies," each of us climbs onto the back of a motorbike behind a Vietnamese man who then takes off for goodness knows where, and at a fairly fast speed, down the road and out of sight. Some of our group members are much larger in physique than the lithe and wiry Vietnamese. This presents a comical sight, as the villagers agree. We are

---

129. It was not until later that we found out that the Communist officials, in preparation for our visit, had arranged ahead of time for this motorbike entourage. We had mistakenly assumed that it was a spontaneous, hastily arranged accommodation. We often were spared the grinding difficulty entailed in getting approval for every planned stop and making the logistical arrangements and therefore we often were oblivious to the terrific behind-the-scenes support that had been provided ahead of time throughout our itinerary. A knowledgeable tour agency is essential to pre-plan the trip and to be available in-country to troubleshoot as events unfold. Again, Vietnam-Indochina Tours deserves our perpetual gratitude.

an amusing and fast-moving parade along the one-lane dirt road between streams and fields of crops and small homes. At almost every home that we pass, there are people sitting or standing outside. If they happen to look in our direction, they do a double take. Then they laugh, quite loudly, point, and make noises that indicate this is just about the funniest sight they have seen. (

Since then, I've seen it on video, myself, and I quite agree.)

When we reach the destination, we are introduced to a very distinguished elderly man in a Vietnamese suit and hat. He leads us along the dikes through the rice paddies (mostly in the blazing sun) for perhaps a mile or so. Finally, we come to a river about 40 feet wide. From this point onward, we will need a boat to get John to his former battle site.

Can Giouc Battlefield

John was extremely lucky: he was able to locate and return to the exact location where his Vietnam War experience happened. This was possible due to a remarkable set of circumstances that won't apply to most returning veterans; most cannot expect to be able to find the exact spot of the battle and actually interact with former enemy soldiers who fought in that very same battle. Also, we have an outstanding translator in Mr. Cong. He is able to help everyone communicate in a full and comprehensible way.

John has an exact, detailed map and coordinates, something that most vets won't have unless their salient experience happened to occur during a major battle. He fought at a distinctive battle site and date — well known to the Vietnamese and to the US forces. The battle location is adjacent to a village that was there during the war and still exists today. The village was a VC stronghold; the former VC and their families and descendants were living here 30 years ago, and continue to be here today.

Furthermore, at least two former VC combatants who still live in the village were in the very same battle that John remembered so vividly. Indeed:

When a boat is found, which is essential to ferry John the last mile or so to the former battlefield, it turns out the pilot is one of the men who fought in the same battle. He is able to describe what happened, his description converging closely with John's memory, albeit from the other side of the same battle.

"This is where the US boat landed and where the helicopter landed."

"This is where our machine gun emplacement was located; we had one full battalion of National Liberation Forces stationed here." (That is far more than what the American force had been told.)

The boat is only big enough for the pilot, Mr. Cong, John Young, Dr. Leslie Root (John's longstanding therapist) and Yaron as cameraman. The rest of us wait while John and the other three go off in the boat for an hour or so to find and visit the battle site.

We are told later that the pilot of the boat related the following to John.

"I was 30 years old at the time of the battle; six members of my family were killed by bombs and artillery. A woman who was wounded during the battle and was given food by some of the American soldiers is still alive and lives in that same home very close to the battle site.

"Our VC forces were fully aware that the Americans were coming; we were extremely well prepared and placed. We waited until the Americans came within one meter of our hidden entrenchments before opening fire."

We wait by the river. Finally, the boat reappears. John looks lost in reflection, contemplative, silent and serious. From my vantage point, where I have remained at the closest location to where the boat would be coming, I am able to get two remarkable pictures of John returning. After they land and we greet them, we all pile onto a larger boat to go back down the same river.

John points out some landmarks, and we disembark to hike a short distance. We are taken to a small memorial, located out in the middle of a rice paddy, commemorating together the battle that John and these two former VC had been in.

We get back on the boat and are transported to a site near a road. Our motorbike hosts take us back to the village. Once again, the sight of 25 Westerners being ferried along on motorbikes is the highlight of the day for adult and child bystanders as we zoom by.

An Emotional Encounter: Roy and Charles Meet Two VC Veterans

Because of concern that they would hold up the rest of the group, due to physical disabilities or physical conditioning, a few group members started to hike back to the road ahead of the group instead of waiting at the river for John's boat to return. This group included both of the other veterans, Ray and Charles, who had not yet returned to their former battle sites. Based on the 1989 trip, I thought that Roy and Charles might also have had at least a little difficulty in fully "getting into" John's visit. This may have played a role in their returning early and not being as focused on John's return as the rest of us were.

I get back to the village with the rest of the group. Roy and Charles come up to me, excited to talk about something that happened back by the road. They were invited to sit down at a table and found themselves in a sort of conversation with two former VC.

Charles: We were sitting there. One of the former VC points to a scar and says, "From Americans." I pull up my pant's leg and show them the shrapnel wounds on my legs, and say, "The VC did this to me."

And Roy and the other VC did the same. And we all laughed.

I'm A Veteran, Too, Right?

On our way back to the hotel from John's battlefield, in the very small mini-van, I am sitting close Yaron and Littlejohn. Littlejohn says that he is sorry that he at times doesn't relate to me as a veteran on this trip but strictly as a faculty person. I respond that it seems OK to me; that I have been a therapist and projected myself into this role of psychiatric social worker, working with psychiatric veteran casualties — in 1968, 1989 and 2000. And I think that it is OK. I thank Littlejohn for his sensitivity.

But his comment is one of perhaps only two comments from any group member about something that I became increasingly aware of as the trip went on. I kept telling myself that, of course, it was not appropriate on this trip for my vet status to be seen in the same light as John's, Charles's and Roy's.

Wow, just as I am re-writing this sentence, back at my university office, I am interrupted as my big laminated map of Vietnam circa 1966 noisily crashes to the floor next to me!

I don't usually have startle reactions, but I sure did this time. A coincidence, or a sign that I need to stop denying my veteran status as much as I do? I start writing again: While it was not appropriate for my vet status to be highlighted on this trip like John's, Charles's and Roy's (no, the map did not fall again), I must admit that, in retrospect, the fact that almost no one commented on my being a Vietnam veteran felt somewhat like a slight, a dismissal of my vet status — even though I understood, rationally, that the focus of this course was on the other three vets. Other than Yaron and Patricia, I don't remember any other students on this trip asking me about my war experience or overtly recognizing my vet status.

My veteran status had been downplayed throughout the planning stages. First, it had never been part of the group's itinerary to visit the area where I had served. Second, I was on the trip as a professional care-giver, as mental health faculty and therapist. Indeed, apparently I also am more comfortable with this aspect of my role in Vietnam. However, I wonder if many of the students overlook the fact that I *am* one of the veterans on the trip due to a lack of interest in the psychological and PTSD aspects of war — which then directly reflects their apparent lack of interest in my role as a psychiatric social work army officer during the war?

And I'll be the first to admit that front-line combat roles are much more central to the vast majority of military history texts and courses than a description of any military mental health, medical or other support activities. (And yet, of course, the way we wage war these days requires nine support personnel in the war zone providing the essential infrastructure for the front-line forces.)

As we ride back to the hotel, I think about John and his experience today, which did appear to have been profoundly moving. It seemed to help him put a number of pieces of the puzzle together, so to speak. For example, he said:

"I now fully understand, in a way that I never could have before, that there was absolutely no way that my unit's military operation could have had a successful outcome, when considering the size and entrenchment of the VC forces we were up against, and how ready they were for us.

"Also, it is absolutely amazing how graciously the entire village received us, and especially the two former VC who had fought in this very battle against me — when I had been part of the enemy force that had attacked this very village 30 some years ago and was responsible for so many deaths of VC soldiers."

Evening Debriefing

Even though it has been a very long and very emotional day, it was important to have a chance to debrief in the evening. This would allow John to at least start sharing and processing the profound events of today, in relation to a battle that he has been reliving over and over again for 20 years. This was the battle in which John has stated repeatedly that he lost his youth and innocence. We began with a 20-minute selection of film highlights provided by Yaron, so that we can all get a sense of what happened while John and the others went off on their own.

John mentions that while they were on the boat, they were taken to the home of a second VC, 76 years old, who sat at a table with him. He told John that he had retrieved one of the US chopper pilot's helmets, and that he continued to use one wing of the helicopter to dig rice.

There was an American canteen holder there on the table; John was told that this, too, was from that battle. The VC had been a POW for five years (1970-75).

John is amazed and grateful that former enemy soldier and their village have been so gracious in hosting him and the group. He becomes very emotional. He relates that he and his unit were under heavy fire, had already suffered many casualties, were pinned down and had effectively been prevented from inflicting any significant damage on the enemy due to their fortified and secluded positions. He was consumed with feelings of helplessness and rage, and had no readily available targets to discharge that rage towards.

Shane then asks John a great question: "Did you get any closure out of your meeting today, meeting with the two former VC you had fought against?"

John makes an initial and affirmative response, and I think, "Great, this is exactly the kind of processing of emotions that I and Leslie have been hoping would be happening on this trip, although we haven't seen much of it yet." But apparently, the mixture of military history and military mental health objectives of the group were not that easily combined, for as soon as I had that thought, another student interjected: "I hope it is not a diversion, but can you tell us about the battle itself?"

John launched into a 30-minute military history lecture, including detailed battle and tactical information. Several other students and faculty chip in with battle/terrain information questions. Let's face it: I was having as much difficulty accepting what had now turned into a history-class portion of this trip as the others were having with the "psych" aspects. Obviously, this course is focusing much more on history and much less on PTSD/psychological aspects; some 18 of the 25 participants in the group share something during the military history component of the debriefing, so I seem to be in a minority with my concerns.

A Former VC Validates Charles' Attitude During the War

The video is powerful, especially the part showing John's interactions with the two former VC, and then Roy's and Charles' accounting of their interactions with several former VC back in the village.

Charles says that while he was growing up he "was taught never to hate anyone, and so I am not surprised that the VC we met today did not hate us. I guess they and I have the same kind of attitude. 'I fought for my country and you for yours, we both followed orders to kill, and we did it.' Hate had nothing to do with it."

This attitude seems to be one of the salient, priceless outcomes of returning to Vietnam. To me, this experience alone is sufficient to justify all the energy and expense of a return trip.

Flashback to 1989

Actually, Charles' experience is similar to what Dave Roberts and I experienced in 1989, meeting with several active duty Vietnamese military at the Nha Be base, where the Vietnamese colonel toasted us with the stirring words: "I was a soldier, you were a soldier, and we fought. Now, the war is over, and we can be friends."

Can this be true? What proportion of American and Vietnamese combatants share this viewpoint or even want to share it?

I am relieved that there is almost none of the intense negativity and tension that permeated many of the meetings with former NVA soldiers on our 1989 trip, not to mention the extremely negative reaction from many vets back home in 1989 that we were "betraying" other vets, those who were living and those killed in action, by meeting with the enemy.

Reflections on the Meeting with the Village Officials

I was very uncomfortable about the woman official and her apparent attitude during today's meeting, given that others had greeted us so graciously. I found out later from someone in the group who understood Vietnamese that the tone and content of her presentation had, indeed, been much more polemic and severe than the interpretation provided by Mr. Cong. The claim of ten US killed for each VC casualty seemed to be just a hint at the exaggerated content that apparently was present throughout her talk: a discrepancy that John pointed out to the group in a later discussion.

I noticed that Charles seemed to be having a negative reaction too, but I avoided exploring that right away as the immediate debriefing was primarily for John, and for the students' reactions to the day and to John's experience.

However, the next morning at breakfast, Charles showed his insightfulness and compassion:

"I did not feel so positive as John did about our reception at the village. However, if John had guilt over what he had done in that battle, and if today helped him with that guilt, then that was good."

Drinking and PTSD: A Mental Health Intervention

Andy, Leslie and I had a late-night ad hoc meeting, with one of the veterans and two of the students, John Littlejohn and Yaron. The veteran, who appeared to have had too much to drink, had been talking with Yaron and Littlejohn, and he had shared a very heavy secret with the students — but swore them to secrecy about it. Yaron and Littlejohn were extremely uncomfortable with this and asked us how to handle the situation. It seems that on another occasion, while drinking, in the US, the vet had contemplated suicide — this, of course, was important information as we were responsible for his well-being on this very emotional trip. Would his current use of alcohol lead to any suicidal impulses during this trip? We needed to know when (or if) ever he had such thoughts, and how strong was his current commitment to life?

With the veteran's permission, we hold a discussion including both Yaron and Littlejohn. I take the lead, as I am responsible on this trip for any mental health interventions with the veterans. We discuss the veteran's denial that his drinking was a problem on this trip, the possible negative interaction between alcohol and pain medications he takes regularly, and whether there is a need to help him to develop a dual alcohol and psychiatric relapse prevention plan. He agrees not to drink anymore during this trip and says that he will let me know if he finds himself weakening in this resolve; and he willingly commits to talk to his physicians soon after he returns home.

Also, he agrees that he needs to get very specific medical advice regarding any possible contra indications to using any amount of alcohol in combination with his prescribed medications. He agrees to a detailed self-care plan during our remaining time in Vietnam that we negotiate with him. Finally, we all agree that if any of the four of us sees him breaking his resolve to abstain from alcohol while in Vietnam, they will first mention it to him and ask if he is aware that he is violating his commitment to abstain, and second, they will let me know.[130]

This was a very heartening meeting, since everyone showed so much caring for the welfare of the veteran and since he was responsive and agreed to a plan to take better care of himself. Also, the two history students and he had obviously developed a mutually caring relationship. The students proved to be an invaluable support and resource for the veteran. And, they intuitively had great peer counseling instincts of sensitivity, awareness, and good judgment.

On a broader level, the potential problem of drinking and the potential of accompanying suicidal impulses or cognitions during such an emotionally difficult experiment must not be overlooked. Students, who may be prone to excessive drinking themselves, might unwittingly put a veteran at risk by directly or indirectly encouraging him or her to drink when he or she should not. Finally, this is a matter that must be discussed with all group members prior to any return trips.

DAY 4. MAY 18. VISITING THE FAMILY OF A CATHOLIC PRIEST NOW IN MISSISSIPPI

An all-day USM program is on the schedule, e.g., presentations by faculty. However, the students of course think their time would be better spent "in the field"; they are quite antsy to get back out into Saigon. They are right; we adjust the remaining all-day scheduled times to a four-hour block and leaving the remaining time free.

Andy: didactic on history of war in the delta region

John Van Sant: overview of Vietnam's cultural history

Leslie: grief and the grieving process

Ms. Trang provides us with a listing of recommended restaurants.

Visit with the Family of Father Truong.

I find myself unable to sleep; I have so many thoughts and feelings going through my mind, particularly about our most wonderful visit last night to the family of Father Truong. After getting up several times and making a few notes, and going back to bed but still unable to sleep, I finally give up getting any more sleep (this happens

---

130. I am very grateful that this veteran gave his permission for me to share this information; he understood that this is an important issue not only for himself but for many other veterans.

several times during the trip), and sit down to make detailed journal notes about what had happened earlier this evening.

This is a priceless day. Leslie and I go to visit with the family of Father Truong in the Catholic district of Saigon, to meet his parents, and younger brother and two sisters. I had met Father Truong at the St. James Catholic Church in Gulfport, MS, a few weeks ago. He had immigrated from Vietnam only a few years earlier and was ordained as a priest in 1999. My daughter, Helani, and Father Truong had established a close pastoral relationship over the past several months. When Helani mentioned to Father Truong that I was going to Vietnam, he asked if I could film him saying a Sunday Mass to take to his family in Saigon. I readily agreed.

And so, this is how I came to visit with his family in Saigon. I invited Leslie to go with me. We take a taxi to the home of Father Truong's family. Father Truong's mother is the most versed in English, and carries on the bulk of the conversation with us. She is a remarkable woman. Her religious faith is so strong, her energy and drive, her concern for her family. She reminds me of my mother. She is strikingly beautiful in her expressiveness, her remarkable smile and laugh, her connecting through eye contact and touching us on our arms and hands as she talks.

There is a gentleness and a graciousness and richness of family life and happiness that emanates from them all. They are poor, money-wise; I believe they live on about $20 a month from the father's retirement and income from tailoring, and yet they are rich beyond measure. Father Truong's mother says that she worries every day about her son and prays for him, because he is so far away and alone in America. The family has agreed to have her husband emigrate next to America, so that he won't be alone: even though it will further split the family.

At first, we are sitting in the small, sparsely furnished living room with the parents and son, drinking tea. I should say, Leslie and I are drinking tea; I don't remember anyone else drinking tea, but being attentive to pouring us more tea. It is not until a little later, at the dinner table, that I realize that anytime we get to the bottom of our tea cup, or have only a little food left in our plates, we are immediately served more. And so, belatedly, we learn that the only way to stop the drink and food from coming is to deliberately leave a substantial quantity in our bottles or cups and plates. But, that realization coming a bit late, we are really stuffed.

Now, we turn to the video from America. After about 15-20 minutes of getting acquainted, I lay the videotape on the serving table, and I give them an envelope from Father Truong (with money inside). Now, I remember that Father Truong had told me that they often watched a video of Father Truong's graduation from seminary and his return for a visit to Saigon; I get the feeling, now, that while they are sitting and politely talking with us, they are really eager to see the video. As soon as I say, "Why don't we look at the video?" they immediately take us into the adjoining room where they have their meals, sit us down at the round table already set for dinner, and put the video into their VCR that faces the dinner table.

They sit raptly watching it. And, as much as Father Truong's mother obviously wants to watch the video, she also is busily going in and out of the kitchen; she and her youngest daughter are finalizing the meal preparations. And, I know that they must be having some language difficulty in understanding everything Father Truong is saying during the mass, as he of course is speaking in English. Following the mass, I had continued filming Father Truong as he spoke in Vietnamese to his family. He gave them a visual and explanatory tour of all of the various pictures,

121

wall hangings and articles in his office, the various rooms in the rectory, and a walking tour of the church grounds.

And now I can just see them, in my mind's eye, watching and watching again this virtual-reality visit with their son, and I regret that one can only capture so much on film.

As soon as this video is done, they immediately get out their video of Father Truong's ordination and visit back to Saigon in 1999. We all watch it during dinner. It is a very impressively crafted video, with Vietnamese music, sub-titles and special effects. (I am a little ashamed at my home movie, which is rather primitive in comparison.)

Leslie and I have two large plates, while each of them has a small bowl. Obviously, we are provided with their best dinner ware. And while we are sitting at the dinner table, we are surprised when Father Truong's mother invites us to their oldest daughter's wedding this coming Sunday (May 21). This will be the first marriage for any of her children, and she repeatedly states that they would be honored to have us there.

As we are getting near the end of dinner, the fiancé arrives on his motorbike. He pushes it in the front door and parks it in the front part of the room where we are sitting, and he sits down and joins us. Shortly thereafter, the oldest daughter arrives on her motorbike from work and pushes her motorbike into the house, too.

All too soon, we get into a taxi (they had arranged this with a neighbor who drives a taxi). Father Truong's mother repeats, "We will remember this day forever." Never mind that I had to miss my own daughter's high school graduation to be on this trip — everything about this expedition has been overloaded with emotion. However, I am somehow reconciled just a little by knowing that my daughter Helani is with Father Truong in Mississippi, while I am visiting with his family in Vietnam. A wonderful connection that we all were sharing together, 10,000 miles apart.

I share that notion with them, and I emphasize how much Father Truong is loved by the parishioners at St. James. In fact, at the conclusion of mass that was filmed, Father Truong announced that this video was for his family in Vietnam; and as he stood in the back of the church and received various parishioners as they were leaving, several of them introduced themselves, on film, making very positive comments about Father Truong.

Flashback to 1968

"I Am The Lord Thy God; Don't Have Strange Gods Before Me." I could not help but flash back to the lie that American military personnel were taught about the Vietnamese during our "cultural orientation" provided by the military prior to our departure to the war zone: a message by which we could justify whatever we had to do to get through the Vietnam War: "Oh, the Vietnamese people don't care about life and death like we do in America; they believe in reincarnation and so death isn't something to grieve at all."

As if, somehow, the loss of a family member didn't hurt. Yes, another example of "dehumanizing the enemy" as a way to wage war. They have different beliefs than we do and somehow the taking of their lives isn't such a bad thing! And, here in Vietnam 2000 I witness a Vietnamese mother, as gracious and full of love for her family as any mother can be, doing everything she can possibly do for them, or even for those who come, from the "enemy" country, in their name.

And this was not just because they were Catholics; it also was the case for North Vietnamese, as Bao Ninh makes clear in his poignant book.

Yes, even among the enemy:

"My mother was here one fateful morning when an official arrived bringing a death certificate for my brother, her first son. She took the news badly, although she had feared and expected it. She was buoyed only by the expectation of her second son coming home soon. But a few hours later another courier arrived with a second death certificate telling her my other brother, her second son, had also been killed. Mother collapsed in a faint, then lapsed into a coma. She hung on for three days without uttering another word, then died."[131]

Oh, it hurts that we, while at war, and so many Vietnam veterans even now, decades after the war ended, can't and won't see the Vietnamese as feeling, caring, wonderful and vibrant *people*. And that so many American soldiers could either hate the Vietnamese so, both then and continuing until now — or have absolutely no feelings whatsoever about them. This is part of the corruption of our very moral fiber that a number of Armed Forces personnel must engage in by dehumanizing people in order to function and survive in battle. Is this not an inevitable component of living through and participating in this monstrosity we call War?

National Security as a Top Priority: A Juxtaposition of Geography and History

Mr. Cong tells us that the top priority of the Vietnam government must be national (domestic) security, "because we are too small and poor and weak, especially compared with China. Our country has been invaded so many times by foreigners and we have been at war for so much of our history.... We have been shot by arrows so many times that when the Vietnamese people see the image of the curved tree branch, we think of the bow."

DAY 5. MAY 19. CU CHI TUNNELS, TAY NINH AND THE CAO DAI TEMPLE

Morning visit to the Cu Chi Tunnels and the Ben Duoc Temple. In the recently completed Ben Duoc Temple are the names of nearly 50,000 NLF soldiers from the immediate surrounding area who fought and died here.

Continue on to Tay Ninh, home of the esoteric and colorful Cao Dai sect; attend their high-noon service; the sect fuses elements of Catholicism, Buddhism, Christianity, Islam and native animistic beliefs into a unified whole. Return to Saigon. Afternoon USM program.

Flashback to 1989

I was at the Cu Chi tunnels in 1989. At that time, seeing the tunnel system was both interesting and very emotional. Two of the veterans in our group had experienced the tunnels during the war: one who had been stationed in Cu Chi and a second who had a traumatic experience in a VC tunnel. None of the three vets on this trip

---

131. Ninh, 48.

served at Cu Chi and so I am not particularly interested to see the tunnels now. However, they are a remarkably extensive and creatively engineered feat, and the group thoroughly enjoys exploring the tunnels. We are led by a young Vietnamese woman, dressed in vintage VC clothing, to a covered pavilion. She gives us a brief orientation with the aid of a large graphic that pictures the Cu Chi Tunnel system at the time of the war.

Then we are shown a film that appears to have been made in the middle of the war. This film has a pro-VC spin, since "it is the victors who get to write the history." It emphasizes the bravery and cunning of the VC forces against the American oppres-sors. I did not enjoy watching it in 1989, and I don't enjoy watching it in 2000. While almost our entire group seems to be intently watching the film, three of us Vietnam veterans end up in the rear of the pavilion. Our body language betrays us: we've seen and heard enough and are ready to move on. Compared to 1989, the tun-nel site has been much further developed as a tourist destination. There is a glossy brochure, nicer pathways, easier access into and further development of rooms in the tunnel system, a substantial gift shop and even a firing range where visitors can (for a fee, of course) shoot AK-47 rifles. What a combination: Communist propa-ganda and tourism.

Tay Ninh and the Cao Dai Sect

We take a two hour bus ride to visit the temple of the Cao Dai sect who, we are told, combines the elements of Catholicism, Buddhism, Christianity, Islam and native animistic belief into a unified whole.[132] What a novel and wonderful idea: is it really possible (or desirable) to combine all the religions into one that worships the same higher power? The Cao Dai sect has been accused of being commercialized and focusing on attracting a larger following. Visitors are guided up the stairs to a

---

132. I thank Courtney Frobenius of Vietnam-Indochina Tours for providing the following additional information. The Cao Dai sect, and the Hao Hoa Sect, are fundamentalist Buddhist sects which hold that believers can communicate directly with Buddha without the requirement for monks; they played a significant role in the 20th century history of Vietnam in the Mekong Delta. While the Hao Hoa were based in Chau Doc, a place south of Tay Ninh astride the Vietnamese/Cambodian border, the Cao Dai had an axis between Tay Ninh/Saigon and Ben Tre Province (the three "branches" of the Cao Dai Church, with Tay Ninh being the largest). The Cao Dai and the Hao Hoa both were funded by the French and fought against the Viet Minh and later with the Americans against the Viet Cong, albeit to a lesser degree. They were kingmakers of southern Vietnamese politics as were the re-settled Catholics from the north from 1954-1956. The founder of the Hao Hoa was brutally murdered by the Viet Cong and bits and pieces of his body were scattered throughout the Mekong Delta.

Both of the sects represent a southern Vietnamese tendency towards the "new" and away from the old. While in the north Mahayana Buddhism holds sway, the south has balanced elements of the Cao Dai, Theravada Buddhism, the Hao Hoa, and protestant religions. There is a strong Catholic presence yet today — much stronger than in the north. The south was initially colonized by fleeing Ming Chinese in the late 17th-18th centuries with the permission of the Nguyen Court. The south has always been a mite new, a mite different, a mite more "out West," a haven for people leaving the grinding poverty of the north to explore and seek out new ways. The south was simply fertile ground for new religions.

narrow balcony with birds flying around: I guess the Catholics don't have a monopoly on mother nature mingling with the church service. Of course, it is very hot and humid We are free to watch the service from our vantage point, which leaves the main floor free for the regular participants. Some 150 or 200 persons, in several differently colored robes, enter and kneel down in organized rows, as the service begins. I find myself becoming quite perturbed by the number of tourists, both Western and Vietnamese, who make considerable noise throughout the service.

Too Many Interesting Activities

Once again, we are running behind schedule. The group is tired by the end of the bus rides and walking at the various sights. Thus, we agree to cancel the planned afternoon USM program and reschedule a scaled down version for the next morning. Even this doesn't placate several of the students; they don't like to get up early, but we want to have our shortened USM program and still have adequate time for Charles' battlefield day.

I insist that the group meet early the next morning anyway. I feel the burden of being responsible for the mental health component of this course, which is much less on the agenda than the history component, and do not want to be cheated of the little time that we have. And of course it is essential not to short-change Charles on the day he returns to his former battlefield site.

DAY 6. MAY 20. VET CHARLES RETURNS TO THE BIEN HOA ARMY BASE

Morning: Lecture on the trauma and the survival modes that are common in a war zone. Orientation to Vietnam tour, search and destroy missions and Bien Hoa area (where Charles went on many search and destroy missions)

Categories of Trauma and Survival Modes in a War zone

I give a presentation on several of the types of trauma that soldiers can be exposed to, deliberately tying my lecture into the one day of battle that John had described to us in detail. I use concrete examples from John's description of battle to exemplify: (1) various types of trauma and survivor modes, i.e., observing death and dying, bereavement over loss, being a perpetrator who kills or maims others, being a witness or observer of trauma happening to others, being or feeling responsible for trauma that occurs to others, physical injury or disability, and (2) primary survival modes in a war zone, i.e., detachment, tunnel vision, risk/thrill addiction (see *A Vietnam Trilogy* for a thorough discussion of the various types of survival strategies in the war zone).

Charles Brown: Bien Hoa, Search and Destroy, and Racism

Charles J. Brown, Sergeant First Class, 1967-68. Company C, 4th Battalion, 173rd Airborne Brigade. Two Bronze Stars. Two Purple Hearts.

Charles gives an informative talk about his upbringing in Hattiesburg and his joining the Army and making it his career. Charles served for a number of years on active duty prior to going to Vietnam; he was a more senior NCO; and he is a racial minority — African-American. Charles tells us two powerful race-related anecdotes (however, I don't remember that anyone ever commented about them, then or later):

"Something that has stayed with me all these years [he pauses to compose himself] — graffiti on a wall in Vietnam:

'I'd rather have my daughter or sister marry a gook than a nigger.'

For those who understand the depth of the hatred, and rage, and denigration that so many combat veterans felt for "the gooks," there could be nothing more hateful to say to a fellow American in Vietnam — nothing.

Charles then tells us something that happened in 1962-63, before he went to Vietnam, between the Cuban missile crisis and the racial crisis when the University of Mississippi ("Ole Miss") was being integrated. Even though he was honorably serving his nation at the time as a career military NCO, this apparently means nothing when the matter of his race comes up again:

"I was stationed in Kentucky, and needed a ride home; a [white] soldier who lived near my hometown said, sure, he'd drop me off on his way home. Then, a few months later, we again both were going home and I asked him if he could give me a ride, and he said, 'No, I can't, my wife is with me.'"

The white soldier, his "comrade in arms," was too uncomfortable to have him along now that his wife was present.

Later, Charles talks about the dangers he faced at home because of racism versus facing the dangers of war in Vietnam: "I could go to Vietnam, where they gave me a gun, or I could stay in Hattiesburg without one — but where I also needed one."

Because time is running short, Charles agrees to continue his orientation on the bus ride to Bien Hoa, about a 90-minute ride away. On the bus, Charles describes search and destroy missions and his role as a platoon sergeant. We emphasize to Charles that we will stay in the Bien Hoa today for as long as he needs and wants to; *this* is *his* day.

Charles's Return to Bien Hoa

Mr. Cong takes us first to a park near Bien Hoa. This location is high on a rise and offers a distant view of a remaining water tower at the former Bien Hoa American military base. As Mr. Cong explains, once we go in the bus closer to Bien Hoa, it won't be possible for any pictures to be taken, as Bien Hoa is an active Vietnamese military base. And so, he has brought Charles and our group to this park, where Charles can take pictures if he wishes to.

There is an absolutely spectacular lake dotted with towering rocks and trees, right next to the main highway and yet extremely secluded. And there, off in the distance, over the rocks, is the former Bien Hoa water tower, perhaps a mile or so away. Charles is quite surprised, as he had never known of the existence of this lake and large rock formations, even though he had been stationed almost next door to it.

Charles then discovered that there was a Buddhist temple at this park that overlooked the lake and the former Bien Hoa base water tower off in the distance. He took the opportunity to light some incense in a ceremony.

Charles later described his experience: "Here was an opportunity to pray in a temple of your former enemy. And from the trip, understanding the Vietnamese people and their nature as it relates to their religion and their relationship with their ancestors. It was a moving experience for me." As Charles lit the incense, he said: "For those who served in the 173rd and lost their lives, the men who served their country — both enemy and friends." Charles became very emotional. "I didn't know I had such an emotional burden inside of me until I was there. . . "

As we linger on the heights, looking at the Bien Hoa water tower in the distance, and admiring the lake, ten Vietnamese Army cadets visit the park. Conversations ensue, through the translation services of Mr. Cong. Several of the young Vietnamese are pleased to have their pictures taken with our female students (some things seem to transcend cultures: uniformed young soldiers and attractive young women always seem to find each other!).

We leave the park and the bus weaves around along a small road through a section of little houses. Mr. Cong explains that we are roughly circling the perimeter of Bien Hoa, but at a distance where we can't see even the perimeter fence. However, when we get to what Mr. Cong says is the closest we can get to the former back gate to the Base, we stop for a few minutes. We are strongly warned not to take cameras off the bus or to take any pictures. This is a restricted military area. Charles gets out with a number of students and walks over to the road that leads up to the back gate. He gives a brief talk about his tour in this area.

I decide to remain on the bus, and secretly take a picture from the bus window of Charles with the group standing by the roadside. This will provide Charles with at least one photo of his closest approach to the Bien Hoa base. So here is a photo of Charles, an African-American veteran large in girth and in height, standing out in the crowd of attentive white college students, animatedly talking with them in peacetime Vietnam, 2000, about Bien Hoa during the war.

Bien Hoa Area: Markedly Different than during the War

When they come back to the bus, we go away from "downtown" Bien Hoa to see if we can find any terrain that is similar to where Charles' search and destroy missions happened during the war. We had planned to have Charles walk us through a search and destroy patrol in a field. Unfortunately, we have no success in finding *any* open terrain that is recognizable after 30 years. There are homes throughout this entire area, which used to be countryside. (Of course, the same trend has happened throughout the US in the last 30 years.) I am worried that Charles may be very disappointed, because Bien Hoa looks so different, so much more urbanized, and because he is not allowed to get onto the base. But he surprises me again:

Charles: "Something like this, so close [to Bien Hoa]. I had no idea of this picturesque location so near to the base. This is an historic moment for me that I had never planned to see. My heart fluttered when I saw the old main gate again: pretty breathtaking. And the progress that this country has undergone in such a short period of time, I'm impressed."

Ray: "Charles, how do you feel about having visited Bien Hoa and finding everything so changed? Was that disappointing?"

Charles: "I'm glad that it isn't the same, because I only have bad memories of the way it was."

Flashback to 1989

This comment propels me immediately back to our 1989 trip. On that trip, there were quite divergent reactions to finding that old battlefield and duty sites had changed dramatically. About one-half of the vets were extremely disappointed that the reality of peacetime Vietnam 1989 clashed with their long-held memories of war-time Vietnam. In contrast, the remaining vets were relieved, like Charles, that peacetime Vietnam offered such a dramatically different picture than the horrors of war. While I don't think it is possible to predict which of these polar reactions a returning veteran might have, I make a mental note to myself: it really is important to at least alert veterans prior to making a return trip to the likelihood that (1) their former battlefield sites may look dramatically different and reflect little if any similarity to their war-time memories — if we can even find them!, and (2) previous veterans who have returned have displayed a dramatic range of reactions upon making this discovery when they finally reached the location of their former duty stations.

The Biggest Supermarket in Vietnam

On the way back to Saigon, we stop briefly at "the biggest supermarket in Vietnam," the Cora Shopping Center just outside of Saigon. The group relaxes and does a little shopping or eating. Picture a typical modern supermarket that perhaps occupies about one-third of an enclosed mall. The entire front of the supermarket and its check-out lines open directly (no walls) to the main corridor of what we would call a mall.

There are perhaps 20 or so stores spread out to the right and left, and in front, of the supermarket. These include a Kentucky Fried Chicken; yes, there are several KFC franchises in Vietnam, but no "burger" chains. The air conditioning works very well and the mall seems to be quite a gathering place, and the customers appear to be much better dressed than most other places.

Note on Group Dynamics

Each of the three veterans is kind of "doing his own thing" on this trip. Indeed, each vet seems to be relating to certain combinations of students and faculty, rather than bonding as a group of veterans. Perhaps this is for the best; it reduces the insularity "as veterans," and contributes to promoting meaningful relationships between veterans and non-veterans.

A Tattered Huey Helicopter: Photo Opportunity or Ugly Reminder?

The students are taking pictures of an old Huey that is on display in a very tattered condition.[133] Roy walks by and I hear him say: "I wouldn't take a @#! picture of that helicopter for anything." Just how I felt about the Hueys at Cu Chi yesterday!

---

133. The "Huey" was indispensable in saving tens of thousands of American lives during the war, whether it was to insert a team into a remote area, drop off troops at various landing zones, evacuate wounded soldiers, extract soldiers from dangerous situations. Yes, the Hueys were our best friends in the daily medical and military tactical miracles. There is no more prominent or universal reminder of the Vietnam War to 3.14 million vets than the Huey helicopter and the brave and skilled crews who flew them.

However, today I swallow my negative reaction, and, with mixed feelings, take a picture of the Huey with Charles and a student talking in front of it. Charles seems quite involved in his conversation and obviously is not bothered by standing next to the helicopter. I, on the other hand, am definitely bothered. The Huey had obviously been damaged, and is in decrepit condition. I suppose one would hardly buff and polish the attacker's vehicle. Especially since he lost.

In fact, what difference does it make, since we all know who won anyway; would I feel any differently if it had been restored to pristine condition? Different veterans do react differently to the many stimuli here in Vietnam.

Vietnamese saying: Vietnamese grow rice; Laotians watch rice; Cambodians listen to the rice.

On the bus, returning from Bien Hoa, John remarks about his return a few days ago: "Yes, there will never be another juxtaposition of time and place and people (as happened at my old battlefield)!"

I'm thinking: what Charles experienced here today is what 95% of vets coming back to Vietnam will experience regarding their old duty sites: everything has changed, the vegetation, new housing, roads, etc., all to the point where very little is familiar looking anymore. My hidden snapshot (from a distance) of Charles and the group near the rear entrance to Bien Hoa Air Base really captures what it will be like for most vets. And that's not necessarily bad, is it?

DAY 7. MAY 21. CATHOLICISM AND RELIGION IN VIETNAM, RACISM AMONG US TROOPS, AND MEETING A PROUD FORMER ARVN

The all-day program of lectures and seminars we had scheduled was sacrificed and we gave the group a free day until late afternoon, then a lecture on PTSD treatment by Leslie.

Flashback to 1968

What about the US wanting to "win the hearts and minds of the Vietnamese people?" I find myself thinking back to William Beaumont General Hospital in El Paso, Texas, and asking to attend Vietnamese language school before going to Vietnam. My request was denied even though I had offered to have my active duty commitment extended an additional six months (which was the length of the language course). The reason given was that my Social Work MOS (military occupational specialty) didn't justify it. Of course, I was a social work officer; what possible good would it be to know a bit of Vietnamese! So much for the military pronouncements that we were to make it a priority to "win the hearts and minds of the Vietnamese people" as part of the counter-insurgency effort against the VC and NVA.

A Catholic Wedding

At 7:15 AM Leslie and I leave in a taxi for the wedding of Father Truong's oldest sister. This is about a 35-minute ride to the southern part of Saigon, in a Catholic district. Ms. Trang, one of our two guides, was kind enough to find out for me that the schedule for the wedding day would be as follows:

8: 00 to 10: 00 AM: gathering at the house of the parents of the bride

10: 00 to 11:00 AM: wedding

11: 30 AM to 1: 30 PM: reception

We arrive at Mr. Trinh's and Mrs. Tranh's house (in Vietnamese custom, the spouses retain their family names) at 7:50 AM. Their home is on one side of a narrow road with other homes, and across from them is a bustling open market. The road is teeming with shoppers. As we are looking for the house, we are spotted by someone standing in a doorway; there are no other foreigners anywhere in sight. Father Truong's mother rushes out to greet us and usher us inside.

There are perhaps a half-dozen guests sitting in the living room area when we arrive. Leslie and I prefer to remain in the background. However, that proves to be quite impossible. We find ourselves being gently but insistently pushed or pulled to the front and obviously the place of honor. And so we are seated at the main table, right next to a table where the grandmother and the grandmother's daughters are seated. At our table are several older men.

I found out later from Father Truong, back in the US, that this was the first wedding that anyone could remember since 1975 that had been attended by Americans. This, plus the fact that we were PhDs also was very prestigious; PhDs are extremely rare in Vietnam, much rarer than MDs. And then there was the fact that my daughter and I knew Father Truong back in the United States. Therefore, we truly were considered to be guests of honor.

I had asked a number of Vietnamese back at the hotel what was a proper gift to give at the wedding? Everyone had stated that money (cash) was very appropriate, from $10 to $15 dollars US. However, I also was told that it depended on the economic status of the families. In addition, since we were Americans, I assumed that we ought to give more than the range that had been suggested; and I had a hunch that, even if we were expected to give more, no one would say that to us.

This was a common experience during the trip; it was difficult to get what we would consider an open and frank answer from the Vietnamese. It became obvious that, when responding to requests for advice or information, Vietnamese would be very polite and cautious; to the point that I found myself asking the same information of several people and trying to gauge what was appropriate by the range and consistency of their answers.

For example, I had asked if we should give the cash in an envelope; and, if so, any special kind? One person told me that an envelope from the hotel, plain white, with the hotel's name and return address on it, was fine. Another Vietnamese told me that red was a traditional color for the envelope. A third told me that red was a Chinese tradition and that an envelope with a card in it would be appropriate. In all cases, the advice received was consistent on three points: to use an envelope, to use US dollars, and to write our names on the envelope so that they would know it was from us. Since I was unable to find a card that seemed appropriate, I decided to use the hotel envelope. No doubt the hotel stationery added a special cachet. And I noticed that all of the envelopes being given to the bride and groom seemed to be either white or pink, so I got over worrying about the color red.

At about 9:00 AM, the groom and his entourage arrive outside the house. They are all dressed in white, and each has a gift in his hands. They are standing, single file, with teems of shoppers bustling by. Then, at some signal that I don't see, they enter in a procession and deposit their gifts on a table set aside for that purpose.

As we are sitting there in the living room, a funny thing happens involving the mother-in-law and Mrs. Tranh, the mother of the bride. As part of one of several presentations and speeches given in the living room, the mother-in-law approaches the bride and places a gold necklace around her neck. We later find out that it is common for Vietnamese to collect their wealth in gold jewelry, or to bury it in gold bars in their homes, rather than depositing money in the bank.[134]

Then, Mrs. Tranh goes up to her daughter and also puts a necklace around her neck. In contrast to the single thick gold strand from the mother-in-law, this striking necklace consists of a number of thinner gold strands; quite naturally, since this one has been placed on the bride's neck after the first necklace, it pretty much covers over the first necklace. The mother-in-law, seeing this, goes up to the bride and lifts the first necklace up so that now it is on top of the mother's gift necklace.

Leslie and I think, "This mother-in-law is going to be trouble!" I guess our mother-in-law stereotypes are pretty universal.

Later we follow along as part of the procession from the house to the church, about a five minute walk through the very busy market. I try to slip back from the front of the procession. However, as Mrs. Tranh is walking up the aisle of the church she notices us and breaks away from the procession, hurries back to where we are standing, and insistently brings us up to walk with her and her husband in the front of the procession. I start resisting, then realize that it's not up to me. Mrs. Tranh is one persistent woman!

She then gently but insistently pushes me into the very first pew, immediately behind where the bride and groom will be sitting on two chairs. This spot also happens to be immediately next to the afore-mentioned mother-in-law. As Mrs. Tranh is pushing me into the front pew, the mother-in-law pushes me back towards the aisle. Mrs. Tranh is insistent and her will dominates; we sit down right next to the mother-in-law. And so here we are, conspicuous as jewels in a crown, and highly self-conscious.

The church is a classic, cathedral-type structure, long and somewhat narrow with very high ceilings and tall columns. There are two sections of perhaps 25 to 30 rows of pews. The walls are an off-white plaster, with wooden kneelers devoid of any padding. The choir singing is as harmonious as the weather is hot. Dressed as I am in tie and long-sleeved shirt, I am sweating profusely. All of the windows are open, as well as the doors; the few fans offer little relief, but the birds flying around inside the church provide a somewhat distracting novelty. Parts of the church are in some disrepair. This is a little jarring, considering that this is not a tiny village church but a church of impressive size in Saigon. I find out later on that only quite recently has the Communist government begun to allow parishes to put money into improving and repairing churches in Vietnam.

---

134. The Vietnamese have traditionally mistrusted banks and kept their valuables hidden in their homes; this has been quite problematic for many who have emigrated to the US. Knowledgeable criminals have preyed upon Vietnamese families; they invade their homes to terrorize them to find out where their valuables are hidden.

Now that we are seated directly behind the bride and groom, I notice what appears to be a price tag on the necklace she received from the mother-in-law; could it be that the tag was left on it on purpose? The ceremony ends; in fact, it was a double wedding, with a completely separate wedding party occupying the left side of the church while we are all on the right side.

As we leave the church one of the girls accompanying the bride sees the tag on the bride's necklace; she reaches up, pulls off the tag, and throws it on the ground. Later, I was told by Ms. Trang that it probably wasn't exactly a price tag but a tag that specified the weight of gold in the necklace, which in effect was a measure of its value.

We proceed back past their house to another, larger street and then to the outdoor restaurant where the reception is being held.

At the reception, we are seated at the head table where four priests and five members of the parish council sit — and two Caucasian-American PhDs. The priest sitting next to me, who performed the wedding mass, apparently is the only one at the table who speaks any English; not much, but definitely much more than we knew Vietnamese. We have several short pleasant interchanges. At the same time, Leslie and I are walking a tightrope between wanting to respect their culture and hospitality but wanting to avoid upsetting our gastronomical systems, as well.

Having been warned that the water can cause diarrhea in some Americans (so much for vegetables that are washed, ice cubes, etc.) we are careful not to eat the luscious-looking greens, and accept our beverages warm. It seems to be expected that I will drink a bottle of warm beer, and I nurse it for the next hour. Leslie surprises the entourage at our table by also partaking of a beer. I hear later that to drink beer with the men in public like this is a big taboo for Vietnamese women.

Later, I find out that this is one of fifteen Catholic parishes in Saigon. I am impressed by how the family is linked with the community, i.e., the "public" display for the wedding with bright pink banners surrounding the front of the home; the "public" arrival of the groom and entourage outside of the home, standing in a line with their gifts before coming in, the procession of the entire wedding party walking from the home to the church and after the wedding from the church to the reception. Courtney Frobenius and Trang were married in a Buddhist wedding that also was very public.

The Uneasy Co-Existence of Religion and Communism

I spoke about religion with several Vietnamese we meet in the Mekong Delta and in central Vietnam, and learned that the Communist government has been gradually loosening up controls and prohibitions concerning religion and churches since the early 1990s; for example, as one Vietnamese said: "To the Communist government, it is not acceptable for there to be "Vietnamese Catholics." This connotes that one is Catholic first, and Vietnamese second. However, now it's OK to be a "Catholic Vietnamese." Being Vietnamese must be first or primary, with one's religion secondary."

That made me stop and think. At first, it struck me very negatively; I had forgotten that in America and other countries, too, there has always been a concern whether Catholics are more loyal to the Pope than to their own nation. What is right? Catholicism in Southeast Asia was linked with the French colonial rule. Indeed, I am told that all religions are suspect by the Communist government.

Others told me,

"Any discussion about religion is avoided; this is a very sensitive subject; please realize that this is only my opinion."

"For about six or seven years now, there is more religious freedom. People can put money to help restore Catholic churches and Buddhist temples. However, if a Vietnamese is a Catholic, he cannot be a member of the Communist Party."

"The government takes the view that: 'Thy Kingdom *not* come. Thy Father stay up in heaven. Catholics are looking for paradise in the sky, while the Communists strive to build a better life right here.'"

For a Catholic priest to be ordained, the application must be submitted to the government for approval. However, there is much less religious discrimination now. Just after the war, a child of a Catholic could not go to a university.

Furthermore, Catholicism was far more prevalent among the relatively educated and relatively cosmopolitan (and French-speaking) elite of the south; very few of the NLF (National Liberation Front, also known as Viet Cong or VC) or NVA were Catholic. At a time when a person's dedication to nationalism and patriotism was in doubt, espousing a foreign religion smells of collaboration with foreign interests. Apparently, the Catholics and former colonial rule (the French) are still seen as one and the same to many Communists. The Catholic population in Vietnam, 10% of the population, is the second largest in all of Asia (the Philippines has the largest Catholic population).

The other religion that does have a following is a kind of Buddhism mixed with a more ancient tradition of ancestor worship. Ancestor worship is a 2000-year-old Vietnamese tradition and is tolerable to the Communists; it is natural to the Vietnamese people.

Former ARVNs apparently could not own businesses from 1975 to about 1990. However, now if they have the money and have the "right connections," they are able to.

Aborted Escape from Vietnam

One Vietnamese told me that he had been an ARVN Sergeant and an English interpreter for the ARVNs, based in Saigon. He spent three years in a "Re-education Camp" after 1975. He and his family had been offered transport to America in 1975 but didn't go because they didn't want to leave their grandmother behind. And so, several years later, they clandestinely arranged to go to Nha Trang, to escape by a boat that their father had arranged. They packed up and secretly went to Nha Trang, a full day's ride away, fully expecting never to return to Saigon. However, the boat wasn't there, and they had to make their way back, again in secrecy, to Saigon; luckily, their home was not yet occupied by someone else and they were able to move back in. Almost all of this family remains in Vietnam today.

We went to a "modern" supermarket: last night, where there was a combination of food, clothing, toys and art artifacts being sold. Just picture a small Wal-Mart type of store, with *all* of the aisles totally packed with people and very marginal air conditioning.

Flashback to 1968

At a Vietnamese restaurant last night, I ordered a full coconut to drink and eat. This brought back positive memories of 1968-69, during the war, on the beach in Nha Trang, buying coconuts from *mama sans* who would cut them open for us to drink. To this day, my mouth waters when I think of drinking fresh coconut milk right out of the husk.

USM Seminar: Psychological Impact of War and Racism versus Military History Tactics and Strategy

Still striving to interject important course content about the psychological impact of war on its participants, I prepare a lecture on the effects of setting individual DEROS dates, so that each soldier's individual tour in Vietnam was scheduled to end on a different date from his buddies'. The individual rotation over and back from Vietnam obviously compromised the carefully nurtured sense of unit cohesion and identification, essential to morale, in favor of promoting individual survival. This was coupled with the horrid results of the military's insisting on a confirmed body count as the way to mark success (resulting in such things as soldiers slicing ears off dead Vietnamese to prove their deaths, at times indiscriminate killing, or counting the deaths of any Vietnamese as a dead enemy soldier, etc.). Did not the body count repudiate the "art" of war and encourage its policy makers and participants to commit criminal-like acts?

Judging from the comments and questions, most of the history students and professors seem more focused on the military tactical and strategic level; the discussions constantly move away from the impact on the psychological health of the warriors who implement those tactics and strategies.

The Race Issue Again

The same dynamic appears when Charles brings up the race issue. Charles mentions a tragedy that happened in Mississippi on January 11, 1966. A black man's house in Hattiesburg was firebombed and he was killed. He had been targeted because of his activism in registering black voters (as late as 1966). His four sons were all serving their country in the military overseas. They all came home for their father's funeral — and then returned to duty overseas.

Charles tells this story with a combination of anger at what happened and pride for the honorable military service of so many of his peers. Is it any wonder that there were racial tensions among soldiers who were defending their country and in harm's way?

Charles also describes the tenor of the times and location where he was raised in Hattiesburg. He wouldn't have dreamed of asking a white woman to dance. "I'd have gotten a Chinese name pretty quickly: Hee Hung Hai. If a black man danced with a white woman in those days, that's what would happen: he hung high."

It is a marvel that Charles and other minority men and women have been willing to lay their lives on the line day after day in the war zone with such traumatic instances of racism at home. And I don't remember anyone making any verbal acknowledgment of the importance or impact of what Charles said. Are people too embarrassed to say anything, or can't they find the proper words? The group returns to a discussion of military tactics.

Contrast Between Saigon Versus Hanoi Military and Political Objectives

A Vietnamese civilian said: "The Saigon-based government and military fought for the 17th parallel and a divided Vietnam." (Some would say that, until near the end, they fought for self-aggrandizement using corruption as a means and were not really fighting for a "country" until after 1971.) "The Hanoi-based government and military fought for a united Vietnam: it was their earthly duty to fight." Andy has been sick for several days and has to stay in the hotel in Saigon and cannot accompany the group to Can Tho. Everyone is worried and he is frustrated not to be able to go to the places that require physical exertion. Whatever he has, I sure hope no one else gets it!

A Proud Former ARVN

During one of our excursions up a small tributary of the delta outside of Saigon, a few of us stop and get out at a small farm. I ask how long the owner's family has lived here, and he says about 20 years. We find out that he was a former ARVN refrigerator specialist, a corporal who had trained in the US. When he finds out that we have four Vietnam vets in our group, he goes into his home and returns, proudly sharing with us copies of his military records that he keeps in plastic covers.

I offer a toast to this gracious, hospitable farmer/veteran. And we four vets have a picture taken with him. I hand him a pen as a keepsake and we shake hands one last time. He gently holds onto my hand as I am letting go; for several more seconds he remains next to me and maintains contact with my hand, Vietnamese style, after our handshake is completed, and says, "I am so glad to meet you, sir." And I feel so good as I sign his guest book, and add my University of Southern Mississippi business card and note on it: Captain, 98th Medical Detachment, 8th Field Hospital, Nha Trang, 1968-69.

He's just one former ARVN who apparently has found some peace and prosperity with his family, way down here on a back waterway of the Mekong Delta. Just one former ARVN, and yet I feel so good to have met him. He's just one, but where there is one, there must be more, scattered throughout the south and center of Vietnam.

DAY 8. MAY 22. MEKONG DELTA, CAN THO

7:30 AM departure for Can Tho, the unofficial capital of the Mekong Delta, via the high-speed hydrofoil through the exotic canals and giant rivers of the world's newest river delta, the Mekong River Delta.

Afternoon three-hour boat ride through the stunningly beautiful rivers and canals of the Can Tho area followed by a two-hour cyclo tour through Can Tho city.

Free evening.

Flashback to 1989

Another contrast between my first and second return trips becomes clear. Sitting with a student, John, at breakfast, I observe that I am having considerably fewer provoking responses to multiple Vietnamese stimuli than on my first return trip in 1989. (Perhaps this is a benefit to veterans of returning to Vietnam multiple times.)

Of course I am still upset to see the disparity in treatment between the winners and losers, damaged US military equipment on display, and the propaganda-laced film at the Cu Chi tunnel exhibit. Even so, I seem to be having fewer such reactions and they are less intense. This, plus the lack of any serious intra-group conflict, has allowed me to pay much more attention to and enjoy the Vietnamese people and culture than was possible on our 1989 trip. I'm reminded that the VVA tour guide in 1989 said, "Some vets have come back two or three times, and each time they heal a little more." Yes, it appears to be happening that way with me.

A Tailor Doesn't Have Good Clothes and Cobbler Doesn't Have Good Shoes

The hotel has provided breakfasts to go. As we are preparing to head out on our excursion, I notice that Ms. Trang is not here yet. Knowing that she is usually very busy helping various group members get ready to leave the hotel, I put aside a box breakfast and write her name on it. Later, trying to explain "burnout" to her, I use this as an illustration: she was devoting so much care to others that she was not able to take care of herself; and I express my concern for her. The group doesn't seem to realize that this must be a very emotional trip for Ms. Trang, too: it is her first return since marrying and moving to the US. In addition, she is being constantly pulled left and right by different group members to help them with one request after another and she has been extremely accommodating at all times of the day and night, help people shop, order tailored clothing. I urged her to take some time off se her family, whom she had not seen for over a year, but she answered: "This is my job; I can take care of me later. That is why they have the saying in Vietnam: 'A tailor doesn't have good clothes, and a cobbler doesn't have good shoes.'"

Discussion with an Educated Man.

"We don't know how to dance; we only know how to march."

Ray: "I find it hard to believe that the war has not had a very marked and longer-lasting impact on many Vietnamese (such as in terms of their attitudes towards Americans)."

Vietnamese: "Of course many Vietnamese have had important and insightful observations and opinions about Vietnam, the American War and its impact on the Vietnamese. Yes, the war had an impact."

Ray: "Then, how is it that almost no one has written about this in Vietnam?"

Vietnamese: "It is still a draft in somebody's drawer. Some want to write about the war, but are unable to do so yet. I will write a book one day, but so far the government wants us to speak with one voice.

"You know, if you go to any places where there is music, that most Vietnamese don't dance or are not very comfortable dancing. We don't know how to dance, we only know how to march. We [Vietnamese] march, we don't mourn; but the South [Saigon] is too soft; mourning, we weaken ourselves from inside. So, after the American War, the winds of the South [modern fashion, music] went to the North and influenced Hanoi, which is now more capitalistic than we are in the South, with the latest motorbikes and fashions."

On the Hydrofoil from Saigon to Can Tho

Everyone is excited. We are getting out of Ho Chi Minh City for a several hour hydrofoil ride south into the Mekong Delta. The hydrofoil is a relatively modern passenger boat with a seating capacity of perhaps 70 to 80 passengers. There are large windows along the sides of the boat, which would allow for panoramic viewing of the passing landscape except for two factors: the water spray and scratches on the windows. There are about 40 Vietnamese passengers with us; we occupy ourselves in different ways. A few sub-groups of students gather together to chat, laugh and relax. A few try to sleep for awhile. Two or three passengers at a time can stand outside of the passenger cabin and experience the water spray and unobstructed views of the passing landscape. At one point, I am standing at the rear, outside hydrofoil, watching as Vietnam at peace is flashing by, and a jarring thought intrudes. Was it really worth over *three million (Vietnamese) deaths* — almost no matter what the original purpose of the war?

Yes, I understand that a people's fate may be one of total and cruel enslavement or extermination, where so many suffer terribly on a daily basis; one could argue that war and the consequent carnage is justified to prevent that from happening. On the other hand, don't governments routinely concoct visions of such extreme consequences in order to motivate people to wage war?

Lyrics from one of my favorite songs, *Me and Bobby McGee*, written by Kris Kristofferson, suddenly play in my head: "Freedom's just another word for nothin' left to lose. Nothin' ain't worth nothin' — but it's free."

Back when the Cold War was at its height, our political leaders tried to tell us, "*Better dead than Red.*" Really? Ask the several million dead Vietnamese and their surviving families. Is the issue really anywhere nearly as clear-cut as we were led to believe in the 1960s? Americans protest against the execution of one man or woman on death row; what could justify the execution, by war, of millions?

The Making of a Quagmire and the Sorrow of War

A Vietnamese told me that he had read David Halberstam's *The Making of a Quagmire*, and he gave me his copy to read. Inside the book, I find these words hand-written on the title page: "Quagmire: 1. marshy ground that gives way under the foot 2. a difficult situation." Sure sounds like the Vietnam War to me.

I start to read an excerpt but find myself quite resistant to continuing. Then I realize why. Now that I am here *in* Vietnam, I find that I want to read something written by a *Vietnamese* author. Someone told me a little about *The Sorrow of War* by Bao Ninh, the only book published in Vietnamese that expresses the personal and realistic views of a Vietnamese about the war, rather than being merely a" political glorification and romanticizing" of the sacrifices of war.

Vietnamese: "The original title was *The Fate of Love*. This author is from the North. If he had been from the South, he would be in prison. But, somehow, this book got by the government censors and it got published."

Ray: "If they found this book to contain what they considered to be very inappropriate views, why did they not banish it once they did discover what views it contained?"

Vietnamese: "Once it was published, it was too late. It could not be held back. 'You can't put toothpaste back in the tube.'"

Last night I was window-shopping in Saigon in the area of the Rex Hotel (well-known during the war and still frequented by foreigners). I notice *The Sorrow of War* on a vendor's table on the sidewalk. I ask how much and he says, "$3." I say "$2," and he says "no, $3." I look at it again, put it back on the rack, look at a few other books and get ready to walk away. I look back one last time at *The Sorrow of War*; the vendor catches my eye and nods in the affirmative. So, I take the book and give him $2. In retrospect, my haggling over a dollar or two seems absurd — although I appreciate that this is a cultural expectation. It may be the best book ever written on the Vietnam War. Indeed, it should be considered a classic personal account about *any* war.

Flashback to 1968

This entire book transaction of course is much more elaborate than just inquiring about the price of something and then buying it or not — as would be common in the US It brings back pleasant memories of having many similar episodes with Vietnamese shopkeepers during the war.

Also, while I don't know it at the time, I am told later that this book is only available in English but it is illegal to sell it in Vietnam in the Vietnamese language version.

Rambunctious Students — An Intrusion or Just what the Doctor Ordered?

I dive into the book while we ride on the hydrofoil, and am completely captivated for the first 30 pages. However, I gradually become distracted by the merriment of the students, who are getting restless and are laughing, talking loudly, and generally making a commotion. How irritating! Do they think they're here to have fun? Here I am, reading an NVA soldier's firsthand account of his ten years in the war. His comrade tells him he is going to desert to go home to be with his mother.

"And, Kien says, 'Listen, Can, leaving like this is suicidal and shameful.' Can replies: 'Suicidal? Killing myself? I've killed so often it won't mean a thing if I kill myself. As for the shame' (Can stood up slowly, looking into Kien's eyes), 'in all my time as a soldier I've yet to see anything honorable.'"[135]

Wow, no wonder the government didn't want this book to be read by the Vietnamese. For that matter, does the US government really encourage the dissemination of this type of literature by Vietnam veterans with similar anti-war sentiments?? Of course, such writings are not banned outright in the US, but they hardly get institutional support.

The students have quieted down, I've written the above journal entry and now I'm ready to return to the book. So, the students' laughter and joviality — an intrusion, or a respite from the depths of war?

Bao Ninh's is just one voice among the hundreds of thousands of unheard voices representing the casualties on both sides of the Vietnam/American War: NVA and VC voices, and those of their families; ARVN voices, and those of their families, in the US and other places abroad where they have fled to; Red Cross workers and other civilians who served in Vietnam, and their families; US veterans and their

---

135. Ninh, 18.

families; and so many dead and wounded and disabled, physically and/or mentally, on both sides.

DAY 9. MAY 23. MORE LESSONS LEARNED

Can Tho.

Early morning river boat trip to the floating markets of Cai Rang and Phung Hiep.

Return to Can Tho.

Check out of hotel and board the hydrofoil for return trip to Saigon.

Arrive Saigon at 5: 30 PM. Free evening.

Well, Vietnam disrupted my personal life in 1968-69, and on my first return trip in 1989. Now, here I am, sitting at breakfast, 7:30 AM, and at just about this moment my daughter is graduating from high school a world away in Biloxi, MS. Without me.

Helani understands, and it is disappointing to her and to me. And, yes, I will be at her college graduation unless I'm in a hospital or dead! But this really hurts. Meanwhile, Father Truong is with Helani back in Mississippi, while I am visiting his family here in Vietnam; and he couldn't attend his sister's wedding.

Another student, Martin, mentions soccer. That immediately catapults my thinking to my oldest son, Armand: Not only am I missing my daughter's high school graduation, but my wife has told me over the phone that Armand suffered a concussion a few days ago during a soccer game and had to be taken to the hospital.)

Social Workers and Psychologists in Vietnam: Welcome to the Unemployment Ranks

Mr. Cong, our tour guide, describes to us how the family first, and then one's neighbors, and then one's village (if the family is unable) are expected to take care of family members with serious physical or mental problems. "You," (he tells me) "as a social worker, and Leslie, as a psychologist, would be unemployed in Vietnam."

For some reason, this reminds me of the fact that I had not received one second of training in war zone psychiatry or "war zone mental health" prior to my arrival in Vietnam, and there was no formal training in Vietnam, either.

Mekong River Delta

We are riding in a boat through lush vegetation and increasingly narrow waterways in the Mekong Delta, our views extremely restricted by the jungle that surrounds us at very close quarters. As the waterway continues to narrow, some feelings of constriction and claustrophobia come up. Imagine making such a boat ride through hostile territory during a war...

These waterways were described during the war as "brown water." I can't help but think of brown-water Navy vets I have known over the years, such as Jim Cordeiro (Honolulu) and Dave Roberts (Gig Harbor, Washington).

Finally, a few students ask me exactly what it was that I did in Vietnam. (No one has made any comment about the lecture I gave on survival modes in the war zone).

Perhaps I really should take an hour or so, sometime after the last visit to a vet's former battle site (Roy), to briefly tell my Vietnam story.

Hotel, Coca Cola, Peasant Woman, Me and Vietnam

Back in my (marginally) air-conditioned hotel room in Can Tho, I am sitting at the desk writing post-cards. I glance out the hotel window. A small white truck goes by, "Coca Cola" emblazoned on the side. I smile at the sight, and write a few more lines. I gaze out the window again, and a Vietnamese woman walks by in the opposite direction, dressed in rural clothing and wearing the traditional cone-shaped, pointed straw hat.

A few moments later she comes back into view, as if to emphasize that, yes, she too is very much an integral part of the landscape: a landscape that in 2000 includes me, a US Vietnam veteran sitting at a desk in an air-conditioned hotel room.

Yes, life is full of wondrously incongruent yet somehow inclusive images and experiences that are integral to my, and our, continuing journey of healing that has brought me back to Vietnam, again.

Flashback to 1989

By comparison to the 1989 trip, which was like being immersed in a very intensive and emotionally saturated marathon group-therapy session, this trip has turned out to be a cultural and historical trip that is judiciously interspersed with emotionally therapeutic moments. And what a difference that is.

Vietnamese versus Americans Going to and Returning from War

I ask a Vietnamese man why American veterans seemed to have greater difficulty readjusting after the war than Vietnamese veterans?

[Vietnamese] "Vietnamese go to war naturally, and in between wars in Vietnam the standard of living is not very much higher than during war. We lived 80 years under French domination, with unstable conditions and the French suppressing the Vietnamese, and during World War II Japan was suppressing Vietnam.

"So, we became very tough surviving over several generations, working in rubber plantations, beaten, exploited and suppressed by the French (not to mention by Vietnamese themselves!), and then going to war against them. So, fighting in the American War seemed like a normal part of our lives. But, some Vietnamese had fought for independence and a utopia, and found out after the American War that a utopia doesn't exist. Such Vietnamese had a 'broken dream' — and they don't like either the Communists or the Westerners.

"And then, we fought the Cambodians. And, there are not so many people like Bao Ninh as it seems that there are American [Vietnam] veterans with PTSD: maybe only the intellectuals in Vietnam have PTSD."

[Ray] "So, you think that having a greater contrast in one's personal life and in the societal conditions that we live in before and that we return to after war, versus what we experience in war time, is a key factor in increasing the risk of getting post-war PTSD?"

[Vietnamese] "Yes, Vietnamese vets generally lived in very poor conditions before, during and following many wars in our country. I think that for US veterans there was a much greater contrast between peacetime and wartime conditions. In Vietnam, after the war, we need to get our daily bread, for survival, and so that is our focus, not so much different than during the war."[136]

Bao Ninh provides a stark viewpoint of post-war life for even the "victors" of the American War, the NVA survivors:

"I can't avoid admitting there seems little left for me to hope for. From my life before there remains sadly little. That wonderful period has been heartlessly extinguished. The aura of hope in those early post-war days swiftly faded.

"Those who survived continue to live. But that will has gone, that burning will which was once Vietnam's salvation. Where is the reward of enlightenment due to us for attaining our sacred war goals? Our history-making efforts for the great generations have been to no avail. What's so different here and now from the vulgar and cruel life we all experienced during the war?"[137]

Vietnamese With Mental Problems: "Sour Fruit" From the Father's Seeds

I asked another man, "What happens if a veteran after the war is having emotional or psychiatric problems?" He told me that the vast majority of the population are villagers, and if anyone manifests any "mental health problems" after a war, first, he doesn't go to see any professional mental health person. Rather, he may go to the temple or to a priest. Second, all of the "invisible diseases" (being crazy, mentally retarded, dumb, deaf) are believed to have come from the sins or problems of the father's generations and are now visited upon the sons and daughters. The father's son (who may be crazy, mentally retarded, etc.), is a "sour fruit" from the father's seeds of life.

Villagers believe that a troubled family member's soul has been captured by someone in the afterlife. An ancestor might be the problem, and you must pray to that ancestor's spirit "to leave my child alone." And so the problems are not seen as deriving from the war or any other causes in one's current life. [As in any traditional society] the words "psychotic," "psychosis," "schizophrenia" are known from the dictionary, not from life in Vietnam. There are no "psychiatric hospitals." If there is a (mental health — or legal) problem, it is handled by the family first; you take care of any troubled family member, at home, until they die; if you have a child with problems, it is because two or three generations back there was a problem that you must now "pay" for.[138]

Ray: "What if the family is not able to take care of the person who is troubled?"

---

136. Similarly, many ethnic minority and other American vets in the US after returning from the war struggled with survival needs, rather than focusing on psychotherapy. Also, there is the viewpoint that life for the Vietnamese in the north remained fairly much the same after the war had ended, but that living standards in the south plummeted. Finally, as Courtney Frobenius suggested, considering the large number of NVA and VC killed in the war, these probably include many of the Vietnamese who might have suffered from PTSD.

137. Ninh, 42-43.

Vietnamese: "It is expected that the family will take care of troubled members; it would be shameful not to. So the family does what it can and the village tolerates the behavior."

Ray: "But what if the family member, for example, is a danger to others?"

Vietnamese: "If someone were violent, they would be isolated so they can't hurt anyone. We also have no need for lawyers.

"[I have been told that this comment reflects the viewpoint of a villager or rural person, and not that of a more educated urban dweller.]

Ray: "But what if there is a legal dispute, such as over the property or boundary between two homeowners?"

Vietnamese: "If there is a dispute between two families, they handle it between themselves. If they cannot solve it, they get the village to handle it. You don't need any lawyer."

Vietnamese Veteran's Convalescent Centers

Veterans' convalescent centers are only for the most severely physically, not psychiatrically, disabled, e.g., invalids, whom the family is absolutely unable to care for. However, again, it is shameful for a family to let the father go to live in a convalescent center. And so, the veteran will be kept at home almost no matter how bad his condition is.

Physically disabled Vietnamese veterans are rated on an "eight" classification or rating system by a group of doctors. A rating of 9 = dead; a rating of 8 = the worst disabilities. Veterans classified from 4 to 8 are eligible to receive care and remain at a veteran's convalescent center if they do not have a family to stay with. If they do have family, they will receive some financial assistance.

It is important to note that the 8 point system is only for NVA and VC, and vets of the Cambodian war —not for any former ARVNs or for any non-veterans. For such people the family, first, and the village, second, are responsible for their care.[139] It seems our eligibility requirements in America for benefits are extraordinarily liberal in comparison. [Courtney Frobenius later pointed out that, while this may represent the perspective of the common rural people, the *Binh Vien Nhiet Doi* hospital in Cho lon does offer mental health treatment. I have also been told that the legal profession is an up and coming profession in Vietnam.]

Can Tho and the Floating Markets; The Return to Ho Chi Minh City [140]

Can Tho is a pleasant change from Saigon. It is of course much smaller, with much less traffic and a distinctly slower pace of life. It is right on a major waterway, the Bassac, one of the two major tributary rivers of the Mekong, with a very pleasant

---

138. For an excellent description and discussion of psychiatric and mental health services and attitudes in more recent times that was gleaned from the perspectives of a delegation of 27 mental health clinicians and scholars who traveled to Vietnam in 1994, see: Johnson, D.R. and H. Lubin, "Uncovering PTSD in the Republic of Vietnam," *National Center for PTSD Clinical Quarterly*, 5 (4) (Fall, 1995), 7-10.

139. After our return from Vietnam,

garden park alongside the water at the beginning of the town. It is a very pleasant place to walk around.

We take a small boat to go to the floating market, a flotilla of medium-sized boats anchored in the middle of the large waterway, filled with fresh vegetables and fruit. They are only accessible by boat. We get right next to several of the boats to examine the fruit. We stop at one larger boat and some of the students buy succulent pineapples, which the two women immediately cut and trim for them. Other enterprising Vietnamese paddle smaller boats amongst the larger market boats, offering cold drinks to potential customers. Several of them pull alongside to hawk their drinks, quite persistently.

The return four-hour trip by hydrofoil, Can Tho to Saigon, is somewhat anti-climactic.

Day 10. May 24. Hue, The Vibrant and Ancient Capital: Echoes of the American War

7:00 AM flight to Hue.

Tour of the former Imperial Citadel, home of Vietnam's last royal dynasty, the Nguyens (1882-1945), Thai Hoa Palace, the Lam Hien Pavilion, the Royal Library.

Early afternoon boat trip to the tomb of Ming Mang, the Nguyen Dynasty's second emperor (1820-1840). Return via boat to the Thien Mu (Heavenly Mother) Pagoda.

(Thien Mu was the home pagoda of a Buddhist monk, Quang Duc, who immolated himself to protest the Catholic-dominated Saigon-based government of Ngo Dinh Diem. The government had refused to repeal anti-Buddhist laws — and Buddhists comprised about 70% of the population! — that had been passed by the French. Eye-witnesses said that Monk Quang Duc sat extremely stoically the entire time that he was burning and that his remarkable composure was a rallying point for other Buddhists.

Mid-afternoon USM program: Group Discussion

We hold a morning meeting and cancel the scheduled late afternoon meeting in Hue to discuss highlights of the trip so far.

Scott: "Really friendly people, very strong family system yet underneath it all seems to be a fear of what this government may do to you."

John L: "The meeting with the former RVN at that farm outside of Saigon; he looked me in the eye and he took my hand. I'll forget a lot of this trip before I'll forget that. And the vividness of the physical scene, the tight waterways and dense foliage, must have been a cause of great fear (for Americans traveling on them during the war) versus now a feeling of being right at home."

---

140. I noticed that I still vacillate between the names "*Saigon*" and "*Ho Chi Minh City*." This is probably a reflection of my reluctance to let go of *Saigon*, and my resistance to accept that it is now officially called *Ho Chi Minh City*. Of course, we discover that many of the people in the south of Vietnam still use the name *Saigon* and not *Ho Chi Minh City*.

John Young: "This was absolutely incredibly unbelievable: a refrigeration specialist former ARVN here in this space. He was so proud to show us those US certificates (of his military training in the US). I have never seen anyone with so much pride."

Ray: "I'm becoming more aware of the fact that sometimes I am reacting here as a Vietnam veteran and at other times I am reacting as a professor/mental health person. Perhaps I need to let you know, when I am aware, if I am reacting/sharing primarily as a veteran. I did find his holding onto my hand for as long as he did to be really touching. What a beautiful man he is."

I am also impressed by the sensitive nature of some of the students. We are lucky to have them with us.

And I wonder at the seriousness, the weight I am feeling as we travel about. Is it the weight of the tens of thousands of Vietnam veterans whose pain and turmoil from this place has plagued them for some three decades...plus the multitude of untold stories of the Vietnamese? I'm pretty sure I need to lighten up a little; but how?

I have just finished *The Sorrow of War*. Part of me is very, very glad that I read it, especially here in Vietnam. On the other hand, part of me wishes I had not read it. It has really pulled me back down into the horrors and insanity and tragedy of war, and the long-lasting stain of its horrid footprint on those from all sides touched or consumed by it. And, of course, there is the Yin and the Yang, the remarkable spirit and impetus for life shown by many war survivors. And one must feel heart-broken for tragic soldiers from both sides like Bao Ninh, who I have heard is "living as a mad ghost in Hanoi."

Then came a tough moment for all of us, as Leslie said her good-byes. She had a baby daughter waiting at home, and we all knew she had planned to leave the group at this stage. Even so, Leslie was ambivalent about leaving early and not completing the trip with us. Of course, we too feel her departure as a kind of rupture. We'll miss her.

Now I think of Angelo Romeo (my college freshman roommate, fraternity brother and fellow ROTC cadet and long-time close friend). Angelo was stationed in Hue at the time that I was in Nha Trang, and we got together once in Hue.

Hue is located in what is now known as "central Vietnam," almost equidistant between Saigon and Hanoi — in "our day," it was 20 some miles from the DMZ. Part of me wants to be here by myself, not having to talk or interact with anyone. I find myself starting to withdraw...and yet if I walk alone in Hue, I will attract attention. I feel like I want or need something, but I don't know what, now that we are in "central" Vietnam, what we used to think of as the "north" of "South" Vietnam.

Flashback to 1968-69

Hue is much less congested and much less hectic than Saigon; a welcome contrast. Riding through town on our bus, this feels more like Nha Trang circa 1968-69. Maybe I'm feeling some nostalgia about a very special time 32 years ago when I was in the same age range as many of the USM students who are here. Wow, now it really hits me — I was just about this age (25) and full of wonder about Vietnam and its beautiful people and land. And so are these students soaking up Vietnam today, but with one major difference. This was a war zone then.

144

However, while I am soaking up the peacetime Vietnam, too, I also am reverberating with echoes and images of a time long gone by. I seem to be letting images back in but at a somewhat more measured pace, a pace of my choosing — or perhaps I am fooling myself once again. I don't seem to be totally willing to let Vietnam back into my heart. Because I am not sure that there is, or that I want there to be, any more room in my thoughts and in my life for Vietnam than I have already allocated to it.

I do believe my cup runneth over with Vietnam. And, of course, as illustrated in an old Shinto parable, one cannot pour any more liquid into a cup that is already overflowing. Or, perhaps my cup is larger than I am willing to admit it to be? I think I need to let Margaret, my wife, more into my heart at this time in my life, more than Vietnam. As if the two, Vietnam and Margaret, may be somewhat mutually exclusive of each other. Of course, many war veterans and their significant others feel that way. At dinner, I reflect. Maybe I've seen too many Vietnam veterans burdened and violated within from the trauma of war and its aftermath. Perhaps I am feeling, too much, their accumulated pain. I feel this weight especially as I'm here in-country in Vietnam, whether it's 2000, and in 1989, and in 1968. I am now thinking that, overall, it is a good thing that I retired from the VA in 1998 — and yet I still very much miss working with vets.

Roy's Evening Pre-briefing: Going to His Battlefield Sites Tomorrow

Roy Ainsworth: PFC, 1967. Alpha Company, 1st Battalion, 9th Marines. Wounded twice at Con Tien. Purple Heart.

Roy: "In 1966 I joined the Marine Corps; 1 March 67 I joined the 9th Marines. I remember very clearly what our Sergeant said: 'don't make friends; and carry only what you need; bury the rest.'"

Ray: "Tell us, Roy, what you are hoping or planning to do tomorrow?"

Roy: "I want to pay my respects to lost buddies, especially Richard Sarakas, my best friend who died in my arms; and to Doc Terry Rudolph, our medic who ran out of battle dressings in the middle of battle due to such heavy casualties; and I have brought a battle dressing to leave here...Also, this is where I lost part of me [wounded and medically evacuated].

"My best friend, Richard Sarakis, was on my right side. I wished the hell that we would get up and start moving. Well, we did get up and start moving, in this open field, I guess we had gone about 50 yards. When we were about 3 yards from the treeline, we got hit with everything, rifle fire, machine gun fire, it was like all hell broke loose.

"The next thing I knew, I saw Sarakis fall. I drug him behind a tank. The corpsman said there nothing we could do for him. So I waited there, holding him, until he died."

DAY 11. MAY 25. VET ROY'S RETURN TO PHU AN

Early departure to the former DMZ. Proceed directly to Phu An, just south of Con Tien. Tour the battlefield of Phu An. Continue on to the Truong Son National Cemetery. Return to Hue for the evening.

Carrying the Weight of 800+ Vets with PTSD

> At breakfast, *The Sorrow of War* is on my mind again. It's hard not to identify with the author, even though I feel the vivid memories and pathos of the war through the 1000+ US vets with whom I've had therapeutic contacts over these many years. I know that there are many more vets seen by other care-givers, and so many more who have not spoken out but are carrying their hurt with them, in all walks of life.
>
> And I just cannot continue to feel that weight so much. It is blocking my ability to enjoy what I am surrounded by. I guess I do have some "compassion fatigue." Even so, as I say that, I think I won't be able to let go entirely of that accumulation of pain. Indeed, I may not really want to. In a way, care-givers give a voice to the voiceless anguish of "The American War." And somehow I feel a little lighter expressing it, and being aware of what I have just expressed.
>
> And I knew so terribly little when I was here, in Vietnam, in 1968-69.
>
> I recall my first Army stint: it was in a nice safe location, far from the field of war. I was assigned to the William Beaumont General Hospital, El Paso, 1967-68. There, as a young, single 2nd LT, I was conducting pre-natal educational classes for pregnant wives of servicemen. My tour in El Paso seemed bizarre and inappropriate.
>
> Then I jump to a recollection of someone else's war, and a vet's psychotic break while picking up body parts. He had a full-blown psychotic break on the battlefield; came out of his psychosis 27 days later. Ever since, he has been haunted by the fear that if he dwells too much on that experience again or even talks about it very much, that he will go completely psychotic — and that this time he won't ever come back out of it.[141]

Another Clash of Styles

> Veteran John Young tells me he is really upset at the conduct of some of the students, who were playing the guitar at a temple in Hue yesterday. He found their behaviors (loud, verbally disruptive) disrespectful of the local culture. In fact, isn't rowdy behavior disrespectful at any religious site, anywhere, or, for that matter, to some extent, in any public place? I hardly know what to say to John since I find them disturbing, too. Or am I over-reacting again to my long-held issues about how the Americans treated the Vietnamese during the war? Isn't it really OK to lighten up a little, Ray, and have a good time here? Perhaps I have something to learn from the students? Should we have talked to them more, before the trip? If Americans really need to be told to keep their voices down in public spaces in general, then it was too much for us to imagine they would be sensitive to the Vietnamese and their culture.
>
> A Vietnamese man was talking with me about the status of doctors and teachers from 1975 to about 1990; they dropped to the lowest status in Vietnam because of

---

141. A very interesting case study of the persistence of such for 75 years in a World War I veteran is found in: Hamilton, J.D. and R.H. Workman, Jr., "Persistence of combat-related posttraumatic stress symptoms for 75 years," *Journal of Traumatic Stress*, 1 (4) (October, 1998), 763-768. The veteran in question had not exhibited any disabling effects due to having these memories throughout his life. The case study and the ramifications concerning the persistence of war-related symptoms are described in detail in Volume I of this Trilogy.

the Communist cultural revolution and the failing economy. Most people ended up with very little money and food was rationed. Why were doctors and teachers looked down upon? "Because they are pale skinned; while others toil in the hot sun, they just sit in the shade and talk — like the 'bourgeois' [the class of landlords and business owners, who, in the Communist view of things, are parasites living off other people's work]."

The status accorded to various occupations is vividly demonstrated by the rice rations allocated:

- About 30 lbs of rice, the lowest amount: teachers and doctors

- 37 lbs: workers/laborers

- 40 lbs: soldiers

- 46 lbs: high-ranking leaders and very skillful workers (engineers, road construction)

A Vietnamese tells me a joke: "In 1989, the Russians stopped their aid to Vietnam and told us, 'tighten your belts.' And Vietnam said back: 'Send us your belts: we have none.' And so, when the Russians did not send even a belt, Vietnam saw that Russian aid would soon be ending and decided to open up economically to other countries. And the value of doctors and teachers has risen somewhat since 1987."

Quang Tri Province (Former DMZ Area): the "Land of Fire"

Quang Tri Province (which consists mostly of the location of the former De-Militarized Zone or DMZ) is one of the poorest provinces in Vietnam. During the war, both sides would attack and counterattack. It is known to the Vietnamese as "the land of fire." Many physically disabled people live here due to continuing occurrences of injuries from the extensive amounts of unexploded ordnance.

Also, the land is very dry, barren, not nearly as fertile as elsewhere in Vietnam. A major reforestation project has been going on in the DMZ area: Australian eucalyptus trees, which are very hardy, have been planted, and are now 10 to 20 feet high. Not many houses. Almost nothing can be grown in this area except potatoes. However, potatoes need water — for which there is no irrigation.

A man tells me, in private, "No one moves to Quang Tri Province, but many move away and seldom return to live here." And so, in many ways, the former DMZ area is still a "no-man's land." I hear the echoes of war continuing to shout out particularly loudly in this part of Vietnam.

At the edge of Quang Tri City, we stop at an abandoned Catholic Church. It was heavily damaged in 1972, when the city was destroyed. Even though it is abandoned, the government apparently won't let anyone use it for any other purpose; probably the several Catholic families in the area would complain. Of course, in 1975 the government could not have cared less what any Catholics (excuse me, Catholic Vietnamese) thought.

We stop as the Hanoi-to-Saigon train goes by. It is a 40-hour train trip. Perhaps most impressive is the fact that this rail link symbolically and literally demonstrates that Vietnam, indeed, is one country.

A consequence of having returned to Vietnam previously since the war: on this second return trip to a peacetime Vietnam in the year 2000, I am finding myself flashing back both to 1968-69 and to 1989. In contrast, of course, in 1989 I found myself flashing back only to the war. Each return trip will add experiences that compete more and more in a veteran's mind with the war experiences, so that the disastrous images are supplanted (or will now co-exist), to an increasing degree, with less hurtful images. Judging from my experience, the theory is working.

I meet a former ARVN air traffic controller. He is a cyclo driver; this seems to be a common employment for many former ARVNs.

I'm not nearly as melancholy today as I have been the past few days. It is just another change in mood elevation on this roller-coaster ride.

Flashback to 1969 and to 1989

During the war (1968-69), I was a designated care-giver for psychiatric casualties, and on my first return trip in 1989 with eight veterans with PTSD, too. Theoretically, I started out in the same role on this trip. However, in the year 2000 that role turns out to be in little demand. I am relieved.

Also, on my two previous "tours" in Vietnam I was not in a position to talk or share about my role as a care-giver. I was too caught-up in being needed as a care-giver on-site. Furthermore, in 1989 the focus, and naturally so, was on the eight veterans with PTSD, and the fact that I, too, was a Vietnam veteran seemed to be an afterthought almost lost to everyone, including me.

However, on this trip, I am more in touch with my feelings about my role as a Vietnam veteran, too; and surprisingly, I find myself somewhat resenting being slighted in that regard, as I see it, by most of the group. I am one of the three professors for the trip. And, we have been quite naturally focusing on the returns of John, Charles and Roy, to each of their respective battlefield sites. And Nha Trang, where I served during the war, is not anywhere near any of the pre-arranged locations on our itinerary. But I am beginning to feel an urgent need to talk with the students, at least a little, about my Vietnam war experiences. And, I get a surge of tears and sadness that erupts up into my mouth and eyes, as I remember...gently taking valuables off the wounded GIs, for safekeeping, in the 8th Field Hospital E.R., as part of my duty as the AOD. Will they never stop coming?[142]

Am I a "Proxy" for Many Vets Who Can't or Won't Return to Vietnam?

I just got it. I've been feeling like I'm here primarily as a proxy for many other vets, much more so than "being here primarily for me." And, perhaps, that is why I am finding it so very difficult to be "lighter" in mood on this trip, like most of the group members. Even so, I really am much lighter than I was in 1989.

At Dong Ha, we stop to get our local guide, who is a native of Quang Tri Province and is knowledgeable of the history and various battle sites in the former DMZ. He has been contracted to help us find the battlefield sites in Phu An and Con Tien where Roy served. This is Roy's day.

---

142. See *A Vietnam Trilogy*, 2004.

The Former DMZ: Still a Killing Zone

Our local guide informs us that from 1975 to now about 5,000 local people have been killed by land mines! Foreign experts (German and US) estimate that it will cost about $17 million and 20 more years to remove all remaining unexploded land mines. Will such funding and effort ever actually materialize?

Also, apparently because of Agent Orange, the chemical defoliant that the US sprayed heavily here in the DMZ, there reportedly have been about 8,000 abnormal children who have been born in this area. And only about 200 are alive today. Roy's son was born with a lung disease; he wonders if that is not also an effect of Agent Orange?

We stop at a bridge at the Cam Lo River (Cam Lo is a very old name, and it is a place where hill people came to trade; fresh food and ivory, too, to barter and exchange). Roy remembers this bridge and the river site. However, he remembers that the place on the river where his unit disembarked from their boats is somewhere further down the river. The guide suggests we go ahead a mile or so to park the bus. From there we will have to walk about a mile to get to the possible area where Roy's unit was ambushed. It is very hot and humid, as always, and dusty, as we walk along a hilly dirt road through open fields, trees and some farm-land.

Roy scans the environment in all directions, desperately searching for a familiar sight.

This reminds me of my own reactions in 1989, as I became vigilant and scanned the environment as Jake LaFave and I were approaching the sites where we were stationed in Nha Trang.

Roy sees one area, off to the north of the road, that reminds him very much of the spot he is looking for. He says that it is not the exact spot of the ambush, but that it is very similar in appearance. He agrees, if he is unable to find the exact spot, that he would want to come back to this area to spend some time and do what he had planned to do at the actual site.

I am walking alongside Roy, and am in a serious, somber mood. We finally reach a small village: a village that Roy tells us did not exist during the war. Roy is being filmed as he talks about what he is looking for. Several members of the group are laughing and talking loudly; I tell them to be quiet or to move away if they don't care what is happening with Roy.

Our guide talks to some of the villagers; he deduces that the battle site that Roy described is probably a mile or more away through heavy underbrush. No one really seems to know; they weren't here at the time. The villagers near John Young's former battle site had lived there before, during and since the war. There is no way that Roy, who has serious physical disabilities and walks with a cane, will be able to hike to a spot that may not be right anyway.

Close Enough

And so, Roy decides to go back to the location we had passed earlier. This is Phu An — it will do. I ask everyone to stay back while Roy and four others go ahead— the two cameramen, John C. and Yaron, and Shane, a student and son of a Vietnam veteran, and Adam Ray (who Roy asked to accompany him and film him with Roy's video camera at the site). Four people are enough to be with Roy at this time.

Also, a number of Vietnamese have followed us and gathered with our group — a not uncommon event during this trip. They include children and several laborers who work in the rubber tree grove that has been planted nearby. The presence of the rubber tree grove is another indication of the changes since 1967: there were no rubber trees in this region during the war. The guide confirms this, adding that this is another attempt by the government to try to develop some crops in the DMZ.

Roy looks for the best place to do what he has planned to do: to leave a modest memorial for his buddies who died in the ambush. He finds a spot that looks very similar to where the ambush occurred three decades ago. He kneels down, drops his cane over his left leg and reaches into his back pack. He pulls out several articles.

"This is Doc Rudolph . . . Phew." He carefully places the photo of "Doc" Terry Rudolph (Alpha Company's corpsman) at the foot of a small bush, and he places with it a battle dressing that he brought from home, signed by all the (remaining) men who had been there with him. "I can see all of them. And they all had a prayer for the other guys, for those KIA, before they signed the battle dressing. . . This is for all my brothers . . . who died."

"It was just like one big flashback, everything came back." Roy takes off his hat, lowers his head, makes the sign of the cross, prays silently for a short while, crosses himself again, and raises his head and looks around. "Somehow it all seems so . . . My marines, Doc's marines . . . [he adjusts the articles he has placed by the bush, and then puts his hat back on]. God bless you, boys." And he walks away.

After rejoining us, Roy tells me that he feels that he has, indeed, accomplished his mission at Phu An. Yaron asks if Roy would like to go back to the memorial spot now, with all of the group, and say a prayer together? Good thought; Roy agrees.

It is a very special, reverent moment. Roy and our group of students, veterans, college professors, and about ten Vietnamese approach the spot that Roy picked out. Suddenly, Roy kneels down and makes the sign of the cross; many others kneel down too by the make-shift memorial, in the very hot Vietnam sun, honoring and remembering Roy and his fallen comrades.

Later, Roy says: "I actually got to come back and say goodbye. I've been trying that all my whole life, and it had just not seemed right. Cause there were a lot of guys I didn't get to say goodbye to, and I got to say it today. And thanks to all of y'all for our support. Made my day. Something I'll never forget — take to my grave. But I'll be with my boys . . ."

We get back to the bus and drive a short while further, again stopping. This time we are going to *Con Tien*, the highest point of land for miles around. There are commanding views and fields of fire in all directions. This is where Roy was wounded, not once but twice during the same fighting, and from where he had to be medically evacuated.

(Please note the spelling: *Con Tien*, not *Con Thien*. Mr. Cong, our outstanding guide, emphasized to us that "Con Tien" had been misspelled during the war, and that misspelling had been repeated in subsequent historical writings. He strongly urged that we note the correct spelling. Yes, sir, Mr. Cong — at least in anything *I* write, it will be "*Con Tien*.")

"We were under heavy attack from incoming. I was wounded, and Doc treated me. I was told to stay back, out of the fighting. However, I couldn't just sit there. So, I went back to my post to join my buddies. However, I then got hit with another round of incoming shrapnel. This time, my wounds were too bad for me to be able to continue fighting. I had to be med-evaced. . . I lost a piece of me, several pieces, on this hill."

Now we are walking perhaps a mile or two, up a narrow, rough dirt road, really more a trail. There are freshly tilled and planted fields in all directions, along with banana trees, green forests and vegetation. Then, we spot the deserted bunker/command post at the highest point on the hill. We leave the trail, and walk through freshly tilled fields and then into tall grass. Finally, we reach the concrete bunker/command post. It is overgrown, abandoned, damaged — and it still commands a remarkable 360 degree view: towards the sea, the south, west toward Khe San and the mountains of Laos, and to the north and towards Hanoi. There are one or two laborers in a nearby field. And all is quite peaceful, serene, quiet.

Roy is struck by how different the terrain looks. He says that he probably would not have recognized the location but the guide pointed out the bunker still standing at the summit, hidden among the tall grass and weeds. Roy described how the entire hill top had been cleared of all vegetation and was a dusty, brown spot that the American forces manned; a remarkable contrast to the green fields and freshly planted crops.

Several members of the group want to climb up on top of the bunker. It is a difficult climb, and requires members helping each other. Roy says, "I want to climb up on top, too — and if my doctor saw me doing this, he would kill me." Standing on a lower wall of the bunker, Roy discards his cane and reaches up to find a handhold. Students up above reach down to grasp his hand; students and a professor at the bottom give him a boost and help Roy to reach the top of the bunker. He stands up on top, quietly triumphant, drinking in the 360 degree panoramic view of today — and of 35 years ago. Roy is back at Con Tien, and on top of the world.

We go back through the fields, and back to the trail, a rocky, meandering, hard dirt path that narrows to a few feet wide near the top. We are spread out, mostly single file, and I find myself walking alone. Then, in the midst of the beautiful silence I hear, coming up the trail, voices. Suddenly two young Vietnamese girls come into view, pushing their bicycles, smiling broadly and waving. They say, in English, "hello," as we pass each other — me going down and they going up, here in what the Vietnamese call "The Land of Fire," a few hundred meters from where Roy Ainsworth, 9th Marines, got hit not once, but twice, by incoming NVA shrapnel, 33 years ago. Another time and surely another place — even if it was right here...

Here's to you, Roy, and to the many very brave men who fought in this horrific war zone, this Land of Fire.

Truong Son National Cemetery

We are told this cemetery holds about 11,000 NVA. I ask if there a cemetery around here for ARVN forces? The guide says no, and smiles.

Personally, I'd seen enough cemeteries honoring those who had fought against us, the former NVA and VC. I want to see and honor those other Vietnamese casualties with whom we fought side-by-side. And so I stay near the bus, while most of the group tours yet another National Cemetery for some of the 1.6 million NVA dead. And what is there for the 800,000 ARVN dead?

Several group members ask the local guide if it is logistically feasible to get to the actual DMZ boundary that separated north from South Vietnam during the war. The guide says yes, and several group members, including Roy, go. When they come back, Roy is beaming:

"Well, for the first time I got to step into North Vietnam. I stood at the boundary line, with one foot in North Vietnam and one foot in South Vietnam."

Of course, what was "North" Vietnam is now "central" Vietnam; and what was once "South" Vietnam is the south of Vietnam — Ho Chi Minh City and further south. This change in description of the geographic sections of Vietnam makes me feel a little disoriented.

Returning from Phu An and Con Tien

We observe some unwritten driving rules:

1: There is no center dividing line that has any meaning to anyone.

2: Use your horn, constantly.

3: He who hesitates is lost; don't look back, don't slow down.

4: Size does matter — there definitely is a pecking order. It is based on vehicle size and whether the propulsion is by engine or foot-pedal. The bigger vehicles own the middle of the roads; smaller motorized vehicles are squeezed more to the right side, and pedal-driven modes of transportation are relegated to the right edges.

Slower vehicles move over very grudgingly and only very slightly, leaving just enough room for the larger vehicle to miraculously squeeze through. Horns beep constantly, as a warning that someone is coming through who is faster than you, and you react by subtly moving towards the right, if you move over at all.

I am remembering the Darwinian rules of road driving in war-time Vietnam: the bigger the vehicle, the faster you can go because the quicker everyone else gets out of the way. I learned this in Nha Trang; I had found that, when going on our MED-CAPs to Xom Bong Hamlet, driving a deuce-and-a-half (two and one-half ton) truck through town was a quite different and quicker experience than driving a jeep. Not quite like Moses parting the waters, but there is a mild similarity.

And now, in the year 2000, there is a creative use for the roads that competes for room with vehicles, all along Highway 1, leaving Hue and going northward. At many places alongside the three-to-six feet of asphalt at the left and right edges of the "highway" farmers have spread out freshly cut grain to dry. There seems to be a "gentlemen's agreement" that passing traffic will avoid, mostly, running over the grain.

At breakfast, Mr. Cong tells us that when he was in Con Tien a year before, he was able to walk directly up to the top of the hill and to the bunker. Yesterday, (about one year later), we had to take a very circuitous route and around heavy vegetation and newly tilled and planted crops.

So the landscape had changed that much in one year. That puts into perspective the changes in the terrain that vets returning 30+ years later will find in Vietnam today.

Yaron has previewed his video of Roy from yesterday, and is able to show a segment of Roy's battlefield visit as part of the debriefing that evening back at the hotel. Roy emphasizes, with delight: "The first time I ever crossed the border to North Vietnam was — yesterday."

During the War American forces were prohibited from crossing into North Vietnam; and yet, there they were, like sitting ducks at the DMZ, facing waves of NVA troops who had no similar politically-driven prohibition on entering into and retreating back out of the DMZ. What an absurd way to fight a war.

Roy tells the group that the DMZ also was known as the "Dead Marine Zone." "And the nickname of our unit [due to the heavy and constantly recurring casualties incurred] was 'The Walking Dead'."

Talking about his day, Roy says, "I definitely found some degree of peace, although I will never have total closure over what had happened during the war."

And, of course, he wouldn't. Who would? Yet, he seemed to make a very important step earlier today about a series of events that have haunted him all these years. And that is a primary objective that we had hoped would be accomplished on this trip.

Military History Synopsis: The Story of Hue, the DMZ and the Tet Offensive

Andy gives a stimulating military history presentation concerning the DMZ and the military activities surrounding Roy's and surrounding units at the time of Roy's Vietnam tour, as well as Hue and the Tet offensive of 1968. This presentation brings home the strength and tenacity of the military force that the Americans and ARVNs were up against, especially in the greater Hue/DMZ area. The lecture is, of course, all the more compelling as we are just about to go into Hue, where the battles over several days resulted in 159 Marines KIA and 345 WIA; and the enemy casualties estimated at 1,290 KIA.

Two NVA Battalions were in the area, unbeknownst to US intelligence. I might note that this was just one of countless examples illustrating why the term "US intelligence" was widely considered to be an oxymoron. The NVA sent five additional battalions to the area, and then the Marines did, too. The battle lasted three weeks, and was covered extensively in the US media. The Marines go back to Con Tien, and the NVA go back as well: a savage (DMZ) zone of attrition, similar to the fighting in World War I.[143]

The civilian Vietnamese deaths in Hue were also dramatic. Andy mentioned that conservative estimates are that there were some 3,000 civilians alone murdered by the NVA. Andy emphasized that the US and allied forces feared that if they did not prevail in Hue, the VC would slaughter Hue civilians who had been supportive of

---

143. Some of the other salient facts mentioned by Andy during this very interesting lecture about the Tet Offensive at Hue: Until January 31, 1968, Hue had been an "open" city reportedly frequented by both ARVN and VC forces. Then, 8,000 troops attacked the unprepared city (largely defended by out-manned ARVN forces) as part of the Vietnam-wide Tet Offensive of 1968. The Citadel was occupied and the surrounding populated areas on that side of the river. Again, due to lack of accurate intelligence reports as to the size of the enemy force that had invaded Hue, a single company of Marines was sent into Hue to (1) get to the unit of surrounded marines, and (2) to retake the citadel! Ultimately, three Marine battalions came in, plus the ARVN forces who were assigned to retake the Citadel. The specter of mass slaughter (if the US were to pull out quickly across Vietnam) kept us in the war a lot longer.

the Allied cause. The US media and the American public paid little attention to the propensity of the VC to murder civilians during the war, in contrast to the furor and condemnation raised over isolated incidents of American forces having purposely killed innocent civilians. Indeed, the Viet Cong's retaliations against locals presumed to have supported the wrong side have never received anywhere near the attention as the reports of alleged or confirmed acts by American personnel in Vietnam.

Andy also notes that the Tet Offensive of 1968 was coordinated to use the New Year's celebration period as a cover. Hanoi had used this same trick 200 years ago against the invading and occupying Chinese forces in Hanoi. It had been "understood" that both sides would honor a cease fire during the time of Tet celebrations each year (think of a wild combination of July 4 and New Year's Eve that goes on for several days throughout the entire country).

And so, while the ARVN forces and civilians were celebrating the week of Tet, feasting and setting off massive fireworks, the NVA and VC added the firepower of their Tet offensive; the huge noise and flashes of NVA incoming fire were disguised long enough to give the NVA a critical tactical advantage.

One Vietnamese told us about his uncle, who had been a high ranking ARVN officer and chaplain in Hue. He was caught up in the Tet offensive. He went to a nearby hamlet that was friendly to the Saigon-based regime. Some villagers from a religious sect disguised him as a "seriously wounded" person, all bandaged up from the head down, for three weeks, limited to drinking soup through a straw.

Because of the Tet offensive of 1968, all Tet celebrations were prohibited until 1972. In 1972 there was an "Easter Tide offensive" by the NVA that also required massive evacuations of Hue. Truce or cease-fire agreements were only seen and used by Hanoi as tactics to reach their goal (of eventual reunification of all of Vietnam); they would honor or violate any agreements in order to accomplish their ultimate goal of total independence — anything goes, at any price. No concern about body count, weapon count, uniforms, etc.: only reunification. Of course, the US has a well-earned reputation for breaking treaties and pulling out of international agreements to this day.

One Vietnamese quotes Ho Chi Minh as saying "We can fight this generation, the next generation, and the next: let the French, or the Americans, bomb all of Hanoi, all of Haiphong, We don't care. Battle figures and percentages mean nothing, only that we will fight until we are independent." This was in contrast to the Saigon forces, where a Vietnamese says that the ARVN government "had no goal, just to finish the game and not score — and make money."

Vietnamese "Rubber-Time"

I am somewhat obsessive about starting things on time, and this turned out to be a difficult task with 25 people each marching to her or his own drummer. And so I found myself getting antsy many times as group members would stroll in 10 or 15 minutes past the starting times for USM presentations or tours. A local man in central Vietnam briefed me on the local concept of time: "Vietnam-time is elastic, but never early. So, when you give the time for something, you need to know if that is 'rubber time' or the 'exact' time."

Combat Exposure Levels

Bao Ninh, author of the *Sorrow of War*, was in the war for a remarkably long 11 years. The average US soldier's tour was 12 or 13 months. Of course there were a number of American soldiers who served two or three tours — and Americans who served multiple tours were significantly more likely to develop PTSD than veterans who served one tour.

This reminds me of the early Combat Exposure Scale that was developed in 1984 to provide a quick-screening for possible PTSD.[144] This scale measured how much combat a Vietnam veteran had been exposed to; and the higher the level of exposure, the greater the likelihood of such exposure being associated with developing PTSD. If the veteran endorsed the most severe item (having served three or more tours in Vietnam), that response was associated with a 100% chance of a positive diagnosis of PTSD. And even taking cultural differences into account, or the fact that the Vietnamese were fighting in their own country, Bao Ninh and many other NVA and VC soldiers (not to mention South Vietnam forces!) fought for as many as eleven continuous years!

As I am grappling with that idea, I realize that unlike US forces, the NVA and VC had no respite, no rotation back to a safe home and country after serving a year or so tour of duty. Also, they had far less in the way of organized Rest and Recreation breaks in or outside of Vietnam.

This thought takes me back to the airfield in Nha Trang in 1968, waiting in a line outside next to the airstrip, to board a C-130 to go on R and R, when the airfield starts receiving incoming fire. The absolute absurdity of this experience, in a war zone, has remained with me.[145]

Then I recall my ROTC class at Dickinson College in Carlisle, Pennsylvania, in spring 1965. Our instructor says, "Look around the room; within one year, well over half of you will be in Southeast Asia." Gulp.

My second-year field placement as part of my MSW studies at the University of Southern California was at the Sepulveda VA Medical Center, where I am assigned to be the caseworker for a severely disturbed young Marine veteran who is consumed with the obsession that he must "return to Vietnam to prove that he is a

---

144. Lund, M., D. Foy, C. Sipprelle and A. Strachan, "The Combat Exposure Scale: A systematic assessment of trauma in the Vietnam War," *Journal of Clinical Psychology*, 40 (6) (November, 1984), 1323-1328. The CES consists of seven items, ranging from "stationed in Vietnam" (the lowest exposure) to "served third tour of duty in Vietnam" (the highest). Individuals are assigned a combat exposure scale rating based on their highest scale score, following what is known as a Guttman scalogram procedure. This psychometrically validated scale shows a very high percentage of PTSD positive diagnoses for the three highest score items: *Wounded in combat* = 63% PTSD positive diagnosis, *Responsible for death of enemy civilian* = 77% and *Served third tour in Vietnam* = a 100% PTSD positive diagnosis. While obviously not as sophisticated as other scales, it works well as a rough clinical assessment screening tool. As the authors state: "The use of a Guttman scale (assigning the highest possible score) to assess perceived trauma is designed to reduce the effect of post hoc reporting bias to which additive rating scales are susceptible."

145. Scurfield (2004), *A Vietnam Trirlogy.*

man" — that he was not someone who had "deserted his buddies" by suffering a psychiatric break-down in the midst of battle and subsequently being medically evacuated out of country (see *A Vietnam Trilogy*).[146]

Even that experience was scant preparation for what I would soon be facing in Vietnam. I had all of three days of weapons' familiarization on a rifle range — during a snow storm. And I never received ANY orientation or training in war zone psychiatry.

Charles' description of his tour, in which he strictly went out on search and destroy missions, was basically the opposite of my tour. Their objective was to go out into the countryside, to seek and find the enemy and initiate combat: to engage with and destroy them. The mission of the psychiatric team was to deal with what the war brought in to us: partly through rocket attacks, but mostly through the hearts and minds and souls of the American psychiatric casualties who were evacuated medically to us from throughout I and II Corps.[147]

Sometimes, as we travel about, the sound of the sam-pan boat motors reverberating off the water remind me of the sound of a Huey helicopter during the war. Whomp, whomp, whomp: but they're motors on sampans, in the year 2000, propelling peasants through their days of labor on the rivers of Vietnam; and there is no threat of being shot at. There is a proliferation of motor-propelled sam-pans now.

ARVN Cemeteries

The next time the Hanoi government asks a Vietnamese tourist guide why any Americans visiting Vietnam want to visit a former ARVN cemetery, I wish the guide would say, "Because, as the Americans told me, the ARVNs were their comrades in war." But the government knows that. Indeed, if the ARVN are seen as traitors, why am I so surprised and angry and sad that they are not honored? Still, Americans arranging a tour to Vietnam owe something to them. Groups can at least apply for permission to visit one former ARVN cemetery (or, don't get permission, just go on your own). Vietnam-Indochina Tours is to be commended for their successful efforts to arrange such permission for our group.

DAY 12. MAY 27. HIGHWAY 1 THROUGH HAI VAN PASS TO DANANG AND SOUTH TO HOI AN CITY FOR AN "R AND R"

Morning departure to Danang via bus, stopping at the Hai Van Pass and at Lang Company Beach (small stone and marble factory) en route.

Danang Military Museum and the Cham Museum. (Note: The Cham Museum, founded in 1915, contains the best collections of sandstone sculptures of the vanquished Indianized Kingdom of Champa, circa 4th-century AD through 15th century AD.)

---

146. Ibid.
147. The operations and experiences of our psychiatric team are described in detail from a first-person perspective and from the accounts of numerous psychiatric casualties in *A Vietnam Trilogy*.

Continue on to Hoi An. Check in at Hotel. Hoi An is an ancient city which was visited by Marco Polo on his journey to China in the 14th century.

Afternoon USM program.

Former ARVNs As Cyclo Versus Taxi Drivers

During breakfast in Hue. I get involved in a conversation:

Ray: "I notice that so many former ARVN soldiers are cyclo drivers (e.g., pedal-driven carts that had relatively low-paying fares) rather than taxi drivers. Is it because they are not allowed to be taxi drivers, where they would have much higher-paying customers, due to their being former ARVNs?"

Vietnamese: "No, they could be taxi drivers. But, most taxi drivers must work for the government and under the government's control. Many former ARVNs prefer to be cyclo drivers..."

Ray: "Wow, if that's so, that is a commendable willingness to stick to one's principles and have a markedly lower paycheck. Would I be willing to do the same?"

From Hue to Hoi An. Phu Bai Base: "The Helicopters were like Dragon Flies"

As we ride along Highway 1 toward the Hai Van Pass and Danang, the remnants of Phu Bai Base are pointed out to us (without a guide, it is almost certain that no one would have known it was there). The bunkers are still there (concrete bunkers seem to be just about the longest-lasting reminders of the war), and it now is a military training base for young military recruits. A Vietnamese man tells our group: "During the war, US helicopters were like dragon flies, there were so many of them."

Highway 1 to DaNang

"The Street Without Joy": Highway 1 through the Hai Van Pass ("Sea and Cloud" in Vietnamese) was a critical military supply and transportation link during the war between Danang and Hue. Consequently, it was severely defoliated with Agent Orange, as it was an extremely dangerous route that the enemy was determined to disrupt. It was equally critical during the French occupation, and the French author of *Street Without Joy* was killed in Vietnam in 1967.

This is a beautiful route, with panoramic vistas and growing pine and eucalyptus trees that are part of the extensive re-forestation efforts along the route to prevent erosion. Ascending the highway to the top of Hai Van Pass, we come to a large lake. The highway is under construction, repairing serious damage from the last rainy season. The road is a modestly wide two lanes, with many steep and abrupt switchbacks; folks who are queasy about heights do indeed lose their composure. We stop for a last panoramic view to the west, back towards Hue. Then, we continue to the top.

Kudos to the Navy Seabees

My wife Margaret has worked since 1997 at the Gulfport, Mississippi, Construction Battalion Base of the Seabees (with the exception of a two-year stint at the Pascagoula Navy Base). I am reminded of this when our guide acknowledges that the Seabees expanded and built the road and bridges through the Hai Van Pass from Hue to Danang during the war. The Seabee slogan is "We build, we fight."

The Hai Van Pass

As we are driving up to the Hai Van Pass, I think back to 1989. At that time the re-forestation efforts had produced short patches of vegetation. Now, the hills seem to be totally re-grown.

At the Hai Van Pass, we stop to look once again at bunkers, and the sweeping vista down to the Eastern Sea (Pacific Ocean), the shoreline and Danang. As we get out of the bus we are flooded by Vietnamese vendors selling postcards and sundry items. These vendors are extremely persistent, hanging onto their respective targeted tourists as we climb up the steps to the old structure at the top of the pass.

Several of us retreat back to the solitude of the bus. Even there, the vendors continue haranguing us through the windows. They keep it up, walking alongside our bus, still trying to sell us something as our bus pulls away.

Now, I feel relief and I am able to feel some sadness for the vendors. They obviously need the money very badly, and they are trying to sell, not beg.

In 1989, I don't remember there were any vendors on the Hai Van Pass. A dubious sign of progress.

Among the pine trees, next to the beach, as we are driving through Danang south to Hoi An City, our guide points out what used to be the US Marine base at Red Beach #2.

Cham Temple, Danang and Its Connection with "My" Vietnam, 1968

Our visit to the Cham Museum in Danang is somewhat melancholy. Mr. Cong explains that the French had collected artifacts of the Cham culture in Vietnam and put them on display at this museum. Even though the Champa Kingdom existed from the 4th to the 17th centuries in Vietnam, there is not much evidence of that culture or peoples as an identifiable group in Vietnam today and most Vietnamese are not familiar with the history of the Champa culture. Few visit this museum. (Courtney Frobenius told me that there still are a number of Chams living in Central Vietnam today, in Chou Doc in the Mekong Delta, in a Cham Village —Phu Hiep — as well as a number who have moved to Saigon; and some 200,000 live just north of Phom Penh.)

When we arrive at the museum, Mr. Cong starts giving us a tour. In no time, most of the group have gone ahead and walked through the museum and straight to the gift shop in back — or outside. Just a few group members, older people, remain to hear Mr. Cong's presentation about the Champa culture. Mr. Cong notices this, and mildly observes: "It seems that the younger members were able to see and hear, in a few minutes, all that they wanted to — about eleven centuries of Cham history."

Mr. Cong remembered that I had been stationed in Nha Trang (a few hundred miles south from Danang along the coast). I had mentioned to him that I had conducted MEDCAPs to nearby Xom Bong (a small fishing village). So, in the Chan Museum in Danang Mr. Cong shares with me some information about the Cham culture and Xom Bong.

A hamlet is smaller than a village; and Xom Bong hamlet is famous for its beautiful girls, and their training to participate in religious ceremonies and dancing in temples (wish I had known that when I was stationed in Nha Trang!) There is a famous Cham Temple, Po Nag Ar, near Xom Bong Hamlet. And Mr. Cong recognizes my description of circular boats that I saw on the beach at Xom Bong Hamlet: "those are basket boats."

When I was in Nha Trang, I used to take my guitar and sing in the officer's club. However, soon after leaving active duty in 1971, I basically stopped playing the guitar or piano or singing. This was a surprise, especially in that prior to going to Vietnam I had been extremely preoccupied that I might lose a hand or the use of a hand and be unable to play again.[148]

Ray: "Could you say a little about the impact that the French have had on your country, in comparison with the impact of the US?"

Vietnamese: "The older Vietnamese generation is much more negative about the French than later generations. Vietnam was influenced for two to three generations by the French occupation of Vietnam. French schools left a very deep impact."

Ray: "In what ways specifically?"

Vietnamese: "The French impact is still apparent through such tangible components of Vietnamese culture as espresso coffee, French-derived baguettes, theater, sports, priests and the Catholic religion, bridges, architecture and the professions."

Ray: "And the American impact?"

Vietnamese: "The Americans were here considerably shorter [12-15 years]; their influence was not so deep, and you came after the French. Also, Americans 'only came to fight' — so there was more of an influence on the military than on Vietnamese culture and social life. There is a Vietnam-American Association, USIS, but USIS just brings over books that will influence a narrow group of students."

American hot dogs and hamburgers — long gone. Coca Cola has arrived more recently.

I might note that a contrary opinion exists: that Americans brought something that may be less tangible but perhaps much longer-lasting and more deeply rooted: the idea of "freedom." If so, how profound is this legacy today in Vietnam and how is it specifically manifested? To know of the imprint of freedom in the hearts and minds of the Vietnamese people would certainly offer some solace, indicating that the American presence was not insignificant beyond the military impact.

Why was the American impact so little? Well, the US was "only" here for 11 years. [To Americans, that was an extremely long 11 years; and, to be technically correct, there was a small American presence in Vietnam dating back to 1955 and the country was certainly not totally at peace even then.]

History Student Visits the Site Where Her Uncle was Killed

Some of the students, along with veteran Roy Ainsworth, accompanied student Marie (Cheri) Bolton on an important side-trip. Cheri's uncle, Billy Bolton, was

---

148. See Scurfield (2004), *A Vietnam Trilogy.*

killed in Vietnam in 1968, and the family knew the general area where it happened. Cheri had made plans to visit the area. Veteran Roy Ainsworth went along for support and to "represent" Cheri's father, who had wanted to be there with her.

Her fellow students videotaped Cheri as she and Roy stood at the edge of a vast landscape of green, sprinkled with purple violets, that stretched about as far as the eye could see. Cheri then spoke for her grandmother, who still grieves for the loss of her son:

"This [card] is for Uncle Billie. It's from his mother and his family, many of whom he never met. Romans 1:16 says, 'I am not ashamed of the gospel because it is the power of God.' Lots of love, your niece, Cheri, who never met you."

Cheri then shows a quarter that she is holding in her hand. "And I'm leaving a quarter here, primarily because it is a symbol of America and that's what he died for; he died for his country. And 'in God we trust,' on the quarter — that is the foundation that our family is built on, God. And a quarter, you think of a quarter, you can always call home. And it's just a simple symbol, you're always a phone call away . . ."

And Cheri bends over slightly and gently tosses the quarter into the sea of violets growing where her Uncle Billy died over 30 years ago. Roy Ainsworth and she embrace for a moment. Cheri then says to Roy, "I was here to see this for my Daddy, I wish he could have been here, but you're (Roy) here to see it for him. Thank you." And she smiles, her eyes brimming with tears.

Later, when talking about her experience, Cheri said: "It made him so human-like to me. Before, he was just been an uncle who had died. But, especially after the experience of going to the battlefields with all of these other veterans, it made him more real to me, it made it more dramatic. It gave him face rather than just a name. Rather than just Uncle Billie, he was a man, he was someone with dreams and aspirations, and he lost all that . . ."

Attitudes and Cultural Differences

Foreign Language Training: I hear that all Vietnamese students study a foreign language, about 90% English and 5% French. If 90% study English, does that mean that the US influence was greater than suggested? Or is it a statistic that would be matched in almost any country, war or no war, simply because English has overtaken French as the global language and many people with ambition are studying English? I don't know. Students have four foreign language classes a week, 45 minutes each, out of four classes a day, six days a week (or a total of 24 classes); foreign language classes are taken in Junior High (grades 6 through 9) and Senior High School (grades 10 through 12).

The French are not giving in easily, however. As in many countries, they offer a generous scholarship program for indigenous teachers to go to France to study, give free French classes and host cultural programs in Vietnam.

The Communist Party in Vietnam

There are about two million Communist Party members in Vietnam out of a population of 76 million (only about 2.5%). Obviously, here, "party membership" means far more than "which group would you vote for." The Communist Party line, that is, the view that is politically correct, is mentioned humorously — and only in private conversation, of course: "You must be red throughout — from one side to the other."

Mao Tse Tung and Ho Chi Minh are quoted to illustrate the changing attitude among members of the Communist party: Mao Tse Tung: "Better Red than expert" (professions) — this was the emphasis right after the war. Ho Chi Minh: "Better to be both Red and expert" (although still "red" first). This is the emphasis now.

Apparently in 1986 the Hanoi government initiated a policy of reforms that allowed increased cultural and other freedoms. One Vietnamese told me that:

"Fifteen or twenty years ago, we didn't dare to say more to you than 'hello.' Someone would be watching you all time [in case you were a spy].

"Five to ten years ago, I could talk to you, feed you rice, but seldom take you to my house.

"Now, you could come to my house, eat a good meal with my family and stay overnight, and it would be OK."

To an American, this of course is appalling. On the other hand, it's been 200 years since America had to fend off French- or English-speaking foreign agents and military personnel, much less actual combat being waged on our soil by foreign military personnel.

Dogs

There are a lot of dogs in Vietnam, but I never saw anyone touching or petting them. They use dogs as guards only, not as pets. The concept of pets is a luxury that most people in the world cannot afford. In Vietnam, dogs are viewed as animals, and it strikes people as bizarre that Americans often treat them like members of the family.

Ray: "What do you name your dogs? Often, we use person's names."

Vietnamese: "We would only name a dog after a person if we were very angry at someone and want to really insult them. We use sounds to refer to or call our dogs, such as Loulou.'"

Ray: "What do you feed your dogs?"

Vietnamese: "Leftovers. We make sure that there are some leftovers for our dogs, and our neighbors will give us leftovers for our dog if they don't have a dog.

"We don't talk about dogs, nor do we send pictures of our dogs to friends....You have a very peculiar custom of taking pictures of your dogs. To our friends we will send pictures of our family, not of our dogs — that is considered inappropriate! Once an American friend sent me a holiday card, and she enclosed a picture of her dog: not of her, but of her dog! I showed it to my wife. She looked at it in disgust and said, 'Why did she send us a picture of her dog?!' I said, 'Well, that is what they do in America.' She said, 'Ugh,' and threw it away."

Ray: "I hope that this is not impolite to ask, but do Vietnamese eat dogs?"

Vietnamese: "In Vietnam, we eat anything with four legs — except for tables. But dogs are eaten only in the North."[149]

---

149. Of course, the man saying this was not from the north. There still seems to be some sense of cultural superiority!

My Continuing Role as a Care-Giver for Psychiatric Casualties of the Vietnam War

I guess I've remained a medic/corpsman all these years for those veterans wounded in spirit and in mind...And I have decided that today, three days before we leave Vietnam, that for the first time on this trip I am going to give myself permission to do this day for me; I am going to try to not even be attentive in any way to the needs of anyone else....

To even imagine doing this, to put me first for at least a day, was, like my taking an early retirement from the VA in 1998, a symbolic further step in my own healing and my willingness to let go more of the role of continuing to be a care-giver for the psychologically and socially wounded of Vietnam. Since that retirement I had felt a distinct gap inside of me, an emptiness, an aching for the daily contact with the vets that kept me engaged in my work with the VA. Indeed, I didn't realize it fully at the time, but I went through a grieving period over this loss of intimacy with so many war veterans. And the loss of everything that went with the role of being a vet care-giver: the joy, the stimulation, the satisfaction, and the weight — the wave after wave of vets struggling with their journeys of pathos and healing.

And yet, I know that I have more writing and soul-searching to do as part of my personal expression and healing path. And, I wonder whether giving some attention to Vietnamese immigrants on the Mississippi Gulf Coast and to Father Truong will be another fork in the road that I may choose to go along — or not.

Flashback to 1968-1969

Wait a minute. I'm not about to make a commitment, while I am here in Vietnam, about something I am going to do when I get back home. Many vets including me made commitments to our buddies and to ourselves before we left the Nam during the war, commitments that we usually did not keep. And then, when we failed to stay in touch, or greet our buddy's family, the guilt only added to our problems.

Hoi An City and A Much-Needed "R and R"

We arrive in Hoi An City in the afternoon. This turns out to be a poor time to try to hold a USM seminar, so the rest of today and tomorrow become "free" days for exploring. Roy's visit to the DMZ two days earlier completed one of our objectives, and no more battlefield sites are on our agenda. Thus a two-day stay in Hoi An with very little in the way of scheduled activities becomes a "winding down" phase of the trip. It was intentionally scheduled to offer an "R and R" time for everyone, a transition from the very busy and very emotional sojourn that we have been on these past twelve days.

Members of the group scatter to explore this bustling commercial center of arts and clothing and markets, a picturesque, hospitable, relatively laid-back yet bustling and easy-to-get-around town, as well as relaxing in the beautiful old-world atmosphere of the hotel. Everywhere I go, in a restaurant, tailor shop, or crafts boutique, it seems I run into someone from the group. They all seem to be enjoying themselves, poring through clothing magazines to find an example of exactly the design for a particular piece of clothing to be ordered, studying the menu, sizing up the gifts to buy. With most shopping in Vietnam, it is not simply going in, seeing something you want and buying it. The pleasure comes from the full cultural experience that includes exploring the various shops, having initial interactions with the vendors, looking at the wares and engaging in a little bargaining.

I spend the remaining time today and on Sunday exploring Hoi An, casually shopping and relaxing. I walk around by myself, at least some of the time, just to unwind and immerse myself in the city and the culture: something I had not permitted myself to do in 1989. However, I am actually not comfortable being myself and surrounded by people I don't know, especially since I am an obvious outsider. Interestingly enough, I am very comfortable to go almost anywhere if I am with one other person.

It is almost unheard of for me to drop all the "busy-ness" I habitually use to numb myself, for instance when I throw myself into the role of care-giver or provider. Today, I make almost no notes in my journal, a sure sign that I am actually relaxing a little. As I become more immersed in the vibrancy of the streets and canals, I see signs that remind me of "the "old" Vietnam city of Nha Trang — bicycles, cyclos, small boats, walking and motor-bikes — a pleasant contrast to the congestion of Saigon. And, we have an enjoyable evening at the outdoor swimming pool at the hotel. It doesn't get much better than this.

DAY 13. 28 MAY. CATHOLIC MASS IN HOI AN CITY

I must be getting more religious, like I used to be in my late teens, as the years go by. I don't remember going to any mass on our 1989 trip, or even checking to see if any were being held nearby. And here, in 2000, I am going to church for the second time on this trip. The Catholic Church in Hoi An was about a 15-minute walk from the hotel. Two students and I go to the church about 3:00 PM, and sit in the middle of the right side. Lucky thing: it turns out females sit on the left side and males on the right side of the church. We three are the only people in the church who are noticeably not Vietnamese.

I have taken care to sit close to one of the fans mounted on the side columns, which merely waft weakly over my perspiration every few seconds. It was so hot that I came in wearing shorts and of course a short-sleeved shirt; I quickly become aware that none of the Vietnamese are in shorts; outside of the US it is considered quite bizarre for an adult male to wear shorts. Here, almost all of the males have on long pants and long-sleeved shirts. I also became acutely aware that I have never had to kneel on wooden kneelers that have no padding. That adds a touch of real penance. The service itself is pleasant, with beautiful singing by a small choir of females. I count my blessings, and thank God for what I have. And I pray for the Vietnamese people, a people and a country who have had to endure, and for so long.

DAY 14. MAY 29. LAST MEETING IN VIETNAM

Morning program.

Ray: Presentation on active duty tour in Vietnam (finally!), and the readjustment problems of Vietnam vets following the war.

Paul Harris: The history of Vietnam, 1946-1975, "from the Vietnamese perspective."

Andy Wiest: "Legacies of the Vietnam War," and closing.

163

I have already described in Volume I my work in Vietnam as an Army Social Work Officer; and the readjustment problems of veterans are discussed in this book as well. What remains to be told is how overwrought with emotion I became in the course of making this presentation.

This is the first time ever, during any of my three times in Vietnam, that I have actually shared my Vietnam experience in any detail, and even now I had had to press to get some time "to tell my Vietnam story." It had become increasingly clear that I, as well as everyone else, had been ignoring my status as a Vietnam vet. I felt that deprived the group of what I hoped was important educational input as well as depriving me of an important healing opportunity.

Of course, this has been at least partly of my own doing. I had not advocated to include Nha Trang, where I had served, in the itinerary. Also, my role was described, from the outset, as being one of the three professors of the course, which meant helping to oversee the day-to-day program, making several presentations, and being a mental health resource to participants if needed.

The Department of Veterans Affairs had instructed Leslie Root that she could not have any "therapist" role with the three vets on the trip; their objection was that it would cause a "dual role" that was considered problematic to her VA job as Director of a PTSD Clinical Team and ongoing VA clinician to two of the participating veterans. Therefore, it was agreed that I would be the mental health resource for the three veterans, and Leslie primarily and I secondarily would be the mental health resource persons for the students on the trip. Here I was, once again, a designated care-giver for US servicemen in Vietnam. Thus, I in effect had willingly agreed that any "personal" agenda on my part would be distinctly secondary: and so they were, at least consciously.

Thus it was a surprise to me that I increasingly found myself willing and quite determined, albeit or perhaps because it is so late in the trip, to provide the group with some details about my tour and the military mental health role. This would also offer the students the perspective of a fourth Vietnam veteran who differs considerably from John, Charles and Roy in a number of ways. For one thing, I served as an officer, not in a direct combat role, and in a quite different part of Vietnam.

I feel just a little guilty about taking the group's time on the last morning of any scheduled activities in Vietnam. However, there just had not seemed to be an opportune time earlier on the trip, especially as I did not want to detract from the focus on the three veterans who were getting their first opportunity to return to their former battlefields.

I am quite emotional as I give my presentation, although I don't know if that comes across to the group. In fact, I am not sure if anyone really remembers much that I say. After all, people naturally seemed preoccupied and restless, as we were in our last day in Hoi An prior to flying back to Saigon to leave for the US. There were very few questions during my presentation and no one asked me anything about my status as a veteran.

Dr. Paul Harris, a visiting professor at USM from a military academy in Great Britain, gave a presentation on the Vietnamese perspective. One of his key points was that most of what we hear is from the American (that is, "imperialist," or, as we like to say, "global citizen") perspective, with some snippets of Communist views to provide contrast. But there are many different perspectives within Vietnam, and in Europe, too, each of which may have some validity.

Paul raised a number of controversial topics and perceptions, i.e.: that the victory against the French at Dien Bien Phu in 1954 did more harm than good to the Vietnamese because of the tremendous loss of men; that Ho Chi Minh was much more concerned about fending off occupation by China than by the French; that many Vietnamese fought with the French and were very much in opposition to the leadership of Ho Chi Minh; that the Hanoi-based Communist regime, dating back to 1946 and continuing through the American War, always had as its objective the unification of all of Vietnam; that the Communist forces utilized terror as a major tactic since at least 1959, and had absolutely no compunctions about breaking their word agreed to in treaties in that they justified any strategy if it would lead to their ultimate goal of reunification of the north with the south. Much of this was news to our group, as Paul asserted that the focus in the US had been designed to support the notion that we "needed" to intervene.

Perhaps Paul's most contentious assertion was that, because of the Tet offensive, LBJ lost his will to continue the war after the first few months of 1968. Paul added that it is generally not recognized by the West that many South Vietnamese had lost faith in the Viet Cong by then and there were massive desertions from the VC forces to the (US-backed) Saigon-based government forces, followed by counterinsurgency at the village levels. During the Tet offensive the VC had been decimated as an effective fighting force, and in reality "the Communists were in real trouble in most of South Vietnam."

Paul concluded by stating that the US strategy of "Vietnamization" of the war effort (by gradually reducing the American forces and increasing the role of the Saigon-based military) made considerable progress by early 1971-72. But then the Americans dropped out of Vietnam, as they had lost their will to continue. And this rendered all of the suffering pointless! One Vietnamese asked us: "Did millions more people die because the Americans came — and then left us behind?" And while there are no solid statistics, there are estimates that about 60,000 South Vietnamese were killed by Communist forces *after* 1975 —

this is almost identical to the number of Americans KIA during the entire 11-year Vietnam War.

Thought-provoking as it was, it was easy to see Paul's talk as an indictment of the US government (and, obliquely, the Vietnam veterans). Had we "deserted our Vietnamese allies"? This was terribly upsetting to hear, at the end of the trip, even if there might be a considerable degree of truth in it. Is that not a point that perhaps some of us continue to deny — to help make our sacrifices and cost somehow more palatable?

In retrospect, Paul had wanted to give this talk early in our trip, and we, not realizing that he was gong to make such provocative statements, blew it by scheduling him at the end of the trip when there was little chance to discuss it afterwards. We also did not think through the need to offer the three combat veterans a chance to respond with their perceptions about what had just been presented. After Paul's talk, I went to Andy to mention this, as Andy was giving what would be the final presentation of the trip. Andy agreed and added that it would also be good to give both Mr. Cong and Ms. Trang the opportunity to address the group. Unfortunately, things did not go that way, and regrettably we did not provide many people with "closure."

Dr. Wiest gave the closing presentation: a brief overview of the fall-out of the Vietnam War on war veterans, and on Vietnam. Of course, the most telling statistic is that the National Vietnam Veterans Readjustment Study revealed that as of the late 1980s, 15.2% of the 3.14 million male and female veterans who served in the Vietnam theater of war, e.g., 477,281 Vietnam veterans, were estimated to have the full inclusionary symptoms for a diagnosis of PTSD, and another 11.1%, e.g., 348,540, had partial symptoms to meet a diagnosis of PTSD. And this was some 15 years after most US forces had been pulled out of Vietnam.[150]

Andy Wiest also noted that there were 303,704 wounded, and 75,000 seriously physically disabled. This latter number, ironically, is testimony to the marked advances in acute battlefield medical treatment and helicopter evacuation capabilities that were developed and implemented during the Vietnam War. This dramatically enhanced medical intervention capabilities and facilitated timely emergency medical treatment that saved the lives of countless soldiers who would not have survived such wounds in an earlier war. [151]

It is estimated that over 3 million (some estimates range as low as 2.4 million) Vietnamese died during the war, and there are over 1 million missing. This is in addition to the estimated 1.5 million (some estimates range as high as 2.0 million) who fled Vietnam to resettle elsewhere (although many died in the attempt) and the countless Vietnamese families torn apart by dead, missing or immigrant members.

At the end of Andy's presentation, I had assumed that we would go around the room and have each group member briefly say whatever he or she wanted to share, mirroring the "get-acquainted" sharing in our first meetings. But we, the leaders of the group, did not explicitly discuss this.

Veteran John Young is called up next. He gives an emotional overview of his 20+ post-war years since returning from the Vietnam War, through 1993, when "he finally was able to admit to himself that he needed help" and went to the PTSD Clinical Team at the Gulfport VA; this was the beginning of his PTSD treatment. Then, John reads a letter to the group that he had composed before this meeting. He thanks the group for having him speak in Andy's Vietnam History classes at Hattiesburg and for their attention during the trip. Tears come to everyone's eyes. Many group members are full of emotion and eager to speak, this being our last meeting together.

---

150. Kulka, R.A., W.E. Schlenger, J.A. Fairbank, R.L. Hough, B.K. Jordan, C.R. Marmar and D.S. Weiss, *Trauma and the Vietnam War Generation: Report of Findings from the National Vietnam Veterans Readjustment Study* (New York: Brunner/Mazel, 1990). For readers who may be interested in a behind-the-scenes description of the political forces in Washington, DC involving the VA and Congress, see Volume I of this *Vietnam Trilogy*.

151. The same trend is seen in the Iraq War today. Advances in battlefield medical interventions are such that a significant number of wounded military personnel who would have died in prior wars (including Vietnam) are being saved, in spite of catastrophic physical injuries and subsequent physical disabilities. Will the United States, the government, and the communities continue to provide support over the ensuing decades as these disabled men and women cope with life-long medical disabilities caused by war?

Andy then closes the meeting. Everyone seems stunned, or totally caught up in their emotions and thoughts. I was looking forward to this closing process, and from a "mental wellbeing" standpoint it was appropriate if not necessary for each of us to have a chance honor each other and say our good-byes. Not even Charles Brown or Roy Ainsworth is given a opportunity to make a closing statement to the group. And several of us will never see each other again — especially Mr. Cong and Ms. Trang.

People start to drift out of the room, some in tears.

I later see Ms. Trang in the hotel computer room, carefully composing a closing letter to everyone. She then had to go all across Hoi An trying to find a place to get it reproduced. Later that evening, she hand-delivered a copy to each of our rooms.

I feel so bad for Ms. Trang, I insist that she go out to lunch with me. It gives us both a chance to transition from the abrupt and emotionally wrenching end of the meeting. Also, this is a modest token of my appreciation for all of her efforts to make this trip such a success.

I also have an emotional goodbye with Mr. Cong. He graciously notes that it was "a most fulfilling experience" for him, too: that he had never traveled outside of Vietnam, and each of us was "like an open window to the world" for him.

Mr. Cong, throughout our tour, has been a gentleman, sensitive and articulate, and he knows the history of Vietnam. He also is a wonderful host, with that rare combination of being gracious, organized, very well informed — and quite humorous. He demonstrates a heart-felt pride about his country. He would be happy to have more "windows" abroad and I have included contact information for anyone who might wish to contact Mr. Cong.[152]

On the bus ride to Danang to catch our flight back to Saigon, I ask about Amer-Asian children left behind when the US troops pulled out after 1975, and various humanitarian projects. Mr. Cong mentions three programs that have been approved by the Communist government. First, there was the ACP: American Children Project that assisted 20,000 Amer-Asian children and 60,000 family members to relocate to the US, from 1990 to 1995. Second, there was the ODP, the Orderly Departure Program, for those wanting to join their family members who already were in the US. Then there is the HO, the Humanitarian Project: established for former ARVN officers, special sergeants who had been in intelligence, etc. and administrators who had been in relocation camps for three years or more.

I have been told that many older Vietnamese who have relocated to the US have a difficult transition and are not very happy. I mentioned this to Mr. Cong.

His eloquent response:

"There are two volumes in the lives of older Vietnamese who have relocated to the US — their lives in Vietnam, and then their lives in the US. The first volume in their lives is very thick. However, their second volume is very slim. In contrast, for young people who relocate to the US, the first volume of life is quite small, so the second volume can be very big."

---

152. Tran Quoc Cong, 292/5 Hai Phong, DaNang. Vietnam (tel. 84. 511. 823620) Email: cong292@yahoo.com

DAY 15. MAY 30. THE LAST DAY, AND WHAT THE VIETNAMESE DON'T SAY IN
PUBLIC

8:30 AM - 9:40 AM flight to Saigon.
Free day until departure at 10:30 PM to Saigon's Tan Son Nhat Airport.

We arrive back in Saigon around 10:00 AM. Since our plane to return to the US
doesn't leave until after midnight, we check back into our hotel until 10:00 PM.
Now, we have one last block of free time and the opportunity to rest, shop and
explore. I go to the hotel salon and get a haircut — one more experience on the
ground, here.

I find the floor where the barbers are located and let myself be talked into their $16
package special: a shampoo, haircut, full massage and tea; now that's a deal. Now I
am really pampering myself. And I recall other haircuts, steam baths and massages,
from the war time.

I allow myself to feel nostalgic with this reminder of some pleasant times during the
war.

All too soon, it's off to the airport.

"Private" Conversations with Various Vietnamese

It of course is quite speculative to draw any conclusions about anything about Vietnam after a whirlwind tour of just 17 days, even for someone who has been there
twice before. Still, one can safely say that the political climate in Vietnam is considerably less oppressive than it was in 1989. This is especially apparent in terms of
people being willing to talk frankly with Americans (at least in private) and share
their opinions. In 1989, people tended to be extremely careful about what they said,
even in private.

There were still some concerns, however.

Ray: "When I am writing my journal and book, and mention what you just told me,
would it be OK if I identified who you are? I would like to 'give you credit' for what
you have said. But, would that get you into any trouble?"

Vietnamese: "I am just explaining my thoughts about Vietnam to you, I am not complaining. Please don't use my name at all. I don't exist."

Ray: "Could you tell me what would happen if I used your name?"

Vietnamese: "Again, please don't use my name when I say my thoughts to you about
Vietnam or about the government. If you do, it is as if I am at home and I tell my son
that if anyone knocks at our door today, he should say 'my father is not home.' But
instead my son says, 'My father is sleeping and he told me to tell you that he is not
here.' Please, let me remain invisible."

There certainly appears to have been a gradual increase in tolerance of religion,
opening up the economy to foreign investors, an acceptance of outside influence on
music and the arts, and, perhaps most noticeably, a somewhat greater willingness

for certain Vietnamese to interact with Americans in fairly frank communications about "sensitive" subjects. However, this is still a country on the defensive and freedoms of speech and expression are nowhere near the level we in the West are used to. Thus, I have not even indicated the chronological order or the geographic location in which I met many of the Vietnamese whom I have quoted, in order to protect their anonymity.

Re-Education Camp

One Vietnamese told me about a former ARVN sergeant who was sent to a relocation camp for three years. After his release, the sergeant went back to his village. Sometime later, he had too much to drink and got into a "domestic disturbance" (fight) with his wife. The local village officials said that "this is like a slap in the face of the Communist regime" — and he was sent back to the re-education camp for another three years.

Big Brother at the Post-Office

One Vietnamese who has been corresponding with several Australians received several letters and packages from her foreign friends over the last few years. She told me the following.

If a package is mailed to me, I am called down to the post office. The package then is opened by a post office official. If it contains a book, the post office will keep the book for several days in order to review it. I will then be called to the post office and be given the book back — if the review doesn't reveal any inappropriate information in the book. But, the book will be confiscated if it is considered to contain inappropriate information. In that case, it is kept in a special restricted library; only certain government specialists have access to it. Also, I have to be careful. If too many books or printed materials are sent to anyone, that person seems to be "under a cloud of suspicion." The government may think that he or she is a scholar, or a spy. Why is this person getting all of these books? And, if you receive too much written material that contains inappropriate information, you will get in serious trouble. [The nature of the serious trouble was not specified.]

Recommended Reading

The following books were strongly recommended by Vietnamese; of course, these recommendations were provided only in private conversation.

1. Bao Ninh's *The Sorrow of War*: This is such a powerful and poignant book that I quoted from it extensively in the first volume of this Vietnam Trilogy.
2. Tran Tri Vu, *My Lost Years*. The author was eventually sponsored for emigration by a humanitarian organization. He writes about his 2,341 days spent in a re-education camp. It is forbidden to have this book in Vietnam.
3. Nayan Chanda, *Brother Enemy: The War After The War*, is about the years following the fall of Saigon in 1975, when Vietnam and Cambodia were at war.
4. Duong Van Mai Elliott, *The Sacred Willow: Four Generations in the Life of A Vietnamese*, offers a richly detailed history of Vietnam over the past 130 years through the eyes of a member of four generations of one upper-middle class Vietnamese family (originally from Hanoi).

DAY 16. MAY 31. A VERY SPECIAL "IN-FLIGHT WELCOME HOME"

Finally, we get on the airplane and take off from Vietnam. It has been quite a trip. I am surprised that I don't feel more exhausted than I do. However, I must be more exhausted than I realize, as I don't make any more journal entries during the 15 hours flying time. In fact, I haven't made a journal entry since leaving Hoi An the morning before. The plane ride back to Los Angeles doesn't seem nearly as long as it had been going to Vietnam. I have several light social conversations with other group members and then I depart from the group in Los Angeles, where I have family to visit.

This flight was very different from the coming-home flight in 1989. Then, I was under stress from the conflict between several veterans in the group, and between two veterans and me, and I had been shouldering what felt like an overwhelming burden by attempting to be a vigilant care-giver throughout that trip. Then there was the inevitable storm of emotions when I visited Nha Trang and Xom Bong Hamlet, where I had served in 1968-69, and the last-minute demand from the veterans that I abandon my plan to spend several days in Bangkok with my wife and instead return to the US with them.[153] And then came the *coup de grace*: while the whole group was tense and feeling a driving urge to get back to the US as soon as possible, our plane developed mechanical trouble after we left Thailand and were flying over Vietnam (oh no!). Several of us of course then had catastrophic thoughts of crashing and burning in Vietnam — in 1989. The flight was aborted and we had to return to Bangkok. I had to keep shutting out thoughts that was I fated to have this plane crash before it reached California.

Our 2000 return flight was sure better than all that! There was a much more relaxed and spirited mood amongst the group members, with the exception of Andy, who still had whatever bug he had caught earlier.

Flashback to Vietnam, 1969

Getting off the plane in Los Angeles, I am reminded that I had also deplaned in Los Angeles after the Vietnam War in 1969. My parents and sister had moved to Pasadena from Pittsburgh while I was in Vietnam. I have a vivid memory of stepping out of a taxi onto a very busy boulevard in Hollywood, in my uniform, some 48 hours removed from the Vietnam War zone, and being overwhelmed by the visual, auditory and olfactory stimuli. I am in total cultural and psychological shock; the experience is surreal, like stepping out and being plunged into a Hollywood movie.[154]

Because I left the group in Los Angeles, I missed what happened next as the group continued on the plane from Los Angeles back to Mississippi, and only found out about it in a discussion with Yaron Kaplan in May, 2001.

Yaron thought it would be a good idea to have a flight steward make an announcement about the three "very special guests" on this flight and asked her if she could do it. She asked the Captain and he told her No, he did not want her to do that. He wanted to make the announcement himself! And in a few minutes, the Captain comes on the sound system: "This is the Captain speaking. I wanted to bring to your attention that we have three very special guests on this flight, three Vietnam veter-

153. Scurfield (2004), *A Vietnam Trilogy*.
154. Ibid.

ans who are returning from their first return visit to Vietnam: John Young, Roy Ainsworth and Charles Brown. On behalf of the crew, I want to express our appreciation to you three veterans for your service to our country, and to personally welcome you home."

The plane erupts into sustained applause and cheers. Many of the passengers and students are crying, and in response to this totally unexpected recognition and long overdue welcome home, two of the three vets burst into sobs; and yes, even the third vet, usually quite stoic, lets the tears roll down his cheeks, savoring this touching tribute.

This is the emotional, expressive and spontaneous display of support, the rousing "welcome home" that most of the 3.14 million Vietnam veterans never did receive. It came in the year 2000. And even then, it made a difference.

Post-Script: Vietnam 2000

Vietnam vet: "You can't hold this stuff in forever, or it eats you up. It starts coming out, one way or another — for the worse — or for the better. It really is a law of physics, isn't it?"

Chapter 7. Reflections and Impact: Vietnam 2000

Reflecting on our 2000 study abroad course to Vietnam, my memories and emotions overall are quite positive, and not nearly as exhausting and provocative as when I came back to the US from our 1989 trip. The 2000 trip was remarkably benign and lacked any serious issues or controversy; it appears to me to have been a highly satisfactory experience for all participants.

Two sets of overlapping lessons came out of the trip, first, those related to the implementation of a program that combines military history and mental health faculty, curriculum and objectives, and second, those related to the many-faceted impact that this experience had on the students and the veterans. A short list of some of the highlights would include:

- It was an eye-opener to see how badly the losers in Vietnam's civil war were treated — something that we probably hadn't given much thought to. After all, "collaborating with the enemy" is usually grounds for being shot, anywhere, isn't it? Why did I think it would be different? But it tears my heart to know that those who fought valiantly on the side we believed was right and who our country then "abandoned" to a still-continuing fate of even more suffering.

- Also, while the history and mental health goals were mutually enriching, the combination created several competing tensions that need to be addressed.

- It is critically important to set rules of conduct for any group of students going abroad, and to establish guidelines that help course participants to be culturally sensitive when traveling in a different culture. There is no need to further promote the image of the "ugly American" abroad.

Treatment of Former ARVN Soldiers: An Invaluable History Lesson

I found it both remarkable and extremely disconcerting to observe the incredible disparity between how the Vietnamese government treats its dead who served on the side of the Communists versus the stance towards the dead who served the Saigon government. Of course, the former ARVNs had made their choice to support the Catholic-dominated Saigon-based government that involved a foreign army to help it oppose the Communist forces and indigenous Viet Cong forces. On the other hand, I could not help but feel renewed anguish over the part that our country had played in this. Perhaps there was considerable validity to the argument that if we had not entered the war on the side of the Saigon government in the first place, then the Communists would have been victorious many years earlier and the horrific numbers (an estimated 6 to 8 million (!) dead, injured and missing Vietnamese people on both sides of the war) would have been averted!

Furthermore, once we did become engaged in the war, there is a viewpoint that we did not have the political will-power to persevere and commit whatever military resources would have been required to help the Saigon-based government actually win the war. This, of course, was assuming that "victory" was even possible. (Yes, the parallels to issues about US involvement in Iraq[155] and Afghanistan and whether we "are willing to stay the course," not to mention the question whether we even should have been there in the first place, are reverberating loudly.)

Televised news scenes appeared as mental pictures in my head, showing the last American helicopters lifting off from the US Embassy in Saigon in 1975 as thousands of desperate Vietnamese who had allied with us were storming the embassy, trying to reach the last avenue of escape before the Communist forces defeated them completely. And only on these two return trips to Vietnam have I allowed my naivete to recede as I become more aware of the plight of former allies and their families who remained in Vietnam.

Perhaps the stance of the Communist government towards former ARVN cemeteries was a graphic and symbolic excruciating reminder to me that the suffering caused by war, no matter how noble the war might have seemed at the time, has long-standing consequences of a most profound nature.

---

155. The ramifications of such issues on the mental health and morale of deployed and returning Iraq veterans is discussed in detail in the third volume of this *Vietnam Trilogy*.

And then the final irony strikes home. It appears that many of the Vietnamese people, and the Communist government as well, are willing to "let bygones be by-gones" in regard to *Americans* but not to their own veterans of the losing side.

A Competing Tension between History and Mental Health Objectives

We worked hard to achieve a good balance between the competing priorities of those students and professors who were more interested in military history, strategy and tactics and battles, and those with more of a mental-health orientation, and I think we succeeded to a large degree. This entailed not only different bodies of factual information to learn but trying on a very different mindset (that is, a cognitive or intellectual focus versus an emotional awareness), which sometimes was clearly uncomfortable for both groups. That, of course, is part of what education should do.

Thinking from the vets' perspective, at the time I was concerned that this dual-focus diluted or softened the intensity of the trip, but I came to see that it actually offered an important advantage. It made things less intense and less overwhelming. The vets were almost certainly helped not to focus exclusively on war trauma.

Instead, the attention placed on military history and the history/culture of Vietnam gave them more neutral and positive information to add to their painful recollections. I am now convinced that the positive, supportive and encouraging attitude from the students is just what these three particular vets needed at this time in their stress recovery.

Perhaps they did miss out on a unique opportunity to process issues at a deeper level; but you can't have it both ways — and the trade-offs seem *very* worthwhile. In fact, I am reminded how "peaceful" and harmonious the relationships between and among the various participants were on this 2000 return in contrast to our 1989 return, which was practically "vets-only."

Tensions over Having to Participate In Mental Health Debriefings in Vietnam

Several of the history students complained about the debriefing sessions, although over two-thirds of the students stated that the debriefings were very important. Clearly, some people are more comfortable than others with "psychological" discussions. If that is to be part of a group's agenda, and everyone will be expected to participate, this has to be made clear from the outset, before people enroll.

And, some of the students stated that I was "too intense" at times. I imagine that they are correct!

The tension between the two types of goals was reflected in a low-key tension between the history and mental-health faculty, as well. However, this in no way approached the intensity and negativity that characterized various relationships following the 1989 return. It also should be noted that the two mental health professors continued to maintain a close and collaborative relationship after the trip, including collaborating on a study of the extent and impact of African-American Vietnam veterans' exposure to race-related events during the war, and, my relationship with history professor Andy Wiest has certainly remained cordial.

Cultural Sensitivity

Given the increasingly casual way that American culture relates to everything, many Americans, especially young people, do not have a clear idea what kind of conduct the rest of the world expects in public places, especially places of worship or places dedicated to the dead. I bit my tongue on several occasions because it is too late to launch into a lesson in etiquette when you are already at the gate to a temple. Emotions and egos stand in the way; this sort of thing needs to be considered carefully and as dispassionately as possible, at a neutral time. I was also unsure about imposing my degree of seriousness onto students who had paid for an experience. Perhaps they were cheated, though, of an opportunity for several adults to offer some thoughtful coaching at a critical period in their approach to adulthood? The leaders of a group need to think about this type of issue before and during any study abroad program, and the students need to be told upfront that they are expected to accept the leadership of their faculty members.

In retrospect, courtesy is among the topics we should have covered before leaving the US. We could have advised the students, Don't forget your manners. If you are careful how you speak to adults in your hometown, you should be all the more so when abroad. Especially in Asia, but in Europe and Africa too, informality is considered impolite, and could be construed as insulting. Don't expect the Vietnamese to tell you that your behavior is inappropriate; after all, they are very careful to be hospitable and gracious, and would be more afraid of offending you. In Asia, you can never be too polite, or too deferential, or too courteous; or anywhere else for that matter. This is especially true at temples. Even if the temple is an obvious tourist attraction, it still is a religious place

All in all, such concerns came up infrequently and I should emphasize that there was a beautiful inter-relationship between the American and Vietnamese people throughout the duration of the course.

Impact of the Study Abroad Experience

After my 1989 trip, I never looked back at my journal until eleven years later. I began transcribing my journal of our 2000 trip within three weeks of arriving back home. And I found myself so absorbed in it that I had completed my transcription in about a month!

In other words, I have been able to actually sit back and reflect rationally about the trip and the aftermath, in a somewhat detached yet positive manner, more like a satisfied observer than a deeply emotional participant. Is this a sign of some further healing on my part?

"Ray the Vietnam veteran" seems to have found a sense of more peaceful co-existence with my own Vietnam-related demons and legacy. And I notice that I did not say "resolution" but "enhanced sense of more peaceful coexistence." I do want "Ray the Professor" to get a few thoughts in first.

Some of the most profound influences emanated from four compelling features of this study-abroad course:

1. the unique mixture of students and veterans
2. our reception by the Vietnamese people
3. returning to former personal battle sites
4. meeting former enemy veterans.

My Own Reactions to Vietnam 2000

As I have mentioned, this second trip was far less upsetting for me than the first return trip. Perhaps this is a benefit that veterans gain by returning to Vietnam multiple times. Obviously, I still had strong emotional reactions several times that were associated with my war experiences; and these were things that appear not to have affected others in the group almost at all.

Two of the things that bothered me most were the disrespectful treatment of ARVN graves, and the apparent disrespect with which students addressed Mr. Cong. This reaction was infused with my feelings about the negative condition and absence of former ARVN cemeteries, and to my long-standing negative reaction dating back to the war about the inhumane way that many US military personnel treated the "South" Vietnamese during the war. Don't *all* of the Vietnamese people deserve to be treated with dignity and respect?

Also, as 1989, although to a lesser degree, I found myself having a negative reaction to the sight of damaged US war relics on display, especially Huey helicopters. From my experiences during the war, at the 8th Field Hospital in Nha Trang where med-evac choppers flew out and in on a daily basis, and our incredibly emotional and successful helicopter ride therapy project at the American Lake PTSD Program,[156] I had come to revere the Hueys as angels of mercy and sanctuary. To see them on display in such decrepit condition felt like an affront to me and to the American personnel who had fought so gallantly in Vietnam.

The Cu Chi tunnel orientation film, the woman official's talk at the village before our visit to John Young's former site, and everything else that hammered home who won, clearly rubbed me the wrong way, and that's a fact. I don't know what is "right" in this situation, but veterans who are considering making the trip need to be warned ahead of time what they might see, and how they might react.

The other outstanding part of this trip was the return of the three veterans to the locales of their former battle sites and duty stations. As in 1989, it was an incomparable opportunity for each vet to face decades-old memories and issues head-on.

I was intense and had intense reactions to all of the above, but I can safely state that overall, my emotional reactions on this trip were considerably milder in frequency and intensity than in 1989. Consequently I was able and willing to pay much more attention to the Vietnamese people and culture than on my 1989 trip. For example, getting involved in meeting the family of Father Truong was a most memorable experience.

Finally, I note that, ironically, having satisfying personal interactions with the Vietnamese people during this return trip was more similar to my experiences in war time Vietnam than to my first return trip to a peacetime Vietnam.

Group Dynamics

At first I had been concerned that the sixteen students would "drown out" the needs and interests of our three veterans and unduly "dilute" their recovery experience. On the other hand, I assumed it would be positive for the students to learn history beyond textbooks and through the personal testimonies of these three veterans. As it turned out, this mixture was an overall remarkably positive aspect of the experience for both the students and the veterans. For the students,

---

156. See Volume I. See also: Scurfield, R.M., L.E. Wong and E.B. Zeerocah, "Helicopter Ride Therapy for Inpatient Vietnam Veterans With PTSD." *Military Medicine,* 157 (1992), 67-73.

being with the veterans offered a unique door through which to experience the realities of war's impact. In the words of three of the students:

> "The trip would have lacked the intensity without them [the veterans] and would have paled in comparison. It is such an amazing opportunity to have veterans share their experiences."

> "The veterans have much to teach, and we have so much to learn. It showed both groups (students and vets) that the other one was sincere."

> "The combination of students and vets makes the trip more light-hearted, not so serious/somber all the time. Allows vets to open up more to inquisitive students."

I was amazed at how few negative aspects concerning the student-veteran mixture there were. A few students did mention that there was a sometimes conflicting motivation/purpose for the trip for students versus veterans, and the students' concern that they might possibly have "gotten on the veterans' nerves at times."

> "I worried about what to ask the veterans and not make them mad."

> "Veterans may think that students can't understand/appreciate their significance."

> "Sometimes I felt like I was invading their privacy."

However, quite dramatically and consistently, the students as well as the professors provided a validation, an acknowledgment, a recognition to the vets for their sacrifices and their experiences. In turn, the veterans unanimously said their experiences with the students on this trip were *very* positive.

> Roy: "The students were really helpful. They were interested in what, where and how. They were very (genuinely) concerned about us. They made it a lot easier. Their laughing and joking takes your mind off things. And they cared, a lot, and showed real interest in learning about the war through their questioning and listening."

> John: "The students were a delight. Many of them had been through the Vietnam course at USM before and I had prior exposure to them. They were able to relate the actual course material to the Vietnam trip experiences. I admired the students. I have a high regard for their having made the trip at all."

> Charles: "It was very positive being with the students. They could see American Vietnam veterans working together, and could appreciate my contributions as an African-American. There was a willingness by the students to really understand the war and its veterans."

Interacting with the Vietnamese People

Many veterans contemplating a return to Vietnam are worried that the people there will be resentful and unfriendly. In 1989, Vietnam was still shrouded in the mists of political, economic and media isolation by the US, and almost no one had been back to Vietnam who could tell us how they had been treated by the Vietnamese people.

To the amazement of the veterans, the experience of interacting with the Vietnamese people throughout Vietnam were almost entirely and markedly positive.

> Roy: "Mostly positive: The Vietnamese were very friendly, and they were helpful. Seeing the people and how hard they work were positive."

> John: "Super positive! One of the most pleasant aspects of the trip. No instance of unfriendliness. Charles: Very positive: Their friendliness, open hospitality, humbleness, going out of their way, and accepting us."

The Contrast of Peacetime versus War-time Vietnam

> Roy: "Somewhat positive impact: because it looked the same except for the TV antennas."

> John: "Very positive: no signs of war."

> Charles: "Very positive: It seems that the war made it a better country. So then it was good."

Indeed, the land showed even fewer visible scars in 2000 than in 1989. There was a regeneration of lush vegetation that had been killed by the defoliant Agent Orange, and barren brown and dusty (or muddy) military compounds were transformed by greenery and crops.

For all of us, it seems that the combined impact of the positive reception of the people, and the regeneration of the country itself, helped make this return trip a positive one.

Visiting Former Battle Sites

Without a doubt, visiting the battle sites where each veteran had served during the war was a profoundly emotional experience for all of us. Although the emotional impact on all three veterans was substantial, the nature of the impact varied to some degree. Any vet planning to go back should be aware that you cannot predict how you will feel!

> Roy: "Somewhat negative impact: It didn't look the same without the military equipment. On the other hand, it did help a little that it's all changed there now. Made me realize that the buddy I lost is no longer with us. I had had a doubt that he was dead, and this made me realize that he really was gone."

> Charles: "Somewhat positive impact: Seeing the [former Bien Hoa base] water tower had an effect: it had been really visible during the war, and seeing it again was very positive. Also, seeing the main gate, that we had used so often to go and come from the base. The contrast from during the war was considerable: during the war,

we would be somewhat uneasy being outside of the gate, but now I felt more secure being outside the gate.... I was glad that it was so different than during the war."

John: "Very positive impact: The vegetation had changed. Nothing lasts forever. Being on the 'ground' is what matters."

Roy's coming to accept, finally, that his dead buddy really was gone, transcended decades of denial. To overcome this denial might seem to an outside observer to be a logical conclusion that should easily have been realized years ago. However, it is not so easy for a trauma survivor to overcome such a denial and this was a major positive outcome for Roy.

Also, Charles' former military base, in contrast to John's and Roy's, was still an active military installation, but with two very different changes from during the Vietnam War: it was now a Vietnamese military base, and it was in peacetime. These two factors further promoted the realization that one's frozen-in-time war-related memories are indeed of the past, and that the Vietnam of today had moved on and become a quite different place. This is not an inconsequential discovery and it is a great realization to juxtapose with longstanding war memories.

For the students, being with the veterans as they revisited former battlegrounds unanimously was a peak positive experience.

Student: "Visiting the battlefields, learning more about the war was so meaningful. It meant so much more to actually see the vets at the battlefields and hear their stories instead of sitting in a classroom listening to a lecture."

Student: "The mixture of veterans and students made the war more real and the trips to the former battlefields were definite high points of the trip that changed my life."

Roy: "Mostly positive: Very friendly, not hostile, interested in what we thought. We even compared war-scars. They don't have VA services like we have."

Charles: "Very positive: This time in Vietnam, one of the greatest reliefs I had was meeting a Vietnamese soldier, and he hollered at me from a distance, 'You are American aggressor.' I said back, 'You are VC aggressor.' And we both talked about our units. In the middle of our conversation he stopped, and said, 'Come, we celebrate. We celebrate survival.' And when your enemy tells you that, you know you have arrived at an end to unbelievable hostility of each other. When your enemy says, 'Let's celebrate, let's celebrate survival' [and Charles is smiling broadly]... And I have replayed this incident at several talks I have given since being back."[157]

---

157. My very close friend, fellow Vietnam veteran Angelo Romeo, told me of a similar experience described by Roger McCallister. When Roger returned to Vietnam and met some of the former enemy, he said: "Let us celebrate that we were such poor marksmen during the war."

John: "Very positive: It's not a feeling of, we are enemies, but — you and I are sol-diers, we were soldiers, and I was proud to shake hands with another soldier; there was no animosity, I was proud to meet him. However, the time together was terri-bly insufficient. I would like to sit down and talk with them in depth. I feel I have more in common and more automatic regard for a combat soldier, regardless of nationality, than I do for the average American citizen. The remarkable alteration in the veterans' attitudes towards the former enemy, in contrast to during the war, cannot be overemphasized."

As described earlier, during war time, dehumanization of the enemy is a cardinal military conditioning strategy to help soldiers do what they have to do in searching out and killing the enemy. By dehumanizing the enemy, a soldier is able to more instantaneously and unflinchingly react in split-second timing. After all, the enemy are not human beings like you and me, are they? They are vile, cruel, godless, murderers, indeed inhuman. And so it is becomes much easier to "detach" one's emotions from the horror of what one is actually doing and to do what would be unthinkable in peacetime — kill, and kill, again and again.

These noxious beliefs and images of the enemy stay with many veterans fol-lowing their return home, and indeed embellish and fortify feelings that what they did was necessary and, yes, right. As long as the veteran can rigidly hold on to such dehumanizing perceptions and beliefs of the enemy, the horrors com-mitted and witnessed during the war — and the sacrifices — are more tolerable. But, what happens when that rigid, frozen-in-time dehumanized perspective of the enemy begins to crack and thaw?

This can occur, for example, when normalization of diplomatic relations, trade and travel between the two former enemy countries occurs. A country and its soldiers who were demonized during the war now somehow are not so demonic. This can result in internal (psychological) upheaval, as the tranquil-izing qualities of such war-based, rigidly and decades-long held dehumanizing beliefs and detachment start to lose their effect.

And then, by returning to a peacetime Vietnam, combat veterans come face to face with former enemy soldiers — and decades-long attitudes, perceptions, beliefs are shattered — in an extraordinarily positive and humanizing way that emphasized the universality of the experience of war — and apparently this can happen on both sides.

Concerns of Veterans Prior to the Return to Vietnam

All of the veterans had their own personal and very serious concerns about this trip. By and large, those concerns turned out to not be issues once we were in Vietnam. Some of their comments before and after are illustrative:

Roy (speaking before the trip): "My biggest concern is if I will be able to find the exact battle sites at Phu An and at Con Tien, and will I come to feel some closure about what happened at those battles once I do visit them, and will I feel better about my guilt that I could have done something different to prevent my buddy's death?"

[Four months after the trip, Roy stated that his return didn't make as much difference as he'd thought:]

"It's always going to be there. Going back and seeing the place we were 33 years ago had some impact — but didn't provide closure."

[However, eleven months after our return, Roy stated:]

"Returning to Phu An helped a little. It's all changed there now and wasn't even the same area, my battlefield, we couldn't find the exact spot but a spot that looked quite similar. Made me realize he's no longer with us. I had a doubt that he was dead, and this made me realize that he really was gone. On that day being back at Phu An I realized that I couldn't have done nothing different. There was nothing I could do differently."

This indicates that Roy did come to two remarkable and healing conclusions: his doubts that his buddy had actually died were resolved, and he recognized he could not have done anything to prevent his buddy's death. No, these conclusions did not remove the hurt and grief and loss, but a profound new level of acceptance seemed to have been gained.

John (speaking before the trip): "My biggest concern is, to a degree, although it's not likely, that the simple sight and smell of delta country will depress me — a vague worry that I will be frightened somehow — reliving harrowing recollections."

[Four months after returning, John said:] "The above concern was true, but I was really afraid of smelling a rice paddy and having a flashback or fainting. I was crippled with fear. The effect of this trip on this worry was 100% positive. My fear of seeing that country and being crippled with fear are gone. What once paralyzed me with fear, I was able to look at and see as the beauty of a tropical riverine environment. I was positively giddy."

[And 11 months after:]

"Going up a river that was exactly the same scene that 33 years ago would have filled me with terror, would have horrified me, and on this trip I looked at it with joy, with delight. Being on the brown water, increasingly narrowing channel, lush green foliage, and not being under threat. It was a highlight experience...."

John's extremely positive experiences in Vietnam totally eradicated what had been his most pressing concern about returning — *and* provided him with a new set of mental images and visceral highlight experiences about scenes that previously had only been associated with terror.

Charles (speaking before the trip): "I am very concerned about the reactions of the students, that they will think that Vietnam vets are all crazy."

Four months after our return, Charles talked about the students: "Very positive. Students were able to see the difficulties, the sacrifices, the service that a minority may have had to experience during the war [through contact with me on the trip]. Many people in Hattiesburg still don't appreciate or understand the contributions of African-American males in the military in any of the wars."

And so Charles felt very good about taking a step to rectify something that he has a deep and sustained passion about: the largely unsung role and accomplishments of African-American Vietnam veterans.

And then at 11 months, Charles said:

"Having students so involved and interested in a period of our history where most Americans were saying "it never really happened," or really wanted to forget about it, having that type of motivation from young people was most inspirational to me to see them dig in and want to know every aspect down to the foxhole and the muddy stream you had to cross...they inspired me. They gave me a new sense of why I was there and for them to express their interest...they were great. I never met such an enthusiastic group about a field trip. Hats off to them. If this is an example of our American young people, America is in good shape and will be for generations to come."

Returning Did Not Resolve All War-Related Issues for the Veterans

I want to emphasize that returning to Vietnam in 2000 was *not* a panacea. It did not eradicate all the pain and issues that were related to the Vietnam War. That is simply impossible. One continuing issue is the pain over one's loss of comrades in battle.[158]

John: "This trip did not ease my feelings of guilt [over being alive when others died, and over having killed in Vietnam]."

Even so, Roy was able to put this loss into a better and perhaps more acceptable or peaceful perspective. Roy stated that the trip had a mixed (about equally negative and positive) impact on his feelings over the loss of friends in combat:

Roy: "My friend died. I remembered there was nothing that I could do to help him. Going back to Phu An, I realized that there truly was nothing I could do to help him — I had not wanted to admit that."

---

158. The pain that accompanies the loss of such a companion is intertwined with various combinations and levels of guilt, rage, helplessness and grief. On the other hand, the special bonds between comrades in battle is intensely positive and irreplaceable. This is one of the powerful positive/negative aspects of the war experience that contributes to making the impact of war so durable. This is discussed with the metaphor of the Combat Cocktail in Scurfield (2004), *A Vietnam Trilogy*.

This is a profound awareness and conclusion to arrive at after 30+ years of anguish — and it may never have occurred if Roy had not returned to Vietnam.

Core PTSD symptoms, interestingly, seem to be minimally impacted e.g., symptoms of intrusive memories in particular, and isolation, physical arousal or hyper-vigilance.

> Vet: "The trip has had little or no impact on my PTSD symptoms: no worse and no better."

And a second veteran is living about as isolated a life-style as he was before the trip. However, he doesn't view this as negative at all. After all, many of these symptoms of PTSD that clinicians or family may consider to be problematic, i.e., isolation, hyper-vigilance, also were highly adaptive survival mechanisms in the war zone — and many veterans continue to consider them to be positive if not indeed necessary continuing modes of living[159] And who is to say that they are not?

Powerful New Images Stand Alongside (but don't replace) War Memories

> The return to Vietnam in 2000 provided the veterans with extraordinary new images of peacetime Vietnam.

> Roy: "I have a whole different outlook now about the Vietnamese in Biloxi. I don't hate them anymore. I've got respect for them now, because the Vietnamese had a lot of respect for us on this trip."

> Charles: "During the war I did not see the beauty of the country. I had no idea of its beauty, its majesty. It is unbelievable the natural beauty for a country that size. Unbelievable...Thanks very much for a positive picture/memory of a dark chapter in my life."

---

159. See the important work of my friend and colleague, Ron Murphy (Psychology, Dillard University, New Orleans, and formerly at the VA National Center for PTSD, Menlo Park, CA) and colleagues. Their work concerns the critical importance of assessing the motivation and ambivalence of veterans to actually want to change various PTSD symptoms that clinicians typically target as treatment goals to reduce or eliminate. Murphy, R.T., R.P. Cameron, L. Sharp, G. Ramirez, C. Rosen, K. Dreschler and Gusman, D.F. (2003). Readiness to change PTSD symptoms and related behaviors among veterans participating in a Motivation Enhancement Group, *The Behavior Therapist*, 27 (4), 2004, 33-36; Murphy, R.T., C.S. Rosen, R.P. Cameron, Y and K.E. Thompson (2003). Development of a group treatment for enhancing motivation to change PTSD symptoms. *Cognitive and Behavioral Practice*, 9 (4), 2002, 308-316; and Murphy, R.T., C.S. Rosen, K.E. Thompson, M. Murray and Q. Rainey (2004). A Readiness to change approach to preventing PTSD treatment failure. In Taylor, S. (Ed.), *Advances in the Treatment of Posttraumatic Stress Disorder: Cognitive-Behavioral Perspectives*. New York: Springer (2004).

John: "Do I have different images of Vietnam now? You bet: shopkeepers, children selling postcards, and endless smiles from everyone we encountered. They just made us feel good and welcome everywhere we went. That is a life-changing event. Yes, I now have good memories to go along with the ugly memories. My memories of the Vietnam war are leavened now. They are not everything I remember. The positive and pleasant and friendly and warmth in ways I can't begin to describe. It was all good."

By all reports and observations the 2000 return trip was not only an unqualified success. It was identified as a *peak-life experience* by several of the students and seemed to be so for the three veterans as well. Students said,

"You don't know a damn thing unless you make the trip. I sometimes wish I was still there. I felt a purpose for living there that I don't feel so much now."

"The whole experience made me rethink my purpose in life."

"The trip was one of the most extraordinary experiences of my life. I highly recommend it. The only negative aspect was that it was too short!"

"Everyone should experience this trip."

"It made me see how very hard and horrible Vietnam was to vets. It was an irrelevant concept for me before, but actually seeing where the vets had to go in the war and what they had to do made it have meaning."

"This trip changed my life and would be beneficial to all students."

Vet John: "When I had thought about Vietnam in the past, it was always violence, noise and ugliness. Now it's everything it wasn't: peaceful, productive, friendly, and fascinating. We didn't permanently cripple all the people or country. I was on a piece of ground that had changed the whole world for me. I was overwhelmed with my own impressions of taking all this scene in, it all seemed so innocent and peaceful, and it was difficult to imagine that in 1967 an entire American battalion and two enemy battalions fought each other to a terrible standstill, fighting all day and into the night. Hundreds of men died on both sides...so hard to take it in. I just sat down and cried. There are not words for that experience. From only war-time memories to three decades later a place of peace is a very uplifting experience. I feel like I'm the luckiest man alive since going on this trip."

Charles: "I never take first impressions for granted. During the war I was exposed to a country and people I had refused to accept as existing. I had failed to see it (during the war) and it was revealed to me in the truest sense on this trip — the existence of the Vietnamese people and country. And I now understand the term from the Vietnamese people, why they call it 'The American War,' and us the aggressors.

"It was OK: the cities, the country, the people and how they felt about us. I have total admiration for the whole experience. It lifted me to new heights. I had left my local church in 1967, and the Sunday we got back I returned to the church for the Sunday service. And while I was sitting in church, it hit me: I went back, not once but twice, to Vietnam — and I survived! It was overwhelming, the feelings of security and serenity, of peace inside me after the trip. These positive feelings were so overwhelming that I had to get up and leave the church [so as not to show my emotions].

186

CHAPTER 8. PARALLELS AND BENEFITS OF RETURNING TO VIETNAM, 1989 AND 2000 — AND EVEN IN 1982

We are on our return flight from Vietnam, 2000, somewhere over the vast Pacific Ocean. I am reflecting on the fact that we veterans who went back to Vietnam in 2000, and we veterans who went back in 1989, every one of us had one dramatic series of unending reactions throughout our entire return trip to Vietnam. Over and over again, while we were getting to Vietnam, during our arrival there, throughout every day in-country, during our departure, in returning from Vietnam, and long after we were back home, we could not help but find ourselves making comparisons — between the peacetime Vietnam of today and the wartime Vietnam of yesteryear.

I have even more elaborate reactions, comparing my three times in Vietnam over three decades. I remember what Charles said upon arriving at the airport in Ho Chi Minh City and getting into an air-conditioned bus. Charles expressed his amazement at the contrast between this modern large air-conditioned tourist bus and the military buses during the war with chicken wire on the windows.

And as I remember this comparison raised by Charles, I find think back to 1989 when we toured Vietnam in a non-air-conditioned faded yellow Russian-made war-surplus bus.

In 1969:

We arrive at a military controlled airport in Long Binh.

We ride in military buses with wire mesh on the windows to stop grenades.

The bus drivers are active duty US military personnel.

All of us foreigners in-country seem to be military, and there are lots of us.

We are warned: Don't hang out in groups or you will be a target. If you have a choice between going by ground or air transportation, go by air — it is much safer.

Hotels tend to be occupied by the military or not very full of tourists; those hotels that house a military function are guarded by sentries, sandbags and fences.

In 1989:

We arrive at a small, third-world flavored terminal in Hanoi (we are required by the government to arrive in Hanoi and spend several days there before going elsewhere). We ride in an unmarked bus, noisy, rough-riding, bare-bones former military type, with no air conditioning.

The bus driver, who speaks very little English, is silent most of the time, and turns out to be a former NVA soldier. He doubles as our "guide."

We are ordered to keep to a very rigidly-controlled itinerary approved by the government. There are very few foreign tourists and almost no Americans.

We are magnets who attract friendly crowds everywhere we go.

We mostly stay together; we feel more comfortable that way.

Hotels seem to have been improved and are now functioning as non-military public facilities. Most but not all damage from the war has been repaired.

In 2000:

We ride in a well-marked, large tourist bus, in good condition, with decent air conditioning and a microphone and loudspeaker system.

The bus driver specializes in driving and has an aide who rides just inside the front door, a second set of eyes who helps out in heavy traffic or in tight quarters. We also have a trained tour guide who speaks good English and gives us an informative, running commentary as the bus is moving.

There is a noticeable number of foreign tourists, from various countries.

Sometimes we attract a lot of attention and sometimes none at all.

We feel comfortable and safe to be in large or small groups, or to go out alone.

Old hotels have been refurbished and new ones built. The top-rated hotels are quite good and offer a blend of traditional Vietnamese hospitality and services (i.e., haircuts and massages) along with a relatively wide array of gift wares for sale — and modern computer email access to the world.

Even the quality and type of art by Vietnam artisans illustrate the marked changes:

1968: The only art I remember seeing on sale was fairly primitive, often on velvet backing and depicting a Vietnamese scene or Vietnamese people. A broad brush-stroked oil-painting depiction of a rustic village during the rainy season is my prize art possession from my tour of duty

1989: Art had become a burgeoning industry, with traditional lacquer-ware artifacts, more sophisticated paintings and other items for sale, although still realistic or traditional/historical scenes and designs dominating.

2000: It seems that there is art everywhere, including more abstract and surreal paintings, some evocatively suggestive paintings of female figures, lacquer-ware of a much more modern design competing with more traditionally designed lacquer-ware and even a Catholic gift and art shop near the Notre Dame Cathedral in

Saigon. Also, there has been a modernization of such services as wrapping the art for international mailing, and direct mail-order available from the larger stores even after returning home.

As I work to set all my impressions in their proper context, I also turn to the reports of other veterans who have returned to Vietnam. One outstanding example is Lynda Van Devanter, who went back long before I did, in 1982. Reading the epilogue to her searing book, *Home Before Morning*, about an Army nurse in the Vietnam War, I came across very strong parallels.[160] The late Lynda Van Devanter was a friend and companion sister Vietnam veteran nurse activist and advocate who was called before her time — like so many other Vietnam veterans. The epilogue is a 14-page account of Lynda's return to Vietnam in 1982 as part of a delegation of the veterans' service organization, Vietnam Veterans Of America (VVA).

Lynda's description of her 1982 experiences was strikingly similar to my observations of the compelling aspects of returning to Vietnam in 1989 and 2000. I offer selected excerpts below, mirroring the parallels of the 1989 and 2000 return trips. Her experiences are beautifully expressed. And I offer a tribute and acknowledgment to Lynda's — and many other nurses' — life experiences and her passing on to a more peaceful existence in late 2002. May you rest in peace, Lynda and so many other men and women vets who already have left us.

COMPELLING PARALLEL EXPERIENCES: 1989 AND 1982[161]

Some, although not all, elements of "old" unfinished war-related issues for veterans were powerfully impacted by returning to Vietnam — and some issues were not impacted much at all. However, several types of experiences consistently and powerfully impacted all participants on both return trips in 1989 and 2000, and of Lynda's trip in 1982. These common compelling experiences may, indeed, be intrinsic and core features of the impact many veterans may feel if and when they might choose to return to Vietnam.

---

160. Lynda spent most of her tour as an operating nurse at the 71st Evacuation Hospital (a MASH-type facility) in Pleiku Province close to the Cambodian border, where there were many severely wounded casualties. Lynda was the former National Women's Director, Vietnam Veterans of America. For a graphic account of nursing and medical duty in Vietnam, I highly recommend her book, *Home Before Morning. The True Story of an Army Nurse in Vietnam* (New York: Warner Books, Inc., 1983). As a post-script, in comparison to Lynda's book, which is so compelling, I felt inadequate to describe the experiences of nurses in Vietnam, even though I was close friends with several during my tour in Nha Trang.

161. Parallels from 2000 were discussed in the previous chapter.

Interacting with the Vietnamese People

How will they treat us? This was even more of a concern in 1989 than in 2000. In 1989, Vietnam was still almost completely shrouded in the mists of political, economic and media isolation by the US, and there was almost no one who had been back to Vietnam who could tell us how they had been treated by the Vietnamese people; and in 1982 it would have been ever more so.

To the amazement of the veterans, both in 2000 and in 1989, the experiences of interacting with the Vietnamese people everywhere in Vietnam were almost entirely and markedly positive. The only somewhat awkward interactions were with a few Communist officials.

1989:

> Jake: "Very positive. Seeing my guide lady and her child in Cu Chi (Tunnels) had a big (positive) impact on me."[162]

> Bob: "Mostly positive. The smiling faces of Vietnamese children with the absence of fear left a very positive lasting impression. And I have less trouble dealing with local Vietnamese people."[163]

> Dave: "Super-positive. This was a real welcome-home in Hanoi, with the Vietnamese people standing in crowds, waving, smiling, happy — in contrast to the 'welcome home' in the US which was more like 'go away, don't talk, don't feel, don't come near us.' I was apprehensive [when standing in front of a crowd of Vietnamese], but something pulled me towards the kids. And when that happened [positive reactions of everyone in the crowd, both adults and children], I said, 'My God.' It was a wonderful feeling, you know."[164]

---

162. Jake LaFave was very kind to respond to a questionnaire that I mailed him in 2001 about our 1989 return trip. All of Jake's comments in this chapter are from his responses in 2001 to this questionnaire.

163. Bob Swanson and Dave Roberts also were so gracious to respond to the same questionnaire, in 2003. All of Bob's and Dave's comments in this chapter are from their responses to this questionnaire.

164. Smith, Stevan M., *Two Decades and A Wake-Up, 1990.* This video contains very emotional scenes of our 1989 return trip to Vietnam. It can be extremely valuable for veterans to view this film and discuss their reactions (individually or in a peer group) with a counselor or significant other. Underlying issues that may be triggered by the film can then be addressed, and one may explore the motivations for possibly returning to Vietnam, what reasonable objectives one might hope to accomplish, and in general prepare emotionally to gain the maximum potential benefits of such an extraordinary trip.

A documentary is also being produced by the University of Southern Mississippi about our 2000 study-abroad course to Vietnam. Inquiries may be addressed to Dr. Andy Wiest, Professor, History Department, University of Southern Mississippi, Hattiesburg, MS — or to myself at the School of Social Work at the same university.

"For me, it is difficult to find the right words to come even close to adequately describe the impact of this truly remarkable discovery and experience: being a positive center of attention from hundreds of Vietnamese of all walks of life in every city, town, shop, street, restaurant we went to, and in myriad episodes of both casual interaction and more in-depth conversations that were experienced by all of us. And this remarkable acceptance and friendship from the Vietnamese people towards the veterans happened everywhere we traveled — from Hanoi in the north to the southern tip of the Mekong Delta, during large group tours and in myriad individual people-to-people encounters in crowded markets, congested streets and in shops of all types and sizes. All of these experiences were unbelievably and stunningly positive."

Even in 1982:

Lynda: "I stopped a few times and spoke with people at village entrances and at kiosks selling fruit, cigarettes and various and sundry machine parts. They responded with smiles and warm greetings. They asked where I was from, and when I said I was an American, the response was always friendly. I had expected the reverse, anything but friendship, but it was never so. They seemed happy to see me. When Les and Dave went out later that day, they got the same kind of reception....[165]

"I didn't know what to make of it [the friendliness from the Vietnamese throughout the country]. I'd expected them to hate me, and I was finding friendship everywhere. I personified the most recent war they'd been victims of, and still they seemed to like me.[166]

The acceptance and apparent willingness of the Vietnamese people to "let bygones be by-gones" with American Vietnam veterans had an indelible impact on the vets, and on the students in 2000. Enhanced self-esteem and self-acceptance, reciprocal feelings of respect and appreciation, peak moments of joy: all characterized the incredibly positive people-to-people interactions throughout Vietnam.

The Changed Landscape:

1989

Bob: "Very positive."

Jake: "Beautiful country, sandy beaches, warm and green."

Dave: "Mostly positive. No people trying to kill you. People in the streets, hustle and bustle of activity, a nation at peace."

Of course, the discovery that there were few noticeable signs that the war had ever taken place was bittersweet for a number of veterans. This appears

---

165. VanDevanter, Lynda, 368-369.
166. Ibid., 369.

especially so for those veterans who are holding onto the idea that they will rediscover in the reality of peacetime Vietnam that which has been in their minds for decades about the reality of wartime Vietnam.

In contrast, we all were struck by how the land and vegetation were now of a country at peace, and, most pointedly, showed very few visible scars of the presence of war (and dramatically less so in 2000 than in 1989). There was a regeneration of vegetation that had been decimated by the defoliant Agent Orange, barren brown and dusty/muddy military compounds transformed by greenery and crops.

This ability of the land itself to regenerate, and the obvious fruits of the hard manual labor of the Vietnamese farmers, was very healing to most of the vets. This was especially so for those who had been suffering from feelings of guilt about "what I (we Americans) did to the Vietnamese people and country." After all, there were a reported 2.4 to 3 million+ Vietnamese killed during the course of the Vietnam War.

It seems that the combined impact of the positive reception of the people, and the regeneration of the country itself, the land and vegetation, was a remarkably powerful influence on making this return trip a positive one for the veterans.

Visiting Former Battle Sites

Without a doubt, visiting former battle sites where each veteran had served during the war was a profoundly emotional experience. There was a range of impact on the vets concerning how their former duty sites were markedly different in physical appearance than they had remembered them. It may seem to be a rather straightforward conclusion that former battle sites in peacetime Vietnam 2000, and even in 1989, would almost certainly be very different than during the war.

However, such a conclusion ignores the fact that — for the war veteran — vivid memories of combat-zone scenes have been "frozen-in-time" for decades. While that may seem quite irrational in one respect, all veterans still were confronted with the jarring incongruity of their war-time memories with the reality of -time Vietnam today.

1989

> Mary: "I'm glad it has changed [the site of the former Army hospital]. I think it would have been too much if it had not changed, because so much pain passed through this spot. I'm really glad it's changed here. It helps a lot."[167]

For Mary and a number of other vets, discovering that the Vietnam of decades-old war memories and experiences no longer existed, including the transformation of most former battle sites into changed landscape and function, was extraordinarily positive.

> On the other hand, for some returning vets who found their former duty stations quite different, there was a bittersweet feeling that blended the sense of loss of a physical and visual anchor for their decades-old memories and the initial disconcerting disorientation caused by the startling contrast to their memories.

1989

> Ed: "Things appear to be very much different than they were. It was a little distressing, contrary to the images that are still alive."[168]

> It was very disappointing for one veteran, Bob, who was unable to return to his former war zone area due to distance and logistical complexities, and for two other veterans who were able to get close but not to actually get on to the site of their former US Air Force and Navy bases, respectively (because both were now active Vietnamese military bases).

1989

> Bob: "The changes in the terrain of Vietnam had a somewhat negative impact. I was not able to recognize much in Vietnam. Plus, I didn't get to go to my trauma site, Qua Viet, where we spent 53 days in the field, January-March, 1968."

> Jake: "The most negative experience was not finding my side of the base, and not finding the 8th Field Hospital. It was a let-down seeing Russian planes on my base, that my base was being used by the Russians."

> Dave: "The absolutely most negative experience on the trip was that I was not able to get onto the base at Nha Be. It was heartbreaking. I could have walked down memory lane."

> However, for every single veteran on both return trips, the return or attempt to return to one's former duty site was perhaps the most compelling experience in Vietnam — and for almost all the veterans, it was a singularly positive experience.

> Dave: (1989) [In reference to his return to the location of the former Navy base at Nha Be, even though he was unable to actually get onto the base] "All the money in the world couldn't buy this experience."

> Interestingly, being with the veterans as they returned to their former duty sites was identified by the students in 2000 as a highlight experience for them, too. Such

---

167. Smith, 1990.
168. Ibid.

visits were clearly a healing experience, a big step toward the resolution of old hurts — while for some, at the same time, it may have at least temporarily re-opened old wounds and loss. Powerful emotions were felt and experienced; and the outcome was a fuller realization of an increased (but definitely not a complete) sense of resolution and progress along the path of recovery.

Even in 1982

Lynda: "I pushed through the swinging door I'd gone out of almost precisely 12 years ago [at the airport]. I turned and walked back to the windows from which I'd stared out so long ago. The feelings of fear returned in a wave. I felt again the incredible sadness, the fear of all the Vietnamese around me, the longing for home, and the deep-rooted fear that I would never get out of here alive. 'Vietnam sucks,' I thought. 'It sucks so bad that it can suck you back down from the sky. It sucks out your heart and your soul and your mind, and you can never get it back.'

"I was surprised to feel tears dropping on my folded arms. I began to realize that this was not 12 years ago, it was now. I had met and had gotten to know some Vietnamese this time, and they were people, just like me and my family and my friends. I didn't have to be afraid anymore. The tears came washing over me, this time, finally, in relief. It was over. The war was over for me."[169]

Interacting with Former Enemy Soldiers

Meeting former enemy soldiers was an extraordinarily powerful experience for everyone, right up there with the positive reception by the Vietnamese people and the return to former battlefield sites

1989

Bob: "Mostly positive experience. That we all suffered in the same ways, and that I had more in common with an old enemy than people at home. I was able to let go of negative feelings towards the Vietnamese soldiers (on both sides). I've been able to adopt the view of myself and Vietnamese soldiers as professional warriors and not murderers."

Bill: "We came here, and the purpose for this was to heal within myself. Now, if that's what healing within myself means, I'll go to a former enemy and shake his hand, and admit that the war is over and I don't want to have hard feelings. That's the whole thing of my PTSD, all this anger and hatred that I have built up, and I got to let it out. And I got to stop it."[170]

Dave: "Mostly positive. Going to the disabled Vietnamese vets' center was really moving. I asked one vet what happened to his arm. He said it was from a (US-fired) M-16. I thought, how different. It seems to me that the Vietnamese people and the [American] vets had a common enemy — the American government! That's probably why we warmed up to our former foe. We all were taken to the cleaners! I still have very bad feelings towards my government. They really let us down! I don't hate the Vietnamese people; in fact I really like them."

---

169. VanDevanter, 373.
170. Smith, 1990.

Some of the vets were skeptical that the positive feelings expressed by former enemy veterans were genuine (on the 1989 return trip, some vets also were afraid that such meetings between our two country's veterans were a political set-up and that we would be exploited for propaganda purposes), but the vast majority considered this to be a genuine and palliative experience. The Vietnamese apparently are able to "separate the warrior and the individual American" from their attitude towards "the American government," and this offered a very human face to what had been dehumanized in war.

Even in 1982:

> Lynda: "As I once more wondered about the friendly attitude being displayed towards us, Mr. Tach and later that evening Ha Van Lau expressed to us their belief that America's Vietnam veterans were as much victims as they were. They had no love lost for the US government, but they understood there was a difference between the warriors and the war. I was learning more all the time."[171]

Shattering the Dehumanized Myth of the Vietnamese People

Seeing the Vietnamese for the first time as a people, as real human beings with feelings, also was disconcerting for some vets. This new perception contradicted the very powerful indoctrination we had been given before going to war, designed to dehumanize the Vietnamese so that we could kill them without stopping to think that they had feelings and valued life like we did.

However, most vets reported this human-to-human encounter to be uplifting, helping to excise at least some of the legacy of hate that had been carried all these years and directed towards faceless Vietnamese.

VETERANS' PRE-TRIP CONCERNS

All of the veterans planning to return to Vietnam had their own personal and very serious concerns, if not outright trepidation, *about something*. As it turned out, by and large the concerns that each veteran had identified before the trip turned out to not be issues once in Vietnam.

1989

> Dave: "I was scared at how the Vietnamese people were going to treat me. And when I flew into Hanoi, I was scared. There's no doubt about it. But, after the reception that we got, and the people, why they seemed so friendly. I'm going to give

---

171. VanDevanter, 371-372.

them, as an individual, the benefit of the doubt and say "Hi." I'm going to meet them half-way."[172]

Bob: "I was very concerned that I would not be able to come back and feared for my personal safety. The impact of the trip on this concern was mixed positive and negative."

Even in 1982

Lynda: "This time I was going back to something that had been inside me for 13 years, something nebulous, untouchable, unreal, but real all the same. I had known Vietnam in my dreams for so many years. What would it be like now? I had known Vietnam at war for a year, and that war raged inside me for years later.

"Could I finally make peace with it? In a way I was afraid of coming back as different as the first time.[173] The people stared at me as I ran in my shorts, running shoes and a T-shirt bearing writing in English. I smiled at all of them and was rewarded by the same each time. I marveled. They were all the same as when I was here before, but I didn't have to worry that anyone had a knife or grenade behind the smile. We weren't at war and I was safe. It was a revelation for me."[174]

IMPACT ON CORE PTSD SYMPTOMS

Interestingly, the impact on core PTSD symptoms *per se* seemed to have been minimal (various symptoms of intrusive memories, detachment and numbing, and physical arousal or hyper-vigilance). Of course, one return trip may be insufficient for those with severe symptoms; it should be clear from this book that in my own experience, the second trip was much more liberating.

Stevan Smith, who has led numerous veterans back to Vietnam several times, stated that their nightmares and intrusive memories were greatly reduced.

However, many of these PTSD symptoms that clinicians or family may consider to be problematic, i.e., isolation, hyper-vigilance, also were highly adaptive survival mechanisms in the war zone. Indeed, it is clear that many veterans continue to consider these to be positive if not indeed necessary modes of living.[175] However, the continuing presence of painful and intrusive war-related memories was substantial.

---

172. Smith, 1990.
173. VanDevanter, 362.
174. Ibid., 368.
175. Murphy, 2003.

1989

> Jake: "The war memories are still much more pronounced and clear. However, the 1989 thoughts of seeing happiness and changes of life styles by the Vietnamese remains in my mind."

The presence of very recent and positive images will, I believe, work gradually to mitigate the indelible and horrific recurring memories of war-time Vietnam, and over time they may be remembered as often as the negative memories (or more often). No, this certainly is not a "cure," but for many returning veterans it can be a powerful antidote to the unremitting toxicity of war.

> Bob: "My memories are more balanced now, 12 years later (2001). Though still intrusive, my war memories have lessened some in negative impact. My old memories were not replaced by new memories, but the addition of more positive memories has changed the ratio."

> Dave: "For me, it was a great experience. I did get help with my guilt, the hurt I was holding onto about how I might have caused the people of Vietnam. To see how the Vietnamese people had changed from the war, the new images, new picture frames in the mind renewed my strength and understanding to see a new generation of Vietnamese people. On the other hand, it clarified to me that I had a lot of healing to do with my country and government, not with the Vietnamese people. In retrospect, I still need a whole lot of healing with my country."

DOWN-SIDE OF RETURNING TO VIETNAM: CONCERNS AND RECOMMENDATIONS

From all my experience and to my knowledge, return trips to Vietnam have been almost without exception a highly positive experience for veterans. Even so, several very specific cautions and recommendations are in order. Some of these recommendations may seem obvious, to some people, but I would be remiss if I did not spell out to Vietnam vets (and to their families and friends, and clinicians) those who are at most risk.

(1) I strongly advise that veterans with severe PTSD should NOT make such a trip. This is especially so for such veterans, in Stevan Smith's words, "who want to remain unchanged — who want to glory in their anguish. The trip is very hard on the 'professional veterans. Many resort to substance abuse to avoid being changed there." As Dave Roberts mentioned, "Veterans need to make a commitment that they truly want to heal; they may be so jaded from their trauma that they cannot see the beauty and healing that's there."

And, any veterans with significant unresolved PTSD need to be continuing in a longstanding and beneficial counseling relationship. Vets with significant unresolved issues related to their war experiences can, of course, derive benefits from returning; but many powerful and unresolved issues will surely be provoked and — unless they can be dealt with immediately inside an expert PTSD counseling relationship — they will tend to overshadow the positive benefits that were derived.

(2) I strongly advise against any veterans returning to Vietnam who have a current or very recent substance abuse problem. The ready availability of substances in Vietnam, the many bars that cater to tourists, and the possible attraction to use alcohol or other substances in an attempt to cope with the inevitable and very strong emotions that will be provoked during travel in Vietnam can be extremely problematic — and especially so for the "professional vets" as described above by Stevan Smith.

(3) I strongly recommend that veterans with a PTSD service-connected disability be seriously counseled about the possible risks to their disability rating from the Department of Veterans Affairs. Admitting to a major improvement in their condition could place that rating in jeopardy. If they do have very positive experiences and there is a continuing positive impact after returning Stateside, they and their clinicians may find themselves in the awkward position of having to consider minimizing or denying the positive benefits of the return trip or risk a reduction or loss of the veteran's benefits. Is it any wonder that so many veterans distrust the government?

(4) Indeed, veterans who have strong issues of rage and distrust for the government, those who feel they were ill-treated or ignored returning from the war and afterwards, need to be forewarned. Such issues may well be triggered or exacerbated by going back to Vietnam. It can be joyous to receive a welcome from the Vietnamese people and heart-wrenching at the same time. A renewed anguish and rage can be generated by the contrast between the unexpected positive acceptance by the Vietnamese people and the unexpected negative response from the US government (and many civilians). Veterans should be prepared for this double-edged sword and search within themselves to see if such issues towards our government continue to be a dominant issue.

The previous caution is part of the reason why I strongly recommend any veterans with significant unresolved PTSD who are contemplating such a return to be in a current counseling relationship with someone knowledgeable about war-related PTSD; someone with whom they can consult prior to and following such a return trip. The resulting intra-personal and inter-personal dynamics that will be provoked may require considerable sorting-out before, during and/or following the return trip; this requires a full commitment to the process and cannot be a quick fix.

(5) For any veteran contemplating returning to Vietnam, whether or not there is any history of PTSD, I strongly recommend first viewing the film, *Two Decades and A Wake-Up*. This can help make the decision whether to return to Vietnam and can help identify the underlying issues that may be exacerbated by such a trip.[176] By the same token, talking with someone who has actually returned to Vietnam can be quite helpful. However, unless that person has good video footage of the return trip, words and photographs tend to be quite insufficient to convey what it was really like.

(6) Such a trip is always highly emotional, so it is best to travel with at least one trusted companion for support. There is a critical advantage in having a support person who returns home with the veteran, someone with whom the veteran is close, who can fully appreciate and relate to the veteran's experience of peacetime Vietnam. Indeed, having someone to continue sharing with after the trip is an important way to keep these new memories alive, to go over them again and again, keeping them in the forefront.

(7) Active inclusion of the veteran's significant other(s), be that a partner, family members, spiritual advisor or trusted friend, must not be overlooked. Many couples already find the "Vietnam experience" that so absorbs one person and that the other one cannot share is a divisive factor. To plan a return trip that adds to the feeling of being excluded is hardly helpful. This is not to say that the significant other should necessarily accompany the veteran. The veteran will be quite preoccupied and emotional while in peacetime Vietnam, especially on a first return trip, and may not be the most attentive or grounded traveling companion. However, this option should at least be thoroughly explored and discussed before the trip is made; the last thing that vets or their family members need is to have such a trip exacerbate old schisms among loved ones.

There are other ways that partners or friends can be included, during the thinking and planning process, while abroad in Vietnam (inexpensive e-mail access is available), in a send-off/welcome home at the airport, and after the trip. Significant others should be included to the maximum extent possible. This includes open dialogue and problem-solving when feelings of being excluded (on

---

176. Stevan Smith, *Two Decades and a Wake-Up*. A video has also been produced from the extensive footage filmed during the 2000 Vietnam History Study Abroad Course. For information, contact Andy Wiest at the History Department, University of Southern Mississippi in Hattiesburg. andy.weist@usm.edu.

the part of the significant other) or invasion of privacy (on the part of the veteran) arise. And arise they will — unless they are just flat-out denied.

(8) And finally, if a veteran is pondering such a trip, he or she might also read this book or other written accounts of veterans who have returned to peacetime Vietnam.

Third-World Realities

The realities of traveling in a third-world country also must be considered.

While there have been major advances in Vietnam regarding travel resources, paved roads, hotel accommodations, and food, it is still a third-world country.

- Prudence is advised concerning what one eats and drinks.

- Traffic and congestion in the greater Saigon area in particular can be overwhelming, especially for vets who have retired to quiet rural areas.

- Travel arrangements may be disrupted and may be difficult to correct in a timely manner. Assistance when traveling outside of the major traveled areas can be extremely hard to find.

- The heat and humidity have not changed; in this regard, Vietnam is still Vietnam, and there are few air-conditioned establishments to escape into.

- Vietnam is a smoker's delight. Second-hand smoke is everywhere.

- Disability accommodations are practically non-existent.

- If you are used to or prepare for such conditions, then travel in Vietnam won't so problematic. However, one must be prepared to face considerable challenges in making advance travel arrangements. Government approval will be required for many places you might want to travel to, and there will be unexpected glitches. It is essential to go with a travel agency that is familiar with Vietnam, knows how to negotiate with the Communist government to get prior approval for the travel itinerary, and to solve problems on-the-spot. Of course, you also need a fluent translator.

Even with the above cautions and recommendations, travel in Vietnam is physically tiring, and very frustrating at times. Add to that any war-related or personal issues that arise or are exacerbated that one may have to contend with. The value of a well-planned and supported return trip cannot be overestimated.

If, considering all the above, you feel that the attraction to return is compelling: please plan accordingly, be prepared, and **go for it!** You probably won't be sorry, and you may well find it to be a remarkably positive peak life experience.

However, the very fact of being treated as very special persons, being greeted time and again with a sense of acceptance, friendliness, and respect by hundreds and hundreds of Vietnamese everywhere — also has the potential to turn negative once the veteran has returned home.

This is especially true for veterans who lead relatively isolated lives or have minimal social support systems in place. This sea of human acceptance by the Vietnamese of our veterans is so powerful that it can be an elixir, with the irresistible lure of a potent and exotic substance that keeps pulling us back. Most vets who have gone say that they want to go back again some day, and a few expressed being quite preoccupied with returning.

And so, ironically, for some returning vets the bounty of Vietnam peacetime positive experiences and images of today may become a new preoccupation. Admittedly, it offers a positive alternative that can at least partly replace the unceasing barrage of debilitating memories that many veterans suffer.

However, this preoccupation nevertheless may inhibit some vets from moving ahead with their lives. This is much more likely to occur with vets who suffer from severe PTSD and those who have little positive going on in their post-war lives. Of course, it is quite possible that vets can move on with their lives back home *and* at the same time be quite intent on planning for another return trip to Vietnam: there is no reason why the two should be mutually exclusive.

1989

> Bob: [Speaking in 2001] "I have been able to separate out the people of Vietnam, the country of Vietnam and my war trauma as each being important individual parts of me. This has given me more energy to deal with the fear and trauma. The negative is that I still have some unfinished business over there. I would still like to visit my trauma site. The incident at the Hanoi Airport (where I was singled out for close inspection and kept back while the rest of the group left the airport) increased my fear levels to the point where I was not able to fully participate as much as I would have liked to on the rest of the trip. I would like to return again."

Yes, after all, what cannot be accomplished in one trip may take two, or three, or more return trips. And what is wrong with that?

Stevan Smith's perspective through taking veterans back to Vietnam multiple times is that returning to Vietnam in a "group" or therapeutic environment is not any more positive for vets than going by oneself, because what is helpful is "the primary experience one-on-one with the Vietnamese people."

Interestingly, there is the very real possibility that a vet who goes back may find that his relationship with other Vietnam veterans suffers to some degree.

Some vets are quite negative about any veterans returning to Vietnam, as they continue to hate the "Vietnamese" and continue to consider the "Vietnamese" to still be the enemy. Dave Roberts had a compelling observation in this regard:

> These vets are still feeding off the baloney that was taught to them in their combat training to hate and destroy, because they can't or won't come to grip with their own failures. They still believe that we won the war because no one wants or loves a loser. Maybe that's what it's all about, love, it's an easy word. But maybe they have lost that feeling and need to regain it.

Such negative feelings can be projected towards those vets *who have* returned to Vietnam, and may seriously complicate pre-trip peer relationships. And the returned veteran can contribute to this schism if he or she displays a judgmental attitude towards those vets who are skeptical, unable to believe or won't appreciate the virtues of the return visit.

Ironically, the gap between veterans who have returned to a peacetime Vietnam and those who have not mirrors the gap that most Vietnam veterans feel (to some or to a considerable degree) between themselves and anyone who was not in the war; the sense that they could not possibly understand what we went through and, both then and now.

Some of us who have been back to Vietnam are struggling with this attitude exactly: How can anyone who has not returned to Vietnam, or who was never there, ever understand our experience? Of course, if we let that thought stop us from trying to share about it, then it is sure to be true. The more powerful the experience is, the more we may feel, "How could I possibly convey how meaningful this trip was, to someone who was not there?"

Dave Roberts stated that this was exactly how he felt when he got back from our return trip in 1989. "Maybe it's simply that you have to go to the well, if you want a drink."

I, for one, certainly have found it quite difficult to share the experience verbally. And so, this book is turning out to be the way that I am conveying what returning to Vietnam has meant to me — even to my wife and three young adult children. One veteran who went on the 1989 return trip told me that as soon as he had finished reading his copy of *A Vietnam Trilogy*, he gave it to his wife to read. He felt that it would give her a much better understanding about what he went through during the war and afterwards and what happened during our return trip.

One veteran from the 1989 trip said:

"I became so involved with processing the information (from our 1989 trip) with my wife that she felt left out. This created a rift between us that ended in divorce."

It seems that there can be a powerful collusion on both sides, an avoidance of intimately sharing what the Vietnam experience (war-time and peacetime) is all about. Such avoidance can widen the gap between veterans, and between returned veterans and significant others in their lives. For example, the partner of one veteran who returned to Vietnam in 2000 has yet to watch any video footage of his return to his former battlefield. And, the veteran is, of course, quite hurt by this. Conversely, Stevan Smith noted that on his multiple return trips to Vietnam, several veterans took their wives with them, about 20 couples in total. Nearly all had very positive experiences by going back together.[177]

I, too, seem to have been quite reticent to verbally share much about my return in 2000, or my return in 1989, or for that matter my war-time Vietnam of 1968-69. Oh, I can do it in professional presentations, and I have been writing about it in various articles over the years — and now in these *Vietnam Trilogy* books. But sit down and discuss it in any detail with family or friends (who are not Vietnam veterans themselves)? Hardly. And I am unclear how much they would really want to hear this from me. As Dave Roberts said,

"That's the problem. We perceive that they would not want to hear us, or wouldn't understand."

Is it that I (and many other war veterans) consider "my Vietnam" to be a series of sacred experiences that I prefer to keep to myself? Is it that I feel inadequate to express the essence of the experience? Is it that I doubt their ability or perhaps even their interest in hearing and listening about it? Perhaps a combination of all of these; and the result is a persistent barrier between war veterans and everyone else.

(And most survivors of other types of trauma, including sexual assault, child abuse, and domestic violence, find that a similar barrier afflicts them in their post-trauma relationships with others.)[178]

The only two groups of people with whom I have felt comfortable to have substantive Vietnam discussions with (war-time *and* peacetime Vietnam) are veterans and colleagues, both veteran and non-veteran, who also have been

---

177. Only one out of about 20 couples did not have a positive experience together. In that one couple, the wife seemed to be fundamentally unhappy with her life and the trip only exacerbated her bitterness.
178. Herman, Judith. *Trauma and Recovery. The Aftermath of Violence — From Domestic Abuse to Political Terror* (New York: Basic Books, 1992, 1997).

trusted companions in the journeys of so many veterans from pathos to healing.[179]

Final Impressions of Having Returned to Peacetime Vietnam — Twice

Having listed some of the potential concerns that veterans should think about when contemplating returning to Vietnam, I want to emphasize my main point. For all but a handful of veterans, I am convinced that it will be a wonderful, positive experience — and the veteran's deeply held memories, emotions and issues will be impacted in positive ways that no other experience could come close to.

Stevan Smith, who has taken 100 to 125 Vietnam veterans back, strongly concurs. As a Vietnam veteran who is a non mental health professional, Steve states, "I am not at all concerned about the impact of a return trip on a veteran's PTSD. The experience is too powerful and too positive. The overwhelming majority come to grips with their time in Vietnam and the losses they suffered and continue to suffer. It is the war itself — not the country or the people that is the real issue. Once the war is over, the veteran can have many positive experiences returning to the old battlefields."[180]

Our study abroad course to Vietnam in 2000 was, by all reports and observations, an unqualified success. Also, it was identified as a peak-life experience by several of the students and for the three veterans as well.

---

179. "Healing Journey" was the title of a half-hour documentary produced by Phil Sturholm for KIRO-TV in Seattle, WA, about two of the veterans who were part of the 1989 return trip. Also, "healing journey" is part of the title of a very moving three-part video series that I am proud to have been involved with (along with Allan Perkal, Irene Powch and Jim Cordeiro), *A journey of healing: An outpatient PTSD therapy group with veterans of three wars* (Honolulu: National Center for PTSD, VAM and ROC, Department of Veterans Affairs, 1997). To my knowledge, this is the most comprehensive film documentation ever made of the conduct of PTSD therapy with war veterans. It includes veterans of World War II, Vietnam and the Persian Gulf Wars. The companion 66-page monograph (by R.M. Scurfield and Irene Powch) describes in detail the counseling method utilized in the film and provides "talking points" that further explain key therapeutic interactions during the group therapy sessions. Copies may be requested (limited copies still are available free of charge) from Allan Perkal, Media Coordinator, Pacific Islands Division, VA National Center for PTSD, Honolulu. 808.566-1546 or 7.

180. Steve could only remember two veterans out of over 100 who had "bad" experiences, one who reported "seeing MIA's in the Mekong Delta" and the other who became very angry when General Giap would not meet with him in Hanoi. Of course, since no mental health professional assessment of the 100 or 125 veterans was provided, it is not possible to know how many, if any, of these veterans had a diagnosis of PTSD, or simply had unresolved issues related to their traumatic war experiences.

And, yes, our 1989 return trip was fraught with conflict, both during and following our return. And, several of the veterans on the 1989 trip had very severe PTSD. Still, vets Jake, Dave and Bob (plus Stevan Smith, himself a Vietnam veteran who organized and led the 1989 return trip), consider their return trip to Vietnam to have been very worthwhile, even though there was a quite varying degree of impact on their war-issues and the PTSD symptoms that they still continue to struggle with.

1989

> Bob Swanson: "I didn't get to go to my trauma [my former battle site], but I came home with a lot to think about. After 12 years (2001), I look at myself and see a lot of changes that were promoted by the experience of returning to Vietnam. The energy I have is being spent on healing and after-care, a loving relationship with my wife Rita of seven years, and a close loving relationship with my daughters and six grandchildren. These are the true fruits of my labors — the most important gains in my recovery."

> Jim Kessi: "My feelings of self-worth have really gone up. I had a finalization of some issues while in Vietnam on this trip. I accepted less guilt, I guess because of feeling forgiveness by the Vietnamese, and the decision of the Vietnamese to move ahead with their lives. So, now, I'm more serious, determined to move ahead."[181]

> Dave Roberts: "Did I get what I personally wanted to get out of returning to Vietnam? Yes! My guilt and actions during the war are at ease now. I find myself thinking more about the future and some goals that I still have to accomplish. I am at peace with the Vietnamese people. I still have to work on liking myself more and understanding myself, but who doesn't?

> "Seeing is believing, it heals the mind. You can now look at rivers and remember them not as war but as youthful fond memories. Sometimes I am able to let some things go from the war. But, I still remember the bad times. Who wouldn't? It helped to see Vietnam again, and I encourage anyone to go back. It was a great feeling. But Vietnam vets still have to deal with their welcome home from the Vietnam War. America still needs to recognize the Vietnam vet for what we went through in the name of Freedom."

Even in 1982

> Lynda: "I wanted to come back here to find something I had left, and I just found it. It was my youth, my innocence. I know that I can never get them back, but I've touched them, and it's OK. I know where they went. I even think I know what they are. It's so sad. I buried my head in my shoulder and the tears washed away the war."[182]

---

181. Stevan M. Smith, *Two Decades and A Wake-Up*, 1990.
182. Lynda VanDevanter, *Home Before Morning*, 1983, 373-374.

The Most Compelling Impact: Peacetime Memories Alongside the War Memories

The one most compelling and healing benefit that was only available because we veterans did return to peacetime Vietnam is the extraordinary experience of now having peacetime Vietnam memories to juxtapose with the wartime horrors. This phenomenon is reflected in the following quite tangible statistic about myself that is reflected in my daily journal logs from 1989 and in 2000.

In 1989, while in a peacetime Vietnam, I recorded 18 (negative or positive) "flashbacks" to my wartime Vietnam experiences. In 2000, while in a peacetime Vietnam, I recorded 19 (negative or positive) flashbacks to my wartime Vietnam experience — and 21 flashbacks to my peacetime 1989 Vietnam experience. This is a remarkable occurrence. Where once there were memories only of war-time Vietnam, now I have essentially an equivalent number of memories of *both* wartime *and* peacetime Vietnam. Similarly, all the veterans on the 1989 and 2000 return trips with whom I have any post-trip communication have reported similarly profound changes in their memory patterns.

This definitely was not a cure-all experience. However, this phenomenon offers an extraordinary impact, perhaps best reflected in the words of a few of the veterans:

1989

> Jake LaFave: "The war memories are much more pronounced and clear. However, the 1989 thoughts of seeing happiness and changes of life styles remain in my mind. The most positive overall impact was seeing the beautiful country, the happy people and progress in Vietnam in most areas."

> Bob Swanson: "My old memories were not replaced by new memories, but the addition of more positive memories has changed the ratio. The smiling faces of Vietnamese children with the absence of fear has left a very positive lasting impression. And playing guitar and singing Beatles songs with the desk clerk in the hotel at DaNang remains a wonderful memory."

> Dave Roberts: "Surprising images, they dance in my mind. No fear, but acceptance and understanding. Changes in everything; you can no longer fight the war in Vietnam. Because it [the war] just doesn't exist any longer. The people and the country will change you, it grows on you, the peacefulness and the beauty of the ocean beaches and mostly all the children!"

2000

> Roy Ainsworth: "In the war, I was not able to appreciate or see the country's beauty, or meet the people on a one-to-one basis other than as the enemy. Before I

went to Vietnam on this trip, I hated the Vietnamese back home. I found it really hard to deal with them; they brought back bad memories. Before, when I used to see Vietnamese here [in Biloxi], I would think: are they VC or NVA? Now, I don't think that way at all. Returning, it was beautiful to see the country and meet the Vietnamese people, not as the enemy. They didn't hurt us. They just want the opportunity for a better way of life like we do. I have a whole different outlook now. I've got respect for them now because they had a lot of respect for us on this trip. They haven't done anything to us. They shouldn't be hated. I don't hate them anymore."

Charles Brown: "Once in Vietnam, the tenseness of my now 230 pound body, I didn't know I had such an motional burden to be moved until I was there. Then, when we arrived in Tan Son Nhut, getting on the bus at the airport at midnight, seeing the city all lit up, people sitting outside at cafes, something we weren't seeing now as a target like we did during the war all lit up at night. And suddenly we were in the middle of the most populous city in Vietnam — and all is well [smiling]. What a relief! What a marvelous experience that day in contrast to the months I was in Vietnam in 1967. It is unbelievable and one can hardly comprehend the difference — unless you were there. And then, we got to see all the majesty of the country, from one place to another. I had no idea of its beauty. Unbelievable. "

John Young: "Do I have different images of Vietnam now? You bet: shopkeepers, children selling postcards, and endless smiles from everyone we encountered. They just made us feel good and welcome everywhere we went. That is a life-changing event. Yes, I now have good memories to go along with the ugly memories. My memories of the Vietnam war are leavened now. The war memories are not everything I remember. (Now there also are) the positive and pleasant and friendliness and warmth of my return, in ways I can't begin to describe. It was all good.

"The most helpful thing I brought back, in spite of all the ugliness and the chaos that had been part of my first time there, familiar signs of the war, was the contrast. We were met with smiles everywhere. Vietnam had not only recovered from the war, but it is a vibrant, living place and people who made us feel very welcome. It was a very humbling experience."

And my own memories continue including as many (if not more), and much fresher, positive pictures of peacetime Vietnam along with the indelible negative and positive wartime pictures. I am convinced that this benefit, alone, has made my two return trips and that of 11 other veterans, and countless others who also have returned, uniquely invaluable and irreplaceable as a healing element in our continuing journeys to attain a more peaceful co-existence with each of our own personal legacies of wartime Vietnam. And for that, we are indeed blessed.

Would You Go Back to Vietnam again, Ray?

I have had no regular clinical contact with veterans since 1998; hence, their stories no longer trigger my own stories on a daily basis. I really felt the loss of such contact for quite a while. Now, I am getting more and more comfortable and stimulated in my second career — Ray the Vietnam veteran and former VA career mental health professional and therapist is now a graduate school social-work professor. And my internalized Vietnam legacy seems more composed and much less center-stage in my professional or personal life. And then, there came a gentle yet quite powerful reminder.

It is eleven months after returning from our Vietnam History Study Abroad Course 2000. Andy Wiest and John C. are filming individual interviews with veterans Roy, John and Charles, and with the faculty Andy, Ray and Leslie, as we reflect on the trip.

As I watch the others, I feel that these interviews are rather anti-climactic. To my way of thinking, the interviews are very cognitive, matter of fact and somewhat detached. We are looking back at something so remarkable that it defies adequate expression during an interview sitting under the Friendship Oak tree at the University of Southern Mississippi.

When my turn comes, it really does seem very anti-climactic. And then, near the end of my interview, Andy asks, "Ray, do you want to return to Vietnam again?" And after a moment I say,

Ray: "I'm amazed. But, as I think about it now, I may want to return another time."

Andy: "Why would you want to go back?"

Ray: "Because ... I realize that, each time I go back to Vietnam ... I've healed a little more."

AFTER-WORD: VETERANS AND CIVILIANS, VIETNAM, 9/11 AND IRAQ

This feeling of healing a little more with each return trip is consistent with the experiences of the 100+ veterans Stevan Smith has taken back. He also has taken non-veteran civilians to Vietnam and they, too, have found it to be a profound experience; Steve and I now believe that the impact of the "living room war" was quite deep on non-veterans, too.

When I first started writing *A Vietnam Trilogy* in 2000, I envisioned that this would be the point at which I would write a concluding chapter and thus finish my writings about the Vietnam War and about Vietnam veterans. And then along came 9/11, and then America's pre-emptive military invasion and occupation of Iraq. And in the swirl of emotions these events triggered, I realized that all the lessons that should have been learned about the impact of war and violence on veterans and their families have NOT been learned or applied; and over 800,000 Vietnam-theater veterans, as well as others, still sorely need the benefit of those lessons. And now, I could see that we were going to have a whole new generation of Iraq and Afghanistan War veterans and their families, who also would not have the benefit of lessons that should have been learned from the Vietnam War and from Vietnam veterans and their families.

And I found myself yet again feeling compelled to write down my thoughts and feelings as I, like other veterans of other wars, found many of our war-related issues triggered.

There are far too many crucial connections and ramifications about war and its impact, from Vietnam to the Persian Gulf War to 9/11 to Iraq, too many lessons that had never been fully learned or retained, that cry out to be heard.

The Vietnam War was the first "living room war" witnessed daily by the folks back home. The events of 9/11 and Iraq were unprecedented in terms of the massive media coverage as events were happening. The Iraq War has been even more of a "living room war" as television technology, e-mail and cell phones bring pictures and words from combatants in real time.

This will all have an impact on our veterans, our children, and on our country. There is a fundamental truth that many would be content to deny or avoid acknowledging:

> When a soldier goes to war, so indeed does every citizen of our country, for better or for worse. And what our military forces do in a war is not only their responsibility; it ultimately is shared by all of our citizens. And this indisputable yet often unacknowledged fact has marked implications concerning what many veterans need in order to more fully recovery from the horrific impact of war.

And so, I determined to explore more carefully how the experiences of Vietnam veterans and their families, described in this book and its predecessor, relate to 9/11, the Iraq War, and our veterans and their families — and the American people as a whole. Tens of thousands of Iraq War veterans and their families are now joining the ranks of Vietnam veterans and those of other wars.

The picture is not promising: the military estimates that 14-17% of Iraq war veterans report serious psychiatric problems: depression, generalized anxiety and post-traumatic stress disorder. Considering that the acute or shorter-term psychiatric casualty rate in a war is always substantially lower than the longer-term rates, and considering that tens of thousands of US military personnel are having to redeploy to Iraq two or more times due to manpower (and woman power) shortages, they are at greater risk to subsequently develop war-related PTSD in the coming months, years and decades.

Many critical issues and lessons need to be addressed.

- What is it about 9/11 that is so important to our understanding about the impact of war and terrorism?
- What is happening with our psychiatric casualties in Iraq?
- What can family members say and do, and not say and not do, after their veterans come home?
- What can be done about the severe problems of guilt and shame that afflict so many of our war veterans?
- What is going on between active duty military and the DOD, between veterans and the VA, and with their families?

- What are the compelling similarities between the Vietnam and Iraq War in terms of psychiatric casualties that should give us all great cause for concern?

- And what can we do differently than what has already been done, to help both our war veterans and their families?

These issues and concerns are addressed in the forthcoming volume, *From Vietnam to Iraq: Veterans and Families, Post Traumatic Stress and Healing,* which completes *A Vietnam Trilogy.*

Appendix: Outline of Initial Mental Health Orientation Session In Vietnam, 2000

May 15: Ho Chi Minh City. Leslie Root & Ray Scurfield

We know that you all are antsy about getting out of here and experiencing Vietnam. However, it really is important to first go over a few important subjects with you. So please bear with us, and we will get through this as quickly as we can.

I . *Uniqueness of this trip*

A. Participants:

- history faculty
- mental health faculty
- history students
- veterans.

B. Multiple roles:

- teaching
- students (as students and as people who have a life history that has some relationship with Vietnam)
- participant observers (of the vets as they visit their former battle sites)
- support

C. Dual purpose:

- educational, both intellectually and emotionally/experientially
- therapeutic (related to the war)

II. Some Misconceptions to Watch Out For

A. Here to party and have a good time (adventure vs. sacred journey)

B. Vets are fragile and students have to walk on egg shells

C. Emotional responses will be limited to when a vet visits his former duty site

D. Accessing mental health consultants doesn't mean that you have a psychological problem (and explain confidentiality of any conversations with Leslie or Ray)

E. Be careful about saying, "I know," or "I understand" do you really?

Rather, think about saying such comments as: "I'm here with you" or "I'm here for you"

• John adds: If a veteran looks like he is having a serious emotional reaction, Do not say: "How are you?" "How's it going?" "Can I help?"

• Also, even with the best intentions of wanting to be available (emotionally or for support), you may find that you are not . . .

III. Brief Orientation to Exposure to Trauma

A. Impact of trauma:

- Short-term, longer-term; level of severity
- Another myth: "time heals all wounds."
- Also, Chaim Shatan, psychiatrist: the analogy of war memories being "freeze-dried."

B. Continuous exposure to stimuli

- Getting to Vietnam
- Arriving in-country
- Generalizing of war-responses to exposure now in Vietnam, e.g., being in crowds of Vietnamese
- Visiting one's former duty site (not only being emotional and preoccupied while actually there)
- After leaving the duty site and later still . . .
- Leaving Vietnam
- Traveling on the plane going back home and homecoming
- Post-homecoming, e.g, will return trip now become another anniversary date with negative and/or positive associations. Will you become preoccupied with wanting to return to Vietnam and perhaps, for example, be bored or detached back home?

C. Individualized responses/reactions.

- Don't expect everyone to react similarly, or to perhaps even react at all, to the same things that you react or don't react to . . .

- Exposure to the trauma of the Vietnam War may provoke personal reactions to prior traumas in your life where the connection is a strong similar emotional state, e.g., you had a relative or friend die traumatically and now you hear vets talking about losing comrades here in Vietnam.

- Some of you may have not nearly as much interest as others in visiting various sites, such as temples, for example.

- You may get bored, anxious, resentful of being along with the group on some activities . . .

- You may have serious issues with how the days have been scheduled, or the time that we spend in orientations and meetings. We need to talk about any such reactions at the time they come up.

D. Participant observers may feel negative emotions (e.g., guilt, responsibility) while you are observing, or have reactions to your reactions.

And what if you are someone who has not experienced any trauma in your life?

E. Vets may experience negative emotions towards observers (students or other vets) who seemingly don't appreciate or don't seem very interested in the full impact of the war trauma.

IV. Ground Rules

A. Individual responsibility to set and enforce our own personal boundaries vis-a-vis other course participants, e.g., in terms of how we are feeling, any personal issues that are coming up for us individually, pressure to socialize or get close.

B. Avoid using alcohol as a way of avoiding (or unduly escalating!) strong or negative emotions, e.g, anxiety, fear, anger, guilt, sadness, disappointment, shame.

C. Be sensitive towards and supportive of one another. (This trip will be like an emotional roller coaster for many of you, with lots of highs and lows.)

And some of you will be find certain activities more interesting than others, planned or undertaken spontaneously.

D. This is a Third World country.

- We need to make sure that people just don't go running off everywhere.

- The Vietnamese government is *very* sensitive to tourists approaching military installations, for example.

- It is essential that there is coordination among participants, and with us the support personnel.

E. There are specific ground rules about the several group mental health debriefings that we are going to have during this course. We will go over these at the beginning of the first debriefing session.

V. Possible Outcomes of this Trip

A. Intellectual and emotional learning experiences

B. Provoking *other* unresolved negative issues that had been buried . . .

C. Healing experiences or more closure for trauma or some aspects of trauma

D. New positive experiences and memories from this trip to challenge/balance long-standing old, indelible and unforgettable, negative or traumatic experiences and associated memories

VI. What We Missed

Topics we did not cover during this orientation that we later wished that we had — or that we should have covered better during pre-trip orientations

- Cultural sensitivity to the Vietnamese people

- History versus mental health ways of looking at our trip, interests and activities

- Ground rules and expectations around the mental health debriefing sessions

Acknowledgments

The following is an acknowledgment of *very* special people, times and places. First and foremost, there are the hundreds of veterans of the Vietnam War, and many from World War II, the Korean and Persian Gulf Wars, and from Grenada and unspoken covert operations, all of whom have allowed me and my staff to bear witness as they laid bare their hearts and souls, nightmares, anguish, courage, strivings, redemption and perhaps above all, their worthiness; it has truly been a privilege and honor that is breath-taking and humbling.

A very special acknowledgment is due to my wife, Margaret, Director, Fleet and Family Support Services, Naval Construction Battalion, Gulfport MS, and to several vets and colleagues who took the time to review and offer helpful feedback on various chapters: Steve Tice who co-wrote the chapter on medical evacuees; Leslie Root, Roy Ainsworth, Charles Brown and John Young from the Study Abroad course; Stevan Smith, Jake LaFave, David Roberts and Robert Swanson from the 1989 return trip to Vietnam; Courtney Frobenius and Trang My Frobenius of Vietnam-Indochina Tours; Charles Figley and John Wilson. The late Lynda VanDevanter, my friend and colleague, was an inspiration and her book and friendship increased my understanding of the remarkable valor of military nurses and were instrumental to the analysis of potential positive outcomes of returning to Vietnam.

A special tribute to Father Truong Trinh and his family in Vietnam for their hospitality and giving us a priceless Catholic Vietnamese and cultural experience. And, while I have never met or communicated with him, through reading *The Sorrow of War*, North Vietnam Army veteran and author Bao Ninh has been an inspirational influence.

A very special acknowledgment is due the staff of programs serving veterans I directed or collaborated with from 1990 to the present that comprise the primary time-frame of this book. First the Post-Traumatic Stress Treatment Program (PTSTP) at the American Lake VA, Tacoma, WA. [Unfortunately, like many other specialized PTSD units in the VA system, the PTSTP has since been radically downsized.] I was the first director (1985 — 1992) of this innovative program, along with the leadership of Steve Tice, Anne Gregory, Jim Burke, Tom Olsen, Shawn Kenderdine, Lori Daniels, Terry McGuire, Bob Coalson, Casey Wegner and many others.

I was the original director of the Pacific Center for PTSD and of the Pacific Division, National Center for PTSD) in Honolulu (1992-1997). I led the establishment of the first PTSD residential treatment facility in the Pacific — the PTSD Residential Rehabilitation Program (PRRP) in Hilo. My clinical experiences at the PRRP and the support of Bridget Souza-Malama, Jamal Wassan, Emmet Finn, Jim Cariaso and the other great staff were instrumental to my insights about race-related trauma suffered by too many Asian/Pacific Islander war veterans that are described in this book.

At our Pacific Center for PTSD in Honolulu, Navy Command Master Chief Jim Cordeiro, Allan Perkal, Janet Viola and Lori Daniels offered many insights that are incorporated in this book.

My most recent colleagues who contributed to the Vietnam History Study Abroad to Vietnam in 2000 include Leslie Root, former director of the Biloxi PTSD Clinical Team, the former Director of the School of Social Work at the University of Southern Mississippi, Earley Washington, and especially current Director Mike Forster, who supported my involvement. My two former university social work secretaries, with their infectious personalities and can-do attitudes, were invaluable in preparing earlier manuscripts: Tammy Moss and Angela Benvenutti. USM History professor Andy Wiest has been outstanding in teaching military history, and leadership of veteran-related projects; without Andy, there would not have been a Study Abroad course. Also, my thanks to the Algora Publishing staff.

In closing, this book would not have been possible without the support, inspiration and manuscript in-put of my wife Margaret and my sister Tomi-Jean Yaghmai. Our wonderful young adult children Helani, Armand and Nicolas, and my large extended family have been invaluable to my post-war readjustment and hence making this book possible. Truly, I am blessed to have such a wealth of relationships.

INDEX

219

Printed in the United States
52499LVS00003B/316-348